D0610034

Aftershocks
the end of style culture

Aftershocks
the end of style culture

Steve Beard

WALLFLOWER PRESS
LONDON AND NEW YORK

First published in Great Britain in 2002 by
Wallflower Press
5 Pond Street, London NW3 2PN
www.wallflowerpress.co.uk

Copyright Steve Beard 2002

The moral right of Steve Beard to be identified as the author of this work has
been asserted in accordance with the Copyright, Designs and Patents Act of 1988

All rights reserved. No part of this publication may be reproduced, stored in a
retrieval system, or transported in any form or by any means, electronic,
mechanical, photocopying, recording or otherwise, without the prior permission
of both the copyright owners and the above publisher of this book

A catalogue for this book is available from the British Library

ISBN 1 903364 24 8

Printed in Great Britain by Antony Rowe Ltd., Chippenham, Wiltshire

For Victoria

CONTENTS

ACKNOWLEDGEMENTS

Victoria Halford for inspiring the book.
Yoram Allon, Howard Seal and everyone at Wallflower Press for publishing the book.
Stephen Hayward for advising me how to compile the book. John Parker for acting as my agent.
Dominic Ridley for supplying the cover photograph.
Paul Dave for writing the preface.
Stewart Home for his militancy; Kodwo Eshun for his dandyism.
Dylan Jones, John Godfrey, Matthew Collin, Avril Mair; Kathryn Flett, Peter Howarth, Sheryl Garratt; Boyd Tonkin and Philip Dodd for commissioning the journalism.
John Kerrigan and Francis Barker for supervising the thesis.
Terry Jones and Nick Logan for infrastructural support.
The staff at the Cambridge University Library and the British Library for their labour.
Pam Downe, Julia Monk, Roy Hutchens, John Hardy, Nana Yaa Mensa, Janet Lee, George Barber, Mark Waugh, Jack Sargeant, Nick Corstin, Suzi Q, Nick Tantis, Nick Land, Sadie Plant, Mark Fisher, Angus Carlyle, Robin Rimbaud, Wolfgang Tillmans, Paul Claydon, Damian Abbott, Adam Scrivener, Peter Pavement, Hayley Ann, Julie Gask, Jeff Noon, Tony White, James Pyman, Bruce Gilchrist, Jo Joelson, Jim Flint, David Eimer, Deirdre Crowley, Chris Wroblewski, Omaid Hiwaizi, Alix Sharkey, Jo Peters, Jim McClellan, Michelle Stavrinou (RIP), Tim Nicholson (RIP) and others for their various acts of hospitality.
Ken Beard, Dawn Beard, Karen Brooks, Tim Brooks, Clive Dreyer and Annette Dreyer for keeping me safe.

'It is always the same sign that controls appearance and disappearance. It presides over both. In the meantime, you're left to your own devices. There may be events, there may be a history…'

Jean Baudrillard, interviewed in 'Forget Baudrillard' during 1984/85

preface
by paul dave

I am glad that my old friend Steve Beard has asked me to write this preface to *Aftershocks* as it gives me an opportunity, after a break in our conversations of a few years, to think about my long familiarity with his work and to share with others my memories of the ardent and engaged dialogues/monologues from which this work emerged, as well as to mark not only my confessed enthusiasms for, but also to clarify my dissensions from, some of the positions adopted in it.

Our conversations have been pursued for almost twenty years in many different circumstances and places (as students; as insecurely employed, temporarily employed and unemployed writers, researchers and intellectuals; as members of groups of lovers, friends and strangers and from different positions within opposing and overlapping worlds). The first designation for our exchanges was the 'symposium'. I cannot remember how it was we came to adopt this term but I would like to think that it was after Plato's dramatic dialogue on love. As we originally conceived it, three of us – myself, Steve and Jim McClellan – agreed to meet weekly, in London's Soho, hand over written work and discuss it. The symposium folded very quickly and Steve began publishing in the style magazines. However, our dialogue continued and it occasionally produced an exchange of texts, although most of the time we concentrated on constructing a common set of obsessions and a common idiom which we tried, often unsuccessfully, to share with 'members unlimited'. This was principally an oral culture, one rooted in the generous conviviality of the pub and the street. It only acquired a consistency and coherence over many years and it represented an intellectual practice that was unconcerned with any immediate shaping or exchange value within a marketplace of ideas and subjectivities. It was marked by levity, anarchic exuberance and a seriousness which already recognised that our conversation might accompany and gloss a lifetime's work and that it could not be measured according to the deadlines of the culture industry or the artificial restrictions of the academy. In writing this preface I have let myself be guided by this spirit.

When asking me if I would write it Steve told me, with clear emphasis, that he is not a Marxist. I have always understood this to be the case and I have taken his warning as a clue or a prompt to think about the relationship between his work (particularly the concluding sections of this book) and what I take to be some of the correspondingly relevant and important issues in contemporary Marxism. But I must emphasise that all I can do here is to briefly outline these matters as they are brought into focus through Steve's compendious and restless imagination. In doing this I am consciously using *Aftershocks* as a resource for thinking about problems that I feel have preoccupied both of us. The range and lucidity of this book – indicating once again Steve's concern with collating dispersed ideas/creative acts and connecting up and rendering accessible to one another their different audiences and associated practioners – seem to invite the type of response which looks immediately for ways of making use of his ideas. It is the relationship of criticism and theory to substantive social functions and the historical crisis in that relationship that Steve's work often – poised uncomfortably as it has been between institutions such as the academy and the publicity machines of the culture industries – draws to our attention. *Aftershocks* is a text which attempts to reach beyond the enclosure of the academy whilst retaining its mission-statement seriousness and which strains against the marketing and publicity agendas of the style presses whilst seeking to retain the cultural energies of their peripheral contributors and creative constituencies.

Some of the most important general issues that the book raises are those concerning the need for an assessment of the role of style culture within contemporary British culture. In the Thatcher era style culture was carried out of its subcultural origins into wider cultural formations through intermediaries like the style presses (*i-D*, *The Face*, *Arena*). It quickly became a dominant cultural formation organised around carefully displayed, customised acts of consumption which became the measure of both legitimate and permissible social identities. A crucial aspect of this process involved making class politics appear an anachronistic irrelevancy. Notions of collectivity that were rooted in class were pushed aside and emphasis was placed on the contingent, topical and impermanent alliances of individuals to be found in consumer politics.

Throughout the eighties and nineties style magazines increasingly offered themselves as consumer courtesy manuals in which the working classes were viewed as poor consumers – a tasteless historical residue that could be defined in terms of caste categories. (As caste, class becomes the inexpungable trace carried in voice, face, posture and the cultural tastes that are seen as unmediated expressions of this naturalised identity.) Working-class collectives often appeared in these magazines as dangerously atavistic – their profiles were drawn from a social bestiary of slow-moving grotesques.

Class viewed through caste categories is the great historical achievement of the English class system. The latter has also worked to conceal class struggle as a dynamic shaping the course of history and has put in its place the now engrained

image of the English classes as a colourful tableau of fixed and intricately interlocking identities. Caste metaphors capture the sense of an immemorial culture in which
class is a historical curiosity of Englishness.

Style culture and the English class system – a great divide bridged by an un-
spoken alliance. This convergence is at its most transparent in the elaborate taxo-
nomic imagination both depend upon and it has often seemed to me that Steve's
writing seems most exuberant when he is naming and identifying the contemporary
style motley – 'whores, skunk pussies, buggers, crusties, dreads, slackers, dopers,
ravers, squatheads', 'crusties, doleys, squatheads, white dreads, students, New Age
types, ravers, old punks, hipsters'. Paul Smith has argued in *Millennial Dreams*
that there is a dangerous overlap between neo-liberal political discourses and style
discourses visible in the vicissitudes of many of the struggles that have been played
out in recent years between the state and those whose activities do not fit in with
its priorities. That is to say the postmodern social directories popularised by writers
like Peter York, Julie Burchill and Tony Parsons have been adopted by the neo-
liberal state and used to smother the 'class alliances' and 'political relations' of
those remaining resistant to the imperatives of capitalism. The method seems to
be one dependent on containing processes of disaffection and antagonism through
acts of naming and identification which then prepare strategies of control. Particular
groups are named, isolated, and then cued up for relentless disciplinary persecu-
tion. 'Travellers', 'ravers', 'anarchists', 'hippies' are some of the categories that have
been invoked in recent years to justify persecutory legislative programmes whose
overall strategy is to criminalise the effective social expression of dissident collective
consciousnesses. Perhaps the clearest example of this phenomenon is the Criminal
Justice Act.

Aftershocks is, in many places, a meditation on style culture and the postmodern political positions built upon it. The retrospective, introductory sketches of the
years Steve spent writing for a living reconstruct an apparent story of defeat which
can only be sensed emerging painfully and at times unselfconsciously in the writing
as it was produced. But that defeat needs to be thought about and the work presented here, helps us to start doing that.

What defeat? The constant folding of community, collectivity, *gemeinschaft* back
into the 'media simulacrum'. This is a defeat Steve writes about with nostalgia and
pain. He valued these magazines and the cultures that swirled around them. (In the
early days of one of these offices, he says with obvious fondness, 'clubworld people
drift in and out, promo records are spun on the decks, idle chat shifts into print.')
But I also remember how he already sensed the exclusions – the invisible pressure
of the guest list on the stranger was one of the ways he talked about it.

Partly Steve seems to be saying that this defeat was simply the defeat of his
own naivete. What did he expect? After all, as he himself points out, his theoretical
work, halted roughly at the beginning of the period recorded here, had already shown
the 'impossibility' of 'media subversion' and this impossibility, it is implied, had
unheeded implications for his project to 'detourne the style press'. Consequently, he
tells us, he spent ten years 'failing' to prove himself wrong. But equally, in some
senses there is no defeat at all, just a career picaresque with its comic, intoxicating
and sometimes squalid moments along with its familiar and endlessly optimistic
structure. Hermes's fingerprints are all over him here. SB the trickster – wheedling,
mimicking, pitching, spinning, scoring, making moves up and down Soho. SB the

trickster getting 'dumped', ending up with the 'bums' in St. Anne's churchyard, War-
dour Street, but never ending up down and out (or 'killed' like his trickier copy). His
pockets half full of disappearance money, kill fees, and the office small change that
he and others took as wages.

The use of the picaresque then takes us away from the language of defeat and
moves us into the language of ongoing struggle – a larger, shared struggle which Steve's work touches on all the time. A struggle suggesting different, parallel 'projects'
and other alliances, solidarities, commitments and of course various possible out-
comes. These convergences and sympathetic alliances are visible in the journalism.
Often I sensed that they were the enabling context of Steve's research and writing –
the conditions of its bearability.

The passages of retrospective framing in *Aftershocks* (the introductory para-
graphs to the various sections with their elliptical mix of theme/autobiography) often
emphasise this sense of struggle and it is here that I am reminded of my enthusiasm
for Steve's uncompleted thesis *Bloody Banquets*, the second and to date last chapter
of which is printed here. It goes under the title of 'Ejected Metanarrative' and 'Ejected
Metanarrative Footnotes'. As always his choice of words is patiently instructive. This
is work ejected by the academy (Oxbridge). However, the word 'ejected' is also one
which Steve often uses in his work with reference to the fate of the 'Fourth World'
(those individuals and groups who are undergoing a process of desubjectification
under contemporary regimes of capitalism and who as a consequence are dropping
below the threshold of the politically visible world). It is significant then that 'ejected'
is paired with 'metanarrative' as the latter is, among other things, code for Marxism
which has also been ejected both within the academy and outside it.

But what is the relationship between the two ejectees? Class struggle is evoked
in the final paragraph of *Bloody Banquets* (the 'Marxist class narrative') and the
proletariat features (as a 'remnant' of itself). But for me there are difficulties raised
by Steve's formulations. The metanarrative recounted in *Bloody Banquets* is one in
which the proletariat often figures as a disturbingly passive presence. Constructed
out of wandering 'refuse' it is confined, disciplined and then expelled back into a
state of chaotic mobility over a four hundred year period.

The history produced in this part of the book is clearly not traditional history
from above with its chronicles of the palace and the chamber of state. Equally, it
is not history from below. Steve says little in *Bloody Banquets* about the English
Revolution of 1649 and the 'revolution within the revolution' – it is here that the
influence of the gentlemen scholars of Oxbridge who were nominally supervising his
PhD thesis is most marked.

I remember how as undergraduates we both attended tutorials on the early
modern period in which cavalier cultural connoisseurs paraded their neglect of Christopher Hill and their appetite for the history-from-above revisionism of writers such
as Conrad Russell. Steve confessed to being seduced by this Oxbridge intellectual
elegance and was still, in my view, wrestling with its influence when we discussed
Robert Brenner's *Merchants and Revolution* in the mid-nineties.

What then seems missing in *Bloody Banquets* is an approach which brings
together history from above (the strategies of exploitation pursued by the capitalist
class) and history from below (the responses of the oppressed and exploited) and
captures a sense of the dynamic of class struggle in history. Such an approach represents what Alex Callinicos has called 'total history'. I suppose therefore that I am

saying that despite the avowed refusal in *Bloody Banquets* to shut down on class struggle I feel Steve nevertheless constructs a position from where what he calls the 'remnants' of labour ('zombies') seem inherently unlikely to re-connect with any clear historically significant agency or even to be about anything in particular.

This brings me to Peter Linebaugh's work which Steve knows through his contributions to my film *Newgate Pastoral* and through conversations we have had since the publication of *The London Hanged*. These conversations have been rooted in our mutual desire to intervene, in different ways, in the proliferating accounts of the impact of London's past on its present (his historical materialism represents a different approach to the ones found in the work of Peter Ackroyd, Iain Sinclair or Patrick Keiller). A few weeks ago I attended a debate between Linebaugh and Eric Hobsbawm at the University of London's School of Oriental and African Studies which seems to me relevant to the issues raised by *Bloody Banquets*. Linebaugh argued that it is difficult to segment the working class historically or contemporaneously into an elect core who pursue a historical mission and a periphery of 'losers' who are history's ejected refuse. The points of attachment, detachment and reattachment to working class collectives are not fixed but fluid and occur in the context of ongoing struggle with the agents of capitalist exploitation. The lumpen, the unrespectable, blackguardly, 'criminal-criminal' rather than 'social-criminal' are all drawn back by Linebaugh into the transformative fire at the heart of working class experience.

These thoughts suggest one way of articulating the complex impressions created by *Aftershocks*. The balanced optimism of the conclusion to *Bloody Banquets* strikes me as bleak, dependent as it ultimately is, I feel, on the rhetorical skill ('force') with which so many theoretical references are deployed and brought into dialogue and the transfigurative effects that skill seeks to lend to a vision of an abjected proletariat. The embodied bleaknesses ('accuracy') of the journalism and the accompanying account given of it – the painful struggles often elicited from interviewees caught up in the coils of the culture industries and Steve's own admissions of bad faith, naivety and bruising illusion alongside brief but exhilarating experiences of creative collectivity – on the other hand, communicate a different kind of hopefulness. Maybe for this reader it is a sense of agency and authentic struggle that is delivered in these passages. In this respect I think it is interesting that the piece of journalism anthologised in *Aftershocks* – it immediately precedes *Bloody Banquets* and is entitled 'Afro-Shakespearean Psychogeography' – is the kind of piece that so clearly inspired many of Steve's readers, demonstrating as it does his ability to identify significant texts and then to swiftly and suggestively summarise their radical implications. ('While plantations owners sat on their porches doing the accounts and "talking dicks" (speaking with proper diction), the language was changing all around them.') The text being discussed in this review – the *Dictionary of Caribbean Usage* – is one which, in Steve's account and in the quote I have just given, forms a commonality of interest and focus with the work of Peter Linebaugh and Marcus Rediker, particularly their recently published *Many Headed Hydra: Sailors, Slaves, Commoners, and the Hidden History of the Revolutionary Atlantic*.

Looking back at the first volume of Steve's collected writing, *Logic Bomb*, I notice that there is a symmetry maintained with *Aftershocks* – the last section of the book, (called 'Slow Memes') which contains the first chapter of *Bloody Banquets*, is split, as in *Aftershocks*, into two ('Archaic Modernity 1' and 'Archaic Modernity 2').

What captures my attention is that in *Logic Bomb* what precedes *Bloody Banquets* is a review of Peter Lamborn Wilson's *Pirate Utopias*. This book also has intimate connections with the project of Linebaugh and Rediker (in fact the backcover of Lamborn Wilson's book carries excerpts from enthusiastic reviews from the historians of the revolutionary Atlantic and from Christopher Hill). As Steve points out in his review of *Pirate   Utopias* – a review which echoes the one provided in *Aftershocks* on the *Dictionary of Caribbean Usage* in its angle of vision – Lamborn Wilson is arguing that the 'ideals of democracy, public property and free speech' must be reconnected to the struggles of 'outcasts of all nations'. Again, this is precisely the historical project of Linebaugh and Rediker. There is then a quiet antiphonal in the prefatory pieces of journalism provided for the two halves of *Bloody Banquets* in the two collections.

The heads of the Hydra are talking to one another. Hercules gets busy. But for every head he cuts off two new ones grow in its place.

London, April 2001

introduction

Welcome to *Aftershocks*. This is my second collection of essays and journalism. Whereas my debut 1998 collection, *Logic Bomb*, promised to deliver 'transmissions from the edge of style culture', this one can only hope to offer transmissions instead from its end. Style culture is defined for me as a set of resistant signifying practices which in the fall-out from the punk moment of the late 1970s passed through an economy of desire to emerge on the other side of the social divide as powerful commodity-signs. It designates the emblematic path followed by Vivienne Westwood in the fashion-world, Damien Hirst in the art-world, Irvine Welsh in the publishing-world, Norman Cook in the music-world, Nigel Coates in the architecture-world and Gary Oldman in the film-world. All of these figures in their different ways have made the journey from *enfant terrible* to grand old man or woman. They have pulled off a status conjuring trick.

It would be entirely possible to demonstrate how this signifying manoeuvre operates according to the received dynamics of a social antagonism – 'young' versus 'old', 'pleb' versus 'patrician', 'street' versus 'salon', 'modern' versus 'archaic' – whose carnivalesque overturning is the guarantee of its continued survival. But that is not my intention here. I think that there was a break in the culture at the end of the 1980s and the beginning of the 1990s and that this coincided with the transition from a mass manufacturing to a niche information economy. The fact that this break has been hidden from view by the persistence of conservative social formations should not lead us to forget the shock of its lived experience. Before the industrial warehouses became recapitalised as upscale design studios they were squatted as

spaces for a rehearsal of the alternative cultures which were later to become institu-
tionalised. They were temporary night-clubs, art galleries, film sets and autonomous
zones. Before that, of course, they were simply rotting away as sumptuary victims of
a crisis in capitalism that at the time seemed permanent.

The 'end' of style culture for me marks its occult passage through this cultural
break rather than its triumphant return to a familiar social. Some stories are in danger
of being forgotten, some people had no chance to come back home. The pieces
collected in *Aftershocks*, like those in the earlier volume, again combine journalism
for the style mags – *i-D, The Face, Arena* – with a huge chunk of mutant theory from
an abandoned doctoral thesis; this time round, though, there are also occasional
pieces for the Sunday newspaper supplements and other mags. All pieces are offered
up in their original form with only minor alterations for the improvement of sense.
Quite a few which were commissioned and then killed are published here for the
first time. I have grouped the pieces thematically rather than chronologically and
introduced each section with a personal memory blip which attempts to situate the
transformation of my subjectivity during the period under review. The earliest piece
(on fantasy writer Michael Moorcock) dates from 1990, the latest piece (on quantum
physicist Stephen Hawking) dates from 1999.

What job of work does this book do? I think that at the very least it gives some
idea of what it was like to be young, privileged and trendy in the metropolitan London
of the 1990s. At the most I hope it defines the continuing importance of certain
lapsed counter-cultural figures (club promoter Fraser Clark, media buster Hakim
Bey, acid guru Terence McKenna, uber-hacker Kevin Mitnick), while catching other
now celebrated people (musician Brian Eno, actor Harvey Keitel, film-maker David
Cronenberg, new media artist Bill Viola) at turning points in their careers. Inevitably, *Aftershocks* features many profiles of writers I respect and admire (queer
aesthete Cyril Collard, Scottish modernist James Kelman, African-American chroni-
cler Nathan Heard, conceptual novelist Stewart Home). It also tracks back to examine
the emblematic value of key historical figures (Elizabethan adventurer Walter Ralegh,
anti-crime tsar J. Edgar Hoover, avant-garde artist Marcel Duchamp) who were all in
perverse ways divided against themselves (much like the malcontents of Jacobean
revenge tragedy).

Above all, this book documents my efforts to conceptualise the media simulacrum within which my writing practice was caught. In a trend-driven world where
every subject needs a hook to deliver it to the merchandising chain, then every story
has to double up as the next big thing. The crazy thing is that anyone working in
this world long enough soon discovers that anything can be hyped if the angles are
judged right and the spin is got just so. You can even end up hyping yourself. (Hell,
you can hype your own *grandmother*!) There are people out there now hyping their
sex lives, their drug addictions, their nervous breakdowns, their various dark nights
of the soul. It's a whole new media industry. Sometimes it feels like the only game
in town. I think that's why I was so attracted to the totalising discourses (conspiracy

theory, Marxism, occultism) which were wild and crazy enough to offer some kind of critical leverage on this world.

I guess at heart I remain some kind of a crinkly English situationist who wants to have his MTV and critique it too. I am reminded of the story of how high priest of situationism Guy Debord rushed over to London from Paris in the 1960s when he heard that a trained guerrilla combat unit was ready for his inspection in Ladbroke Grove. He was directed to military headquarters on the All Saints Road where he discovered a young guy watching 'Match of the Day' on the sofa with a can of McEwan's Special Export in his hand. Debord raged about this act of passive collaboration with the society of the spectacle and denounced the books on the shelves as ideologically suspect. Meanwhile, the guy explained that the guerrilla combat unit consisted of him and his kid brother and that they were ready to spring into action at the generalissimo's command. Debord, quite naturally, stalked off in a rage.

One thing that became clear to me as I compiled this book was that as a self-appointed intellectual I had been labouring under the illusion that there is a bourgeois public sphere in England. This was probably the result of having my head turned by Jurgen Habermas and other continental philosophers in my youth; I thought their insights had universal application. It was only after ten years of trying to smuggle ideology critique into lifestyle journalism that I realised that what passes for a bourgeois public sphere in England is actually a media simulacrum stencilled over a single national market. It took a return to social systems theorist Niklas Luhmann for me to understand that this media simulacrum simply consists of a series of commodified life-worlds – the fashion-world, the art-world, the publishing-world, the music-world, the architecture-world, the film-world – which persist as networks of social relations. In other words, mum, it really is who you know and not what you know that counts. (Yes, I know, two high-priced universities and a fancy career to deliver me this kernel of folk wisdom!)

The intellectual generalism of *Aftershocks* is therefore atypical of English culture. I hope it has more than curiosity value. The real significance of it for me is the theorisation of Elizabethan theatre as a self-reflexive space which was able to comment on the lived experience of its own late sixteenth-century cultural break; the one which, let's say, inaugurated the passage from a peasant agricultural to a gentrified manufacturing economy. Conceptualising this proto-modern break as the double of the postmodern one I was living through I think helped me to navigate my way through the semiotic crush of the media simulacrum. If nothing else, it made for a good story. But it's often stories that help us to live, isn't it?

What I now understand is that it's the snagged material that gets left behind in the cultural breaks that interests me. Take the events allegorised by the 1998 movie *Shakespeare in Love*, for example. This speculative fantasy dramatises the emergence of William Shakespeare's mature style of romantic comedy (*Romeo and Juliet, Twelfth Night*) from an interval dominated by Christopher Marlowe's blood and thunder plays, Will Kempe's gestural clowning and the popular idiom of brothels and taverns. By the time of the film's triumphal conclusion, Queen Elizabeth I herself has appeared on Richard Burbage's national stage to manufacture a new consensus reality based on the poetic realism of the court. What gets lost in this new dispensation is the play which Philip Henslowe was hoping to see staged at his own Bankside theatre. Despite the movie's rather mean little jokes about the persistence of protomodern social formations (the rivertaxi-driver's devotion to celebrity, the tavernkeeper's pretentious menu, the puritan minister's inevitable hypocrisy), Henslowe's drunken challenge to Shakespeare ('Let us have pirates, clowns and a happy ending or we shall send you back to Stratford to your wife!') still carries a certain popular authority.

Pshaw! Grand old men and women? Who needs them! I hope you enjoy this book.

rock'n'roll paradigms

You are fighting your way across the dancefloor in the old holding tank on the south bank of the Thames. It is hot, close and dark here in the bowels of Clink Street. This is as near as you can get to the collective euphoria of acid house club culture – a 'noonday underground' (Tom Wolfe) which pulls in the slack from the mid-1980s rare groove scene and sends out a delayed trauma signal to the mid-1990s crash sites of darkside drum'n'bass. A whole generation of ravers miss out on this detour and get the Gemeinschaft of anti-Thatcherite cultural resistance reprocessed into the Gesellschaft of Blairite cultural reaction. You are dumped at the limit event of this subcultural turn, doubly exiled from the dominant postmodern order. Hyperconformism now beckons as a survival tactic. Your theoretical position is occult. 'In times of reaction, the intellectual must choose dandyism or militancy.'
(Roland Barthes)

TECHNO PAGAN
arena, 47, september/october 1994

The list of eccentrics, idealists and hucksters who have plundered the sound of black America, repackaged it in London and sold it back to the USA is as long as the history of British pop music. Brian Epstein did it most famously with the Beatles. The infant tycoon Andrew Loog Oldham followed in Epstein's footsteps and did it with the Rolling Stones. And then 20 years later Simon Napier-Bell did it all over again with Wham!

What was the formula in each case? The British Invasion of the States spearheaded by the Beatles and the Stones mixed English prole attitude, continental pop modernism and contraband rhythm and blues to manufacture a 'beat boom' which had its epicentre in London. The 'Second British Invasion' of the mid-Eighties – anybody here care to remember how bands like the Human League, Culture Club and the Eurhythmics plastered black American soul with English panto flash and went into heavy rotation on MTV? – was similarly a product of London nightclub culture.

Is anybody out there ready for a Third Invasion? Fraser Clark is. In fact, he's been ready for it ever since he first cottoned on to the Acid House craze of 1988. A figure from the hippie underground who escaped to Ibiza in the Sixties, dropped acid with the best of them and then held out against the dreadful spectre of Getting a Proper Job for the next 20 years, Clark is a perplexing hybrid of idealist, hedonist and scam artist. He has kept alive the radical social ambitions of the Sixties and is a big fan of changing the System by seeding it with the spores of peace, love and understanding. At the same time, he is a notorious publicity hound who has not been slow to generate press coverage for himself in the style press.

Dubbed by some the 'Timothy Leary of the E generation', Clark gatecrashed the Acid House party right at the start and tried to whip it into some kind of political shape. From as early as 1986, when he founded the underground hippie bulletin *Encyclopaedia Psychedelica* (quaintly described as the 'ultimate Techno-Pagan Love fanzine'), he has been in the forefront of preaching a return to the values of communitarianism and transformed states of consciousness. He has organised shamanistic retreats in the West Country, has invited psychedelic gurus like Alexander Shulgin and Terence McKenna to deliver 'Ambient Lectures' from his Evolution platform in London, established a record label and set up his own club, Megatripolis, at Charing Cross.

In the process he has helped to alter the development of a whole subculture. When the rhythms of Chicago house and Detroit techno first seeped into British nightclubs in 1987 there were all the usual hipster arguments about who'd heard which white label import first. MDMA changed all that. Once everyone was doing Ecstasy, the collective vibe on the dancefloor intensified and the one-upmanship disappeared. Hippie emblems came back into fashion again and the post-punk embargo on psychedelic culture collapsed.

When that happened, a lot of old hippies – especially those who had drifted into a squat-hopping lifestyle on the margins of society – suddenly seemed less like embarrassing cultural leftovers and more like crucial links with a visionary past that had been wiped off the map. Clark was not slow to seize his chance. He grabbed this new youth cult by the scruff of the neck and pumped it full of hippie idealism.

'I'd been waiting for this generation for 15 years,' he has said. 'In the Sixties, if you went into any British town, you'd find only half-a-dozen or so hippies. They were always in a tiny minority. Most were middle-class and educated. When things got tough, they abandoned the ideals and the whole thing collapsed. I look on the ravers as reinforcements.'

He is not alone. In 1989 house culture migrated to the margins of the capital in a series of big outdoor raves which took place beyond the orbital stretch of the M25. The collision with the rag-tag army of fossilised hippies, white dreads and old punks who were bobbing along on the free festival circuit created a mutant sub-culture – labelled New Age Travellers by the Tory press – whose lineage can plausibly be traced back to the Levellers, Diggers and other antinomian religious cults of the 1640s.

Mobile sound systems with names like Spiral Tribe, Armageddon, DIY, Circus Warp and Horsedrawn toured the countryside. Strange kinds of cultural hybrids began to emerge. Paganism plus personal computers. Sacramental chemicals. Hardcore techno and tribal rhythms. Ambient house and Zen Buddhism. Trance dancing. Shamanism rewired through chaos theory. Body piercing and sex magick. It was exhilarating, it was exhausting.

It was a threat to public order. Police crackdowns on the festival circuit soon followed, vehicles and equipment were impounded and the Criminal Justice and Public Order Bill (which makes it a criminal offence for more than ten people to loiter in public with intent to have a good time) was draughted. The vibe moved back to London. Over the last few years, clubs like Megadog, Whirl-Y-Gig, Telepathic Fish and Megatripolis have incubated the techno-hippie underground within the confines of licensed premises. And it has flourished.

Megatripolis has been the real scene-stealer. A typical Thursday night at the club would feature tribal drummers on the main stage in the Cathedral, trippy visuals in the Virtualitiroom and a philosophical lecture by an acid guru in the Techno-Silence Room, with a Glastonbury-style mix of market stalls – selling smart drinks, beads, bongs, illuminated face paint and anarchist pamphlets – patched into the rest of the space. The crowd, meanwhile, would be a mix of crusties, doleys, squatheads, white dreads, students, tourists, New Age types, ravers, old punks and hipsters. Plenty of leather and beads. Plenty of tattoos. Plenty of long hair and goatees. Clark has been desperately trying to come up with a label for this amorphous bunch of fellow travellers ever since Acid House first struck. Born-Again Hippies? Zippies? Techno Pagans? None has really stuck.

And now he has severed his links with Megatripolis and is off to America. The Zippy Pronoia Tour (where pronoia is the opposite of paranoia) represents an attempt to export British techno-hippie culture back to the country which originally spawned it in a grand act of larceny which rivals the chutzpah of Loog Oldham and Napier-Bell. Except for one crucial difference. Clark is not managing a band. He had gone beyond that. He is promoting a vibe, managing a concept, exporting a whole scene. Let someone else provide the music. He'll supply the ideas to go with it. Will it work? Kodwo Eshun, music editor of the *Modern Review*, thinks it might: 'Clark can't be as barefaced as Loog Oldham or Napier-Bell. His hustler terms have to go through a Learyesque process. He has to sell himself as a guru rather than as a promoter. I think there is a crossing of the two things. He's a pop entrepreneur, but he's marketing himself as a pop guru – that's the difference. So in other words he's saying: "What's at stake here isn't just a new thing for the kids to wear this summer; what's at stake is a change in evolutionary consciousness." That's the pitch this time round.' Music journalist Matthew Collin is more positive: 'I think he'll certainly be taken a lot more seriously over there than he is over here. Partly because there's no real ideology in the British sub-culture. There are some half-arsed slogans in there, but there's no ideology behind it apart from going out for a laugh and getting off your head and dancing to some music. Clark has tried to graft an ideology on to it and the Americans will love that. I see him doing something really unexpected.'

Clark is planning a rave in the Grand Canyon as the climax to the Pronoia tour, an event he describes as the 'Woodstock of the Nineties'. Whether it comes off or not is anybody's guess. But it certainly makes more sense as a commemoration of the original Sixties spirit than the rash of '25th anniversary' Woodstock revivals which have appeared on the media landscape this year. Do you want Woodstock the Book, the Movie (director's cut no less) or the Repeat Performance? If it's the latter then all you have to do is mail a cheque for $899 to America Ad Lib and they will send you on a five-day package tour to Woodstock '94 (featuring old stalwarts Bob Dylan and Joe Cocker as well as newer acts like Arrested Development and Cypress Hill) with airport tax thrown in. It is this kind of empty celebration of the past which Clark has turned his back against. He is more interested in making history come alive for a new generation. In this he has been helped by the May issue of the glossy American cybermag, *Wired*, which not only ran a glowing story on Megatripolis but even featured a stereotypical zippie beaming crazily from its cover.

Will the Pronoia tour succeed? Is talk of a Third British Invasion anything more than a pipe dream? One thing to bear in mind is that there is already a thriving underground scene in America quite ready to embrace the cultural virus Clark is throwing their way. There is the post-hippie computing community, the cyberpunk crowd, the disaffected slacker generation. And most of all there is the vast constituency of Grateful Dead fans. Don't laugh. Since the end of the Sixties, Jerry Garcia and Co have compensated for their lack of a record contract by sustaining their career on the road. Grateful Dead fans follow them round the country, swap homebrew tapes of their performances and take lots of psychedelic drugs. They are also into computers. Deadheads were among the first inhabitants of the Internet and already a conference has started on San Francisco's primary bulletin board, the WELL, on the similarities between the trippy mantras of the Grateful Dead and house music.

Fraser Clark landed in New York in June and is sweeping East. Mark Heley did it the other way round. A Cambridge philosophy graduate who was writing for *i-D* about the connections between virtual reality, shamanism and rave culture in 1990, he set up a smart drugs bar and Mind Gym in the Brain nightclub in London, created a buzz and decamped to San Francisco. Once on the West Coast, he introduced house music to the still rather rockist cyber zine, *Mondo 2000*, started a nightclub, Toon Town, and waited for a sub-culture to form. It didn't quite happen. According to Douglas Rushkoff's *Cyberia* (Flamingo), an account of the American cyberpunk phenomenon, Heley gobbled too many chemicals, became convinced one night at his club that he was a shaman guiding the whole event to a successful conclusion and basically went a little bit crazy. 'I experienced some polarities, that's all,' is how he put it. All of which implies that life as the next Andrew Loog Oldham is not without its hazards. But Clark has been there before. Here he was prophesying in *Mondo 2000* two years ago: 'Without a scintilla of doubt, house music is the sound of the nineties.

Zippy youth culture will be booming out of Peking and Baghdad jukeboxes within five years.' When questioned about why house music was going to conquer the world from London, he waxed philosophical: 'Why the Beatles last time? London's the planet's heart chakra and Acid House definitely stimulates the higher emotional circuits. Another reason is that, since the command-and-control virus in Western Culture originally entered the system in Ancient Britain (and Europe), the antiviral revival must be initiated there too. So the Goddess starts her endgame in Britain, where nobody's looking, takes America and Japan by storm, then gets it broadcast from there to the whole planet.'

Nice pitch! This is really the crux of Clark's whole project – the obsession with London. For all his hippie mysticism, he at times sounds like an old-fashioned gentleman capitalist, a swag merchant who happens to trade in concepts rather than stocks and bonds but still thinks that London is the storehouse of the world.

It's a myth, but a potent one. All of which begs the question: what does Fraser Clark want? Does he want to become rich and successful or does he want to change the world? Already the monolithic subcult – 'Acid House' – he wishes to export to America has splintered. There is the 'handbag house' of glossy pop acts like M People and D:REAM. The hardcore rhythms of the still largely underground 'jungle' music. There is even – most ominously for Clark, because it goes against the grain of his whole philosophy – a return to the old-fashioned values of spectacle, musicianship and album deals with 'progressive' white techno bands like Orbital, Seefeel and Underworld.

It may be that the world will change without the need of Clark's intervention. While he is busy setting up his sound system in the Grand Canyon, a revolution has been quietly brewing in the music industry. There has been talk of 'virtual record stores', of punters browsing for records in cyberspace and having the album of their choice sent down the wire and written to disc on a blank CD. Some artists see this as a chance to cut out the record company and deal with their fans direct.

Certainly the Internet Underground Music Archive allows anyone with the equipment to upload their own home-produced music onto the Net without the hassle of dealing with the middlemen. Potential consumers can simply download the music direct. And they don't even have to pay!

This is the shocking thing for the record companies. It is not such bad news for Clark, who is very much into the whole idea of collective self-help. At the same time, it does rather question his self-appointed status as techno-hippie prophet. Once music can be wired all over the world at the touch of a button, it doesn't need to track the old imperial trading routes. It doesn't need to come out of London.

All of which suggests that Clark may be on a hiding to nothing. It's happened before. Back in the Fifties, impressario Larry Parnes booked Eddie Cochran and Gene Vincent to play London but was never able to export Tommy Steele, 'Britain's Answer to Elvis Presley', back to America. Even Malcolm McLaren came a cropper when he toured the States with the Sex Pistols.

If Fraser Clark is as much of a prophet as he thinks he is then he's going to have to ditch the Anglo culture riffs on the Pronoia tour and make much more of a global pitch. That way he could go on to set up an underground communication network to rival MTV. In the meantime, he might just come back from America with some fresh sounds. Which would be good news for everyone.

REMIXOLOGIST #1
arena, 24, november 1990

Brian Eno is lying uncomfortably on the grass in his back garden cupping a hand over the microphone of my tape recorder. It's a thick summer afternoon in the flatlands of Suffolk, a space of slow time and quick noise, banded by the deep blare of traffic, the buzz of conversation and the peripheral scat of air turbulence. A complex pattern of sound waves. Almost a kind of ambient music.

Idle thoughts prompted not only by Eno's continuing interest in the form he almost single-handedly invented in 1979 with *Music for Airports*, but also by the way he speaks about making music. 'Melody' and 'rhythm' are words which rarely enter his vocabulary. Instead, it's all 'frequency ranges' and 'transmission losses'. Or, when you come right down to it, it's music as 'the amplification of the movement of atoms'.

It's this kind of talk which has won Eno a reputation for cerebral remoteness. An egghead with a synthesiser, a techno-monk plugged into the mixing desk. But what I soon learn from meeting the guy on his home turf is that he's surprisingly relaxed, humorous and open. He laughs a lot, curses a fair amount. He even does funny voices. He looks younger than his 42 years, much less austere than he usually photographs. Thinning blond tonsure, alert blue eyes, a compact, mobile frame. Dressed down in shorts and sunglasses for the interview, he could easily pass for a weekending professional businessman. Which, in a sense, he is. He did found an independent record label in 1975 to release difficult material by the likes of Harold Budd, Michael Nyman and Simon Jeffes.

If he's so analytical about his craft, it's only because he's so devoted to it. His ambient recordings, even his film soundtrack samplers, are not abstract exercises in form so much as meditations on the textural crush of sound, the distant embrace of vibrations. Music which shivers at the end of the senses. 'It's a matter of creating a landscape which is credible to its very edges. You want to hear to the limits of your hearing, because then you realise that there are things outside. I like that idea a lot, the notion that there's a continuum of sound which you happen to have landed in somewhere. I like strange balances for that reason, because that reinforces the feeling that you might not be in the best spot to listen.'

This, ultimately, is the big difference between Eno and other avant-garde composers like La Monte Young or Steve Reich. Where they're technical, he's still funky. 'I remember giving a lecture in New York where I was criticising Steve Reich – who I really like as a composer, I must say – for a piece of his called "Drumming". I said that it was a great piece, but if he'd been a pop musician he'd have used good sounding drums instead of such pathetic little bongos. And he would. As it is, it's like a diagram of a great piece. There's no sense of the possible sensuality of the sound.'

Eno keeps on coming back to the vital importance of pop music during the course of the interview. For a man who coolly made the decision not to be a pop star, who quit Roxy Music after their inspirational first album, this is slightly surprising. But maybe he only felt able to appreciate the real meaning of pop once he'd escaped its fake celebrity.

He listens to a lot of Nigerian pop – the expected outre reference – but is still a big fan of Marvin Gaye and Al Green. Insists that pop is historically significant because it's the only musical form to have taken sound seriously as a subject of composition. Like with hip hop's use of sampling and collage: 'I think a lot of hip hop really is very avant-garde indeed. If it had been produced by balding intellectuals like me at Stanford, everybody would be saying how incredibly brilliant it was.'

Which is typical of Eno's perverse modesty. He's already been there with David Byrne. Their New York studio effort, *My Life in the Bush of Ghosts*, was mixing polyrhythms and sampled chants nine years ago and remains one of the seminal pop events of the last decade. But then, Eno's career is littered with casual triumphs. The brace of eccentric rock albums – particularly *Taking Tiger Mountain by Strategy* – knocked out in the mid-Seventies, the three David Bowie collaborations, the input for Talking Heads' best album, *Remain in Light*. He's been so consistently ahead of his time, and so steadily influential, that he can be forgiven for the lapse in taste which led him to produce U2.

But if his experience with the immensely successful rock Irish band shows anything, it's that there's increasingly less misunderstanding between the conceptual scratchings of the avant-garde and the cash register rattle and hum of the record industry. When Eno made what was a very bold decision in the late Seventies to abandon the conventional song structure of what was still – in however mutated a form – rhythm and blues, things were very different. He got crucified. And he still seems to bear the scars.

'It was fucking difficult for a while. I'd betrayed my early supporters by not being the next David Bowie and they really hated me for it. And of course the serious music scene was all sewn up. So I didn't belong anywhere for a long time, I still don't. I don't have a place here. Because England is the worst place to do this, they're such shits. Really, English cynicism is such a disgusting attitude. We really have developed it beyond any other country and it's a great shame.' Up until five years ago, Eno had been living in New York, having moved there from London in 1978. Now he resides close to his family, holed up in an English country pile in the small market town where he was born. Does it bother him to be back in England? 'Yeah, it does actually. It pisses me off.'

Even so, there are compensating distractions. He's collaborating with John Cale in his home studio, producing something 'more rhythmic' than his most recent offerings. Plus he's kept busy working on the video installations which have brought him increasing renown over the last ten years, sculpted exhibits dealing in refracted light and shifting bands of colour.

He's actually only in the country for less than half of each year. Most of his time is spent in transit, leading the life of the post-industrial airport nomad, the vagabond scholar, the multi-disciplinary artist. Any day is as likely to find him organising an installation in Milan or attending an international think tank seminar in New York as pottering restlessly in his back garden.

Eno exists on a range of cultural frequencies, hops between concepts as rapidly as he does aircraft. He is that rarest of breeds, a suburban cosmopolitan, a genuine English intellectual. Someone should give him a university chair fast before he decides to quit our grimy shores for good.

GUITAR ANTI-HERO
the face, 2/17, february 1990

'I know certain authors, including me, who live in stark terror at the prospect of some yuppie Booker panellist moving into the flat next door.' So fulminates Michael Moorcock, greybeard enfant terrible, ex-member of rock outfit Hawkwind and Grand Old Man of the English science fiction avant-garde, in one of the diatribes, 'Literally London', included among the engaging, if rather uneven, collection of short stories, people profiles, reviews, autobiographical notes and odds and sods which make up his latest book, *Casablanca* (Gollancz). You can almost see him stocking up on the literary ammunition in his Ladbroke Grove flat as he girds his typewriter to do battle with those twin forces of Thatcherite evil: Gentrification and Literary Respectability.

Get ye the hell back behind the closed blinds of middlebrow Hampstead, seems to be the stern command of this blazing eyed visionary as he surveys the sorry sight of London's alleyways and back streets, the corridors of its secret imaginative power, being tarted up as a novel adventure playground for the Lit Biz classes. 'Could Little Dorrit or Mrs Dalloway or even a Great Detective be born in these streets today?' he thunders.

He may go over the top a bit, old Michael, especially when venting his spleen over the spray-paint modernism of Thatcher's Britain (he gets similarly steamed up, to less effect, over the Deadly Menace of Pornography in other sections of the book), but this whole issue of the contracting mythical aura of the nation's capital is a significant one. It formed the imaginative hub of the sprawling magnum opus which was his last novel, *Mother London*, and has been a dully gleaming sub-text in the dozens of pulp novels he has churned out since the Sixties.

Moorcock may be interested in juggling the time-worn tropes of heroic fantasy, but that doesn't mean he's interested in escapism; his imagination is firmly inscribed in the bricks and mortar of London – theatre of history, scene of memory. For a science fiction writer, he's not at all drawn to the future; the only new world he wants to explore is the debris of the old one half-buried beneath today's high street. Hence his resentment of the gentrification of Notting Hill Gate, his profound attachment – expressed here in 'Building the New Jerusalem' – to the bomb-scarred ruins of his childhood. For him, London means Dickens and Conrad, not Burtons and Conran.

But this kind of prophetic nostalgia isn't really so surprising when you come down to it. Science fiction could almost be generically defined by its gothic links with eighteenth-century English Romanticism – the same horror of industry and progress, of Blake's dark satanic mills, the same nostalgia for an imaginary English Eden, whether Jerusalem or the New World. Think not just of H. G. Wells' blasted civilisations, but of Conan Doyle's little-known scientific romances, like *The Lost World*, or Mervyn Peake's grotesque dystopia, *Gormenghast* – both big influences on Moorcock (there's an appreciation of Peake included in the volume).

Moorcock is a writer quite at home in the ruins of England's past. The six stories in *Casablanca*, drawn from various stages in his prolific career, are all suffused with a familiar End of Empire lassitude, whether set in a post-colonial Morocco, a post-WWI Europe of half-forgotten urgencies or a Martian dustbowl of crumbling monuments. The same impotent lanquor even shapes the episodic construction of these tales, which seem compressed, half-formed – or half-eroded, perhaps – like the fading memories of ancient superstitions. But it is precisely such entropic fantasies as these which spark the imagination of this gloomy Romantic. Glowing amidst the narrative rubble of each story is the treasure of an enigmatic but compelling epiphany: a Roman Catholic cardinal frozen inside the ice of an alien world, a shred of human skin tattooed with the map of a lost Carthaginian city, an old Royal Albert bicycle used as a time machine. Very strange. But also, occasionally rather whimsical.

Where it all really comes together is with the brilliant novelette, *Gold Diggers of 1977*, a substantially revised version of the story originally commissioned ten years ago as a companion piece to the punk movie, *The Great Rock'n'Roll Swindle*. If Greil Marcus in his recent door-stopping tome *Lipstick Traces* treats the Sex Pistols as a curious example of Dadaist anti-art, for Moorcock they belong squarely in the blinding tradition of English prophetic poetry alongside Blake and Shelley.

A fragmentary collage of jokes, incidental routines and fantasies, *Gold Diggers* is by turns sharp, savage and funny. It revives Moorcock's great Seventies creation, Jerry Cornelius – one of the few credible portrayals of the English rock star as mythical anti-hero (along with Nick Cohn's Johnny Angelo). Last surviving member of the League of Musician Assassins, Jerry recruits his martyred buddies from the rock'n'roll hall of fame, the Cafe Hendrix, and together they gatecrash the Pistols' infamous gig on the Thames and take out the Houses of Parliament with a sonic barrage.

Of course, it all ends in tears. Or as Jerry's fat, wheezing old mum puts it: 'You can bet your chains we won't have anarchy in the UK in our lifetime. Just the usual bloody chaos.' Ah, for the good old days, eh Mrs C?

REMIXOLOGIST #2
i-D, 117, june 1993

Alex Paterson is sitting at his dining room table rolling a joint while reflecting on the success the Orb has brought him over the last four years. 'To be really honest I can't see how we ever got off the ground. But we did. We just had an amazing bit of luck with "Huge Ever Growing" and then, to top it all off, "Little Fluffies". Which are two really good singles. In the future, I can see people thinking of the Orb as those two songs and nothing else.'

He lights up, inhales, releases smoke from his lungs. 'But then we have got "Blue Room" and "Assassin" as well,' he admits. The terrapins splash around in their tank in the corner, the window-box sweet peas are coming on nicely, the crystal on display in the background persists as vainly as any mantelpiece ornament. I take a drag on the offered joint and think that Dr Alex Paterson is an Englishman at home in his castle. Even if that castle takes the form of an ex-council house in Battersea, where candles burn brightly against the slow gloom of a Bank Holiday afternoon.

The story of the Orb is now a recognised landmark of Planet Pop. How Paterson was a roadie with Killing Joke, got a job as an A&R man for Brian Eno's ambient label, rubbed shoulders with the squat nucleus of what was to become the KLF, started dabbling in the Transcentral studio with Jimmy Cauty and came up with an early version of 'A Huge Ever Growing Pulsating Brain that Rules from the Centre of the Ultraworld' in 1989. How he was given a slot as a DJ by Paul Oakenfold on his Land of Oz night at Heaven, bumped into Steve Hillage after playing his 'Rainbow Dome Musick' and later started to gig with the rehabilitated hippie guitarist. How in the interval he teamed up with his old pal Youth from Killing Joke and mixed 'Little Fluffy Clouds' with the help of a young sound engineer called Thrash in the summer of 1990.

According to Paterson's drastically abbreviated view of his own recording career, that's the end of the story. But there's more to it than that. He's missing out how Cauty left the Orb for the KLF and was replaced by Thrash. How the band released their first album, *Adventures Beyond the Ultraworld*, complete with cover art which gently poked fun at the sleeve of Pink Floyd's *Animals* album (instead of inflatable pigs flying over Battersea power station there was a cloud shaped like a turntable). How their second album, *U F Orb*, went to the top of the charts last year only to be slagged off for its cosmic pretensions by old punk rockers (Tony Parsons reckoned it was 'full of shit'). How the 39-minute-long 'Blue Room' got them on to *Top of the Pops*, where they proceeded to play chess in best stick-it-up-yer-jumper fashion. How the release of 'Assassin' seemed to mark a break in the continuing development of the Orb story.

For Paterson, the first few months of '93 have been a period of reappraisal, hard work, and reinvention. The first thing he's decided is that he's not getting a good deal from his record company. It was Youth who persuaded Big Life to sign the Orb when the underground success of 'Huge Ever Growing' became something which Paterson's own indie label, WAU! Mr Modo, could no longer handle. Big Life secured the rights to the Minnie Ripperton sample which forms the basis of the track and re-released it in early 1990. From then on, they have been with the Orb every step of the way. Which looks like being one step too many as far as the good doctor is concerned. He is worried that the existence of WAU! Dr Modo as an independent entity has been compromised by the deal with Big Life. He is also worried about the small size of the royalty cheques he has been receiving. He won't be drawn on the details, but there are rumours that the Orb are about to be signed by another label and repositioned as an act which is more adult-orientated rock than ambient house.

What is certain is that Paterson has been busy. There are some new remixes of Yellow Magic Orchestra, Front 242 and Bill Laswell's Material waiting to come out. Meanwhile, the Orb has two albums in the can. The first, *Orbus Tyrannus*, features as its signature track something called 'Valley', which was recorded in the open air with 'Star 6&7&9' collaborator Tom Green on his parents' Dorset farm along with Simon Phillips. It also includes two tracks recorded in Berlin: a Thomas Fehlmann collaboration called 'Plateau' and a thing with Sun Electric called 'Pom Fritz' (which Paterson refers to as the 'new Fluffy Clouds'). There was also a plan to include a track which featured Robert Fripp. But when Paterson and Thrash went down to Dorset with the ex-King Crimson guitarist for three days in February, he threw them so many 'extremely weird noises' that things escalated and they assembled enough material for a second album, *Hidden in Heaven*.

All of this is presumably going to be used by the Orb as a bargaining chip with any potential new record company. Paterson explains what led to the break: 'We thought we were on the same side of the fence as Big Life. Obviously we weren't. I've got a record label to look after on top of it all. We had two records that were coming out this year and then we were injuncted by Big Life because they presumed they were Orb tracks under different names. This is where all the trouble started. That's what all the Orb stuff came out on in the first place and then Big Life licensed it from us. It's just a big mess really.'

A lot of the major record companies have been rubbing their hands with barely disguised glee at the post-rave development of ambient house. What started out as an ambiguously phrased joke with the KLF's *Chill Out* album three years ago (itself a spin-off from Cauty's Transcentral experiments with Paterson) has now become a serious money-making concern. The Orb have per-suaded a generation of ravers to stop buying 12 inches and start buying albums as much as they have educated musical tastes. And that means higher profit margins. Paterson is hip to all this. He did work at Eno's EG Records for six years (he did the whole yuppie number, complete with suit and pension plan). His spacey blue eyes harden slightly as he gets down to brass tacks. 'Through my experiences with record companies, I know when I'm being taken for a ride. It's not as if we're bread-heads. I've got a nice flat but then I am 33 bloody years old. I don't want to be squatting for the rest of me life. Time to move on innit really?'

The mention of his squatting days is a reminder of the cultural influences under which Paterson has laboured with the Orb. After quitting Bromley art college at the end of the Seventies, he ended up squatting in Ladbroke Grove and Brixton (where he hung out with the likes of King Kurt and Under Two Flags) before going straight and getting his day-job at EG in 1986. The squat culture of the early Eighties was a hybrid affair – part-hippy, part-punk, part-dread – whose environmental soundtrack was dub and whose drug of choice was draw. Paterson got heavily into both.

The fluid dub, drop-out bass, weighty rhythms and trippy sound effects of a typi-cal Orb track all have their origins in the mutoid wastelands of London. The vacant spaces of Ladbroke Grove and Brixton were where the utopian debris left over from the hippie scene was reactivated by the critical fall-out from punk and regenerated by the apocalyptic rumblings of rasta-dom. The result was a new mutant strain of English millenarian culture whose defining moment was the release of Pil's *Metal Box* in 1980.

An old copy of the album (in its original bomb-proof canister) still has pride of place on Paterson's shelf above his dining room table. He looks up at it benignly through a cloud of smoke. 'I was in the lucky position where I sold it for a fiver for draw once and then bought it back off the geezer when he needed some. That's how I used to look at my records at one point. As draw commodities.' He beams.

The route which took Paterson to the squatlands of London was a typically eccentric one. Born and bred in Battersea, he was bundled off at a tender age to a boarding school in Banbury reserved for spoilt brats and problem kids (it was here that he first met Youth). Kingham Hill School was a tough joint which sent a lot of its inmates quietly mad. Paterson coped with it by getting into his head, listening to reggae and playing chess.

The two activities remain linked in his mind, perhaps as different ways of regu- lating internal psychic tension. 'I remember the first day I ever beat me older brother at chess. I cried. Because I thought I'd really upset him. It was like when I bought this reggae album – *Under Heavy Manners* by Prince Far-I – and got him into reggae. I was really chuffed.'

Paterson's brother is now a traveller and part of the reason why he wants to make a bit of money is so he can help him out. Meanwhile, the music of the Orb is extremely popular in Her Majesty's prisons (as, of course, is chess). Funny how things turn out. 'All these prisoners wrote to John Peel after he'd played one of our sessions. I was really touched. It's escapism. And that's what the Orb's about. It's not about commercial pop records, it's about escaping with your own music. And if you physically can't escape then, fair enough, you can understand it.'

The move which took Paterson from Kingham Hill to the cultural playground which was Ravensbourne College of Art and Design in 1976 came with the force of a revelation. It unsprung him completely and maybe explains his interest in the repercussive powers of spaced-out dub. 'I went from a single-sex boarding school to a place where there was a three to one ratio of girls to boys and loads of punks. When I say "punks" I'm not talking about the preconceived ideas that you have. I'm talking about people that were like clowns running around, people who just had completely free ideas of what they wanted to do. They were wandering round wearing ripped PVC, bin-liners, cardboard boxes, pyjamas, anything. Anything that looked out of the norm, the normal everyday thing that was happening in the mid-Seventies.'

He was into disco before he was into punk and used to hang out at the Global Village and Busby's. 'I started getting called a punk cos I was dying me hair orange. But I wasn't a punk, I was wearing soulboy stuff at the time. But then cos I had ear-rings in I was also getting beaten up. You used to get attacked by people for wearing those clothes. Nowadays people can wear whatever they want, you don't tend to get workmen chasing you or a brickie laying into you. Oh, how we had to suffer for the young.'

Paterson has slipped into a Johnny Rotten voice at this point. It's reminiscent of the recent cover of 'No Fun' the Orb did for John Peel, which was the Stooges by way of the Sex Pistols. This has been interpreted as a clever act of postmodern pop pastiche, an imitation of an appropriation. But it is not that at all. It is an act of cultural remembrance heavily inflected with whimsy. The Orb are not ironists, they are humourists. If Fredric Jameson's definition of postmodernism as 'inverted millenarianism' is borne in mind, it becomes clear that the Orb are not postmodern. They do not think that the cultural assets of history have been frozen and that all that is left for future artists is to randomly reshuffle them. They think, obscurely, that history can be redeemed.

This is the source of Paterson's notorious espousal of the whole New Age cosmology of dolphins and UFOs. It is not that he really believes in it (he admits that the punk side of him is in agreement with Tony Parsons on that score). It's that it is the only generally available cultural language which attempts to organise a collective sense of yearning. He trusts the utopian impulse behind it more than he does its imagery. Add that up and what you get is a willing suspension of disbelief. You get whimsy, nonsense, the whole English nursery sensibility of Edward Lear and Lewis Carroll.

As in so many English utopian myths, it all goes back to lost childhood. Paterson grounds his interest in star systems and extra-terrestrials in the science fiction TV of the Sixties, which was a collective cultural experience shared by lots of little boys who otherwise never met. Same time, same channel, same imaginary place. 'I tell you, since I've been doing this the people who have had most interest are people of my age who have actually been brought up watching *Land of the Giants* and *Lost in Space* on a Friday evening after school. It must affect your brain in some way.'

In many ways, the story behind something like 'Blue Room', with its secret NASA holding tank full of captured aliens, is simply a forgotten episode of *Lost in Space*. Once you begin thinking like that then the aural soundscapes of the Orb take on a whole new perspective. All the ambient noise – the astronaut transmissions, running water, Kraftwerk stuff, birdsong, chopper blades, traffic horns, doorbells and barking dogs – are not so much samples in the postmodern sense as illuminated fragments from a collectively remembered past.

Take the Minnie Ripperton vocal in 'Huge Ever Growing'. Everyone knows that. And if you don't, Dr Paterson is there to remind you. The vinyl scratchiness of the sample explicitly signals that this is an act of cultural remembrance (rather than one-upmanship), while the stupid tom-toms, Tarzan jungle noises and goonish nonsense take the melancholy out of the nostalgia and turn it into a bit of a laugh. 'I remember hearing "Loving You" for the first time on the radio in my yard in Battersea when I was living with my mum when I was little, about eleven. My mum turns around to me and she goes, "Gawd, that boy can't get in tune" – 'Mum, it's not a boy, it is in tune, it's a girl". Even then.'

Paterson has often been compared unfavourably to Eno as an ambient musician and remixer. But he is plugged into a living culture in ways that his former boss is not. Eno's references are to avant-garde composers like La Monte Young and Terry Riley whereas Paterson's are to whatever was on in the background when he was a kid. Eno keeps his mind in trim by reading state-of-the-art philosophers like Richard Rorty. Paterson prefers to go slumming with trashy books on UFOs which revive memories of Erich Von Daniken. Eno is interested in games, Paterson in rituals.

What they share (besides a whimsical sense of humour) is a common interest in dissolving traditional notions of cultural production and consumption. Both are in big demand as remixers and both, in their separate ways, interrogate received categories of authorship. When Paterson is hired to do a remix, he pulls out a fragment from the original recording and completely reworks it in ways which often make it indistinguishable from a typical Orb track. The difference is that they get paid for their trouble instead of having to get clearance rights for the original fragment. Take Paterson's ambient hip hop remix of Erasure's 'Ship of Fools'. It was barely recognisable as an Erasure track and the band hated it (although their record company loved it). Or, to look at it from the other side, take 'Little Fluffies'. The Rickie Lee Jones vocal which forms the basis of the single (significantly, she is wittering on about the Arizona skies of her childhood) didn't need to be cleared because the spoken word counts as 'free' noise. But that didn't stop the American singer's management company trying to reclaim it as a Rickie Lee Jones remix.

Paterson is probably more radical than Eno in that he does not insist on his authorial singularity but is prepared to designate 'the Orb' as a collective identity which can shelter any number of collaborators, from Steve Hillage to Jah Wobble, Thomas Fehlmann to Bobby Gillespie. At the time of writing, the Orb has been reinvented in the image of a 'rock band', with Paterson at the turntable, Thrash (who now prefers to be known as Kristian Weston) on keyboards, Nick Burton on drums and Simon Phillips on bass.

The plan is not to go touring so much as to host a series of intimate raves. Paterson likes to think of it as inviting an audience into his studio. Or even viceversa. 'It's like having a mobile studio on-stage. As opposed to recording it, we've got everything laid down so we can actually do remixes of each track we've done now. It's mixing live essentially.'

It's also a way of celebrating cultural communion. The Orb are the missing link between punk and the rave scene. It's no surprise that yet another English subculture has been accepted into the fold of the steadily building hippie-punk whiterasta caravan. What started out as a single utopian event (whether marked by the magic numbers '1967', '1976' or '1988') has developed into a collective material body of New Age Travellers. The Orb make roots music for the dispossessed.

Is there a message to something like 'A Huge Ever Growing Pulsating Brain that Rules from the Centre of the Ultraworld'? If there is, it's a very simple one. It's a broadcast to all the whores, skunk pussies, buggers, crusties, dreads, slackers, dopers, ravers, squatheads. All the inmates of Planet Pop. Hey, you out there! Dr Alex Paterson is calling you home.

hard men

You are going out to drink with your male friends in Soho and drift between the pubs and the clubs. The clubs have door policies and are strictly for media professionals and wannabes, the pubs spill out on the streets. You are standing on the corner outside the Coach & Horses talking about Michel de Certeau, zombie movies and the legacy of Marx. Paul designates collective membership of an intellectual underclass and the other blokes peel off to network and pursue their careers. The two of you are left to deal with the homeless guys who circle the block on the lookout for spare change. Each time they pass by they're older and their tales are more desperate. There's one bastard keeps offering you a nip. You remember interviewing old Soho boho Robin Cook in a ghost pub off Fleet Street. He said: 'You don't look down on the bums crashed out in Dean Street. You get them one in at the bar.'

Harvey Keitel sits across from me in a reception room at the Savoy Hotel stirring his coffee. He is dressed soberly in a dark jacket and trousers. His legs are crossed and his ankles are bare. I am asking him a long complicated question to do with his involvement in the American independent film *Reservoir Dogs*, a winningly hip, abrasively comic and brutally obscene take on the heist movie which has been one of the hits of this year's international festival circuit. It seems as if Keitel is listening attentively to what I'm saying, but then he suddenly starts muttering to himself. 'Damn! I used the wrong spoon.' There is a clatter as the sugar spoon he has been using is ejected on to the table. Then he leans forward and fixes me with a lunatic grin. 'Well, hang me from the Tower.'

   This is a typical piece of Method 'business'. It is the kind of loaded gestural activity which Keitel would have learned was useful for characterising and condensing emotion when he was studying at the Actors' Studio in New York 25 years ago. He learned his lesson well and like many performers, he can't resist the temptation to click into action even when faced with an audience of one in the confining space of an interview. At one point, I lob him an easy question. Why do so many of the characters he plays appear to be men on the edge? He responds by delivering a line from the *Katha Upanisad*, a sacred Indian text on the quest of the hero for knowledge. 'Like a razor's edge is the path, difficult to traverse – so the poets declare.' He pauses for full dramatic emphasis. 'Don't you feel that way yourself?' I respond that I suspect I'm not quite out there on the edge with him. 'You wanna go there?' he demands, eyeballing me in a way that is completely indecipherable. I have to admit that I don't. At which point there is laughter and a triumphant shrug. 'That's just it. Therein lies the hero's journey. There are no guarantees about anything.'

   Throughout our little chat, flashes of impatience, arrogance and self-mockery strobe Keitel's coarse features like so many fluttery distress signals. He works himself up and brings himself down. His hands are eloquent and aggressive. He is fond of making eye contact, not as a means of asserting dominance, more as a way of testing limits and establishing boundaries. He periodically scans his surroundings to check on new arrivals. At one point during the interview, we have to move tables because another hotel guest is sitting too close to him ('Look at this! He's sitting right over here. I can't believe it … this whole room … imagine!'). Keitel may come on like a tough guy, but there is something precious about him as well.

   His brand of machismo was date-stamped by the Marine Corps in the early Sixties. He joined up when he was 17 immediately after leaving high school and it is clear that the experience marked him tremendously. He punishes himself in the gym every day, walks stiffly with his chest puffed out like a bantam cock, and has a firm hand-shake. He appears in good shape for a man of 45. Or he would if it weren't for his face, which looks wrecked. It's as if everything purged from his body – the sag of confusion, the lines of anxiety – has worked its way back into his expression. Although he didn't serve in Vietnam, he does seem damaged in some way.

   This obscure sense of private injury is what fuels the intense energy of his acting. Keitel is quite simply one of the best in the business and he has the track-record to prove it. The list of directors he has worked with reads like a Who's Who of auteurism. There is Martin Scorsese, who first used Keitel as his jangly alter-ego in *Who's That Knocking at My Door?* and *Mean Streets*, the director's two defining New York neighbourhood hang-out movies, and then went on to give him small but memorable parts in *Alice Doesn't Live Here Anymore*, *Taxi Driver* and *The Last Temptation of Christ*. Then there is Paul Schrader, who stuck him between Richard Pryor and Yaphet Kotto in *Blue Collar* as a regular working guy shafted by the system. These films are still those he is most renowned for. But over the years, Keitel has worked for a host of reputable slipstream figures, ranging from maverick American modernists like Robert Altman and Alan Rudolph to European art-house darlings like Ettore Scolas, Lina Wertmuller, Nicolas Roeg and Bertrand Tavernier.

With his dense face and squat build, he is a difficult actor to cast. He has never been leading man material and is often shunted to one side in a moody support role. Most usually, he is a cop (*Thelma & Louise*, *Mortal Thoughts*) or a gangster (*Bugsy*, *Sister Act*). He can fill these slots well enough but, when given the space to really get to work, he is capable of hitting the jackpot. His detailed performance as a corrupt cop baffled by rage and disgust in Roberto Faenza's psycho thriller *Order of Death* was astonishing. He didn't have to shout and scream to grab your attention. All he had to do was sit there in his empty apartment, ritually clipping his cigars and listening to his stereo, and you could feel the guilt coming off him in waves.

It is rare for Keitel to be used at his full potential. He is not a bankable actor and has to fight for parts. At an age where most actors would have made it to the flash-lit slopes of stardom or slithered into the nether-world of cult celebrity, he still feels he has to prove himself. No wonder he finds it hard to relax. Even in the protected environment of the Savoy, with its orderly calm and massive weight, he exudes an aura of barely contained hysteria. I have the distinct impression that the reason Keitel submits himself to the intensive regime of the Method – with its textual analysis, reflection and emotional preparation – is not to psyche himself up but wind himself down.

Not that he has anything to berate himself for at the moment. Two recent films confirm that he is on something of a professional roll. Not only does he get to punch at his full weight in *Reservoir Dogs*, in which he plays an ageing professional thief whose emotions get in the way of his survival instincts when he is hired to pull a diamond heist with five other guys, but he has been given the chance to stretch himself to the full in the harrowing urban psychodrama, *Bad Lieutenant*, which plots the descent of a corrupt cop into an inferno of addiction, despair and brutality.

Both films are highly personal and defiantly anti-commercial. *Reservoir Dogs* is the directorial debut of Quentin Tarantino, a 29-year-old hotshot who despite never going to film school has already begun to generate comparisons with Scorsese. Meanwhile, *Bad Lieutenant* is the latest excursion into the decadent sub-world of contemporary New York to be directed by Abel Ferrara, whose previous credits include such avant-exploitation movies as *Driller Killer*, *Ms. 45* and *King of New York*.

Does it feel like a comeback? 'I would prefer not to use the word comeback,' replies Keitel with elaborate precision. He shifts the weight in his chair and frowns. 'I would prefer to say that now is as equal a part of my journey as the past has been. Because the idea of a comeback can be applied on a very material level – in terms of Hollywood, blah, blah, blah. The more important thing is the idea of a journey. This is a part of it, as was the quiet period when I wasn't getting the work I was hoping to.' Does he regret any of the parts he took during that period? 'First of all, I am a working man,' he replies. 'Like any other working man, I have to pay the rent. Like you do,' he says, pointing to the tape on the table between us. 'I have to clothe myself. Like you do. Feed my children. Like you do. There's no other way to do that than by working and making money. Films like *Reservoir Dogs* and *Bad Lieutenant* I did for very, very little money, at a great sacrifice. And these other commercial films I've done to make some money – that's a part of my journey.'

Keitel's wilful fatalism obscures the level of his behind-the-scenes involvement in *Reservoir Dogs*. Tarantino was working as a video sales clerk when he turned out his screenplay. He originally planned to shoot the thing in 16mm black and white from the back of a car but gave himself two months to try and get financing. His partner and producer, Lawrence Bender, showed the script to his old acting coach, Lily Parker, who, like Keitel, was a member of the Actors' Studio. She mailed the script to her old friend and Keitel was on the phone to Tarantino within a day of reading it.

Keitel was brought in as a co-producer, put together the pieces of a deal for Tarantino and helped him audition actors. In the end, Tim Roth, Michael Madsen, Steve Buscemi, Eddie Bunker and Tarantino himself were recruited as the other members of the gang, while Lawrence Tierney (a veteran Hollywood character actor) is the wheezing mobster who hires them and Chris (brother of Sean) Penn is his doting son. Keitel was also active in rehearsal. 'I asked for a month's rehearsal, we got two weeks,' he remembers. Given that the film is highly speech-driven, a litany of slangy abuse punctuated by gobbets of violence and scored to an incongruous soundtrack of Seventies bubblegum music, he was able to block out the action almost as a stage play so that, as he puts it, 'when it was time for Quentin to shoot, all the problems had been solved in rehearsal and did not need to be solved on the set.'

Reservoir Dogs has been compared by some critics to *Mean Streets*, in terms of its expert phrasing of male manners, its knowing use of pop music and its sheer cinematic confidence. But there are real differences between the two films. Scorsese was attempting to define the moods, rhythms and textures which belonged to the Italian-American culture of his native New York. Tarantino is one generation down the line. He is a deracinated suburban kid whose spirit country is mapped by the cultural accretions of the media. *Reservoir Dogs* lacks the urban density of *Mean Streets*; its most exalted moments have to do with a certain shared expertise with pop culture.

What is interesting is that Harvey Keitel should have been sufficiently alert to have worked with both men. Maybe it has something to do with his own background. He was born in Brooklyn in 1947, the son of hard-working Polish Jews who ran a refreshment stall at nearby Brighton Beach. He decided he wanted to be an actor after leaving the Marines and first met Scorsese as a result of answering a newspaper ad placed by the New York University film student when he was working on his thesis project, *Who's That Knocking at My Door?*. Scorsese has remarked that he felt an immediate affinity with Keitel despite their different ethnic backgrounds: 'I became friends with him, got to know him, and found we had the same feelings about the same problems. Both our families expected us to achieve some sort of respectability.'

It was as a result of meeting Scorsese that Keitel got to work with Robert De Niro, who has been up-staging him ever since. The routines they worked up between themselves are some of the best things in each of the films they have appeared in (let's draw a discreet veil over the banal *Falling In Love*). There's the bar scene in *Mean Streets* where Keitel's natty hoodlum tries to tame the antic wildness of De Niro's hopeless loser. And then there's *Taxi Driver*, the alienation movie which caught the mood of a generation. One of the best scenes in the film discovers Keitel's jittery neighbourhood pimp doing a deal with De Niro's appalled and confused urban avenger (De Niro: 'I'm hip!' Keitel: 'Funny, you don't look hip.'). It's Keitel's business with the folded handkerchief that really makes the scene. He keeps touching his lips with it in a reflex gesture which manages to be obscene and delicate at the same time.

Quentin Tarantino, Martin Scorsese, Paul Schrader, James Toback on *Fingers*, Ridley Scott on *The Duellists*, Alan Rudolph on *Welcome to LA* – Keitel has a habit of working with first-time directors. He also has a reputation for being hard to handle, not because he is capricious but because he is so serious. He needs a long time to study and prepare for a role, he generally isolates himself on set and he is fond of pitching in with his own ideas on how a scene should be played. Certainly, he has the capacity to reduce strong men to tears. Schrader has reported that the tension between Keitel and Richard Pryor was so bad on *Blue Collar* that it nearly gave him a nervous breakdown. At one point he had to grab Keitel and force him to the floor to drive home the message that he should never break a take just because he felt that Pryor was edging him out of shot.

Keitel obviously needs measured treatment. Something which Francis Coppola failed to understand when he wanted him to appear in *Apocalypse Now*. Keitel was originally offered the part of Willard, the jaded vet whose mission it is to travel into the psychedelic heart of darkness that is Vietnam and capture the great white whale that is Marlon Brando's mad Colonel Kurtz. He quit because Coppola wanted him to sign a contract which he considered dictatorial. Having missed serving in Vietnam when he was in the Marines, he was not about to take any lessons in manners from some counterfeit Field Marshal playing soldiers in the Philippines.

Even now the memory rankles and sends Keitel off on some private jag of slightly paranoid ratiocination. 'Listen, obviously to make it for three years in the Marines you must be disciplined, you must be willing to compromise. Compromise. But there's a difference between compromising and being shoved around. You get my point? I'm willing to compromise. I have as much difficulty compromising as the next guy, but I recognise its necessity. But I will not be shoved around. By anybody.' Looking back, you can see he made the right decision. Martin Sheen replaced him in the film, was pushed over the edge by Coppola, had a heart attack and never acted seriously again.

Whereas Keitel is still going strong. *Bad Lieutenant* is as much his creation as Abel Ferrara's. He explains it as an attempt to renew the message of the Bible by updating its imagery. Many of the scenes are his creation and they pulse with anger and despair. He curses and weeps, he does a full-frontal nude scene, he appears out of it for many of the scenes where his character is smoking crack or injecting himself with heroin. Was he conscious of taking risks with this film? 'Risks?' Keitel creases his brow. He stares down at his hands, then raises his head and looks me in the eye. 'If I want to know, I will have to take risks. Anyone who wants to know will have to walk the razor's edge, or else just shut the fuck up, go and be commercial, make your money and shut the fuck up.' He is scowling.

Yes. Well. Let's talk about that option. Shutting the fuck up. 'That option,' he repeats. Suddenly his mood blows over and he starts laughing. 'It is an option, isn't it?' Of course. We are both chuckling by now. 'What I meant when I seemed a little upset before, is that I have no patience for those who don't study the craft of acting. I have no patience for those who don't get involved in telling stories that are relevant to our well-being as citizens, to help us to advance. Yes, there's room for entertainment in the cinema and in the theatre. But it's unbalanced right now. There's too much commerciality, too much entertainment.'

When I naughtily try to steer the conversation to *Saturn 3*, a ludicrous psycho-science fiction movie which is one of the most 'entertaining' things he has ever done, he becomes extremely agitated. 'Let me say this to you – okay? – because I see a road that you're going down. I'm going to say this and then I'm going to get off the subject. That year I did *Saturn 3* I turned down five hundred thousand dollars' worth of work because I felt the films were not socially conscious. You can call my agent from that time and he'll tell you about it. I was down to not being able to pay my rent and I took *Saturn 3*. Does that answer your question?'

Absolutely. Every actor has done schlock at some point in their lives. Only an actor like Keitel could feel guilty about it. Not that he has too much to worry about at the moment. There is a sense in which he is reaching the peak of his career. The comparison with his old rival is instructive. Whereas De Niro has moved into producing films for his studio complex at Tribeca in New York and seems to be pursuing a determinedly mainstream tack with his acting, Keitel is still out there on the edge. The little guy obviously has powers of endurance which are staggering. Who would have known he had it in him?

CYRIL COLLARD
arena, 40, july/august 1993

The Césars ceremony in Paris last March couldn't quite match the Oscars for show. But what it lacked in glitz, it made up for in gush. Cyril Collard was universally acknowledged as the saviour of the French film industry three days after he had died of complications from AIDS. His urgent, amoral, semi-autobiographical and fiercely tender debut feature, *Les Nuits Fauves* (*Savage Nights*), collected four awards and a host of personal tributes. It made you wonder where everyone was when the 35-year-old director was trying to get his film made, for not only did he have trouble getting the finance together, he also had problems casting the lead. It was not as if he were an unknown. A notorious bourgeois apostate, Collard had reneged on his upbringing (Catholic school, engineering college) and fled to Puerto Rico to become a pan-sexual hedonist and have-a-go artist. Unlike many who take a walk on the wild side, however, he had the talent to pull it off. Returning to Paris, he was taken on as an assistant by Maurice Pialat, one of the Grand Old Men of French cinema, and helped him out on three films. He also formed a rock band, shot music videos and turned out a series of highly acclaimed shorts, among them the tele-film, *Taggers*, about the combat between graffiti artists and the law. His big break came with the publication of his first novel, *Condamne Amour*, in 1987, which was followed two years later by *Les Nuits Fauves*. Not a bad track record for someone who was originally destined to become another engineer.

So why all the problems on turning his second novel into a film? Well, the film's protagonist, Jean, is a coke-sniffing bisexual hedonist who commits the ultimate act of sexual irresponsibility: he comes inside a girl without telling her he is HIV positive. You can understand why several leading French actors were put off. But you can also understand that this was not really a disappointment to Collard. Having written the script for *Savage Nights*, composed the incidental score and put his name on the director's chair, he was not exactly going to shy away from playing the lead. It was going to be his film all the way.

Collard was one of the first French public figures to admit that he was HIV positive way back in 1986. But he has always been a difficult figure for the AIDS industry to patronise. Like the religious fundamentalists who stigmatised AIDS when it first appeared, Collard considers that the disease confers a special distinction: 'What happens when AIDS hits you? You feel fear, a profound fear: but at the same time a strange calm comes and takes you in hand. It turns fatality into destiny, in which you can dredge up out of even the filthiest depths those insights into truth, love and lust that console you for your pain.'

It is ironic that the French cultural establishment has attempted to canonise him as another heroic AIDS martyr. His meaning is very different. *Savage Nights* has become a cult film for French youth precisely because of the way it trashes conventional pieties about AIDS. Collard was quite prepared to romanticise his affliction, to make the proscribed link between Illness and Metaphor, to die young and have a good-looking effigy. The man dubbed the 'little prince' was renowned for his narcissism: it would not be surprising to find such Collard relics as film posters and picture-books being flogged in the same Left Bank shrines devoted to the perpetuation of the cults of James Dean and Jim Morrison.

Like a lot of French artists and intellectuals before him, Collard was heavily into transgression. *France-Soir* did the perfect job of nailing his cultural presumptions when it called him 'the spiritual child of Genet and Pasolini, convinced like Bataille that eroticism and death are inextricably linked.' That's an awful lot of proper names to get into one sentence, although the more severely critical may want to linger over the word 'child' more than anything else.

It would be possible to write off *Savage Nights* as 'adolescent' if it weren't so clear, confident and strong. Jean may be a rebel without a cause (in the novel he admits to his frustration that he was born too late to participate in any of the great revolutionary struggles), but he is no male hysteric. His lusts are sudden, precise and exacting and he indulges them without complaining – though never without thinking. Indeed, it is the extravagant links made between gesture, sensation and meaning which make up the madly racing heart of the film. Collard puts it best in the novel (which has just been published in translation by Quartet): 'For certain looks, certain gestures, even if I know their sincerity will only last a few seconds, I'd wait a hundred years.'

Like the novel, the film is a thing of fragments. Set in Paris in 1986, it tracks the tangled personal involvements of Jean as he cruises Paris squeezing hard, fast and sometimes dangerous sparks from its combustible slew of transvestite bars, late-night pick-up grounds and busy streets full of skinheads and Arab immigrants. In the film's most disturbing scenes, he takes a savage pleasure in submitting himself to the pain and degradation of rough (though safe) sex with strangers. These are ambiguous rites of purification whose aftermath is best described in the novel: 'Standing soiled and bruised at the river's edge after orgasm, I felt graceful and light.'

It is as this level of contact – hard, fluid, anonymous – that Jean pitches his game. A professional cameraman who enjoys playing all the angles, he reserves his most acute feelings for Sammy, a moody young blood from the streets, while toying with the affections of Laura, an absurdly young *gamine* whose charm belies her violent temper. But this is no conventional love triangle. Sammy is into beating up Arabs, slashing himself with a knife in front of the mirror and other sado-masochistic rituals. He consents to sex with Jean only because it provides another strong sensation. Laura, meanwhile, is romantically attached to Jean in a way that eventually leaves her rejected, exhausted and dispossessed. She pesters him on the phone and leaves reams of crazy messages on his answering machine until she is breathless.

Carlos Lopez and Romane Bohringer bring a real drive, intelligence and alertness to their respective roles. When Laura learns the truth about Jean's act of sexual irresponsibility, Bohringer brings more to her reaction than is supplied by the novel. She is violent, tender and indignant all at once. When she is then obliged to slip her moorings and play the typical French stereotype of the girl mad for love, you can't help feeling that her character is being punished for Jean's crime. Lopez, meanwhile, finds himself with a role whose ambiguity has been considerably reduced. In the novel it is revealed that Samy is a Spaniard pretending to be part-Arab in order to play on Jean's guilt-ridden revolutionary fantasies. In the film, he is simply a kinky Spanish skinhead.

There is no moral to *Savage Nights*. It closes with an ambiguous act of surrender which we are invited to think is an acceptance of life rather than a defiance of death. But the film has already done all the work here. Its meaning is in its style. Collard keeps a hand-held camera close to the bodies of his actors, jump cuts around the action to capture moments of intensity as they occur, relies on improvisation, energy and accident. Snatches of music from the Pogues, gypsy songs and Collard's own compositions merge with the cries on the street, with the characters' dreams and desires. A lot of the scenes are out-of-focus or over-exposed. Collard is seeking out those looks and gestures for which he would wait a hundred years if only he had the time. Some of it works and some of it doesn't. At its best it has the raw feel and uncompromising honesty of an early John Cassavetes film. At its worst, it's like some postmodern *Un Homme et Une Femme*, all blowsy and portentous.

Collard seems to have been forced on the defensive after his film was completed. In interviews just before his death, he talks solemnly of 'redemption' and 'Judaeo-Christian themes' and generally tries to suggest that Jean becomes a better person as a result of his experiences. This feels like a defence mechanism and it may have been something Collard was forced into as a result of candidly admitting that Jean's wilful act of irresponsibility was something he himself committed just after he was diagnosed as HIV positive. He has said: 'I must admit being HIV positive is much easier now than in 1986. The same story about Jean in 1992 would make him almost a criminal.' Which is surely the whole point. Collard's iconoclastic instincts lead him to isolate an act of transgression which has real meaning and potential (as a symbolic gesture rather than a real act). But then he backs down at the last minute and settles for a little dose of liberal understanding. It's a shame he wasn't there to pick up his Césars. It's an even bigger shame he won't be making another film.

NATHAN HEARD
i-D, 115, april 1993

Whereas Malcolm X went to jail and became a preacher, Nathan Heard went to jail and reinvented himself in a different way. He became a writer. Both bear out the truth of the saying that prison is the black man's university, a place where the circumstances which have led to one person's incarceration can be understood as the inevitable consequence of a whole people's subjugation. Heard was in and out of reform school for most of the Sixties, finally ending up in the New Jersey state pen at Trenton on an armed robbery charge. It was here that he educated himself. He read books on jazz and African-American history, black Muslim writings, anthropological texts as well as the work of Langston Hughes, James Baldwin, LeRoi Jones (now Amiri Baraka) and Norman Mailer. He also began to write. In 1963 he completed the first draft of *Howard Street*, a ruthlessly unsentimental portrait of the violent Newark ghetto in which he grew up. It was published just prior to his release from Trenton in 1968 and was an immediate critical and commercial hit. Which is why it makes sense for the American indie publisher, Amok, to put it back into print. *Howard Street* is set in 1963, just before President Johnson's 'War on Poverty' programme built the bleak housing projects which dominate the imagination of so much black urban experience today. Heard's pimps, whores, junkies and hustlers belong to an older urban neighbourhood culture, whose tenements, dives, back-alleys and main drags express a denser, more intimate and less alienating vision of human social activity. Less brutal, too. Scores in *Howard Street* are more likely to be settled with fists or knives than with guns. Which doesn't mean people don't get hurt. The novel opens with the ritual abusing of a john by a whore and her pimp. Not only is he ripped off and humiliated, he is stabbed in the back, smashed over the head with a beer bottle and, in a final act of gratuitous viciousness, kicked in the groin as he lies helpless. The event immediately enters into the folklore of the neighbourhood, but not into the record-books of the police. Howard Street as Heard describes it is 'as wild and as rowdy as Dodge City or Tombstone ever was, with no Hitchcock or Earp in evidence.' It is a place ruled by its own codes and rituals (which are themselves supervised by a shadowy white power structure), its inhabitants skewered by an economy of delinquency which unites them only in a common culture of oppression. Heard has plenty of stories to tell. The chief story is about Hip Ritchwood, pimp and dope addict, his best whore, Gypsy Pearl, and his straight brother, Franchot, and how they get caught up in a spiral of mutual need and exploitation which ends in a complex gesture of triumph-in-defeat.

Then there is the story of Jackie Brown, political firebrand turned barstool philosopher; Jimmy Johnson, the mixed-up kid who thinks he's Jimmy Cagney; Slim McNiar, the corrupt cop who hates blacks as only a black man can; and Too Loo and Lillie, the majestic drag queens who model themselves on Hollywood glamour icon, Tallulah Bankhead. Heard portrays *Howard Street* in a hard and bright light, zooming in on the details of slang and body language. He is not averse to moralising the action, but he refuses to judge his characters. Instead he objectifies their behaviour as the historic legacy of racial injustice, with black bodies used, abused, exchanged and mutilated in an unconscious repetition of the slave experience. In this, he goes further than other black urban writers like Iceberg Slim or Donald Goines. What he tends to skimp on is the freighted meaning carried by cultural forms like fashion, music, and food. He also overdoes it with the purple prose at times. But these are small criticisms to make of a great American novel.

JAMES KELMAN
i-D, 91, april 1991

Jim Kelman's ears are burning. Captured by the lights of *The Late Show* camera crew, he's patiently listening to the man from the BBC clatter on about Thatcherism, the plight of the Left and the political meaning of his Booker-nominated novel, *A Disaffection*. 'Of course, it was brilliantly written,' the BBC man gushes. 'But the central character was a bit of a misery. He did seem to be all doom and gloom.'

'I thought he was quite funny,' responds Kelman. 'Perhaps you've missed some of the structural ironies in the novel.' Grins back at the camera. At which point, his inquisitor changes tack and launches into a convoluted dissertation on the significance of the European City of Culture campaign for Glasgow last year.

It's like an anthropological exercise in middle-class wish-fulfilment. Kelman is dragged into the media spotlight as if he were some pristine cultural specimen. The Last Living Socialist, Spokesman for Clydeside, Working Class Culture Hero.

'It is irritating to be treated as some sort of spokesman,' he tells me later. 'It's also part of a mystification process. Rather than seeing that there are a lot of people who are involved and active, society would much rather single out individuals. It's easy to dismiss what might be implied or said by an individual; it's always more difficult to dismiss groups and crowds of people.'

Kelman has been cornered in a Wood Green bookshop during the course of a nationwide reading tour sponsored by the Arts Council. A wiry figure dressed in jeans and an olive green jerkin, he has the spoiled, haunted look which comes from years of hard graft. Only his hard, glittering eyes hint at an imaginative toughness.

Minutes after the BBC have packed up their cameras, Kelman is itching for a drink. We decide to head off to a nearby pub, an appropriate location for the interview. Pubs – along with other male resorts like football terraces and betting shops – bulk large in Kelman's fictions. Smoke-filled arenas of willed oblivion and ritual release, they fill out a symbolic Glaswegian topography whose private aspect is defined by narrow rented rooms and dingy tenement interiors.

Imaginative space in Kelman is always pressured, cramped. Characters are usually out of work, are generally skint. Faced with the blank succession of demands which make up their waking hours, they barely have the means to improvize a response. Instead, they procrastinate and obfuscate. They transform the snagged details of their lives into demonic allegories of paranoia and revenge.

This is the source of Kelman's humour – his clear-eyed view of baroque self-deception, his alert transcription of obsessive linguistic compulsion.

It's there in all his work, in the novels (*The Busconductor Hines*, *A Chancer*, *A Disaffection*) as well as the short story collections (*Not, not while the giro*, *Greyhound for Breakfast*). Even in his present collection, *The Burn*, there are a couple of stories devoted exclusively to the theme of paranoia. One man goes for an early morning walk and imagines the police are secretly spying on him, another bumps into some old friends in a bookshop and immediately assumes that they are out to humiliate him.

By now, we're safely ensconced in a corner of the pub. Over a pint of Guinness and a pack of Marlboro, Kelman discourses in clipped tones about the importance of irony to his craft. 'That's one of the hallmarks of the European existential tradition – the irony. Dostoevsky, Gogol. Incredible irony. It's so black. Without the irony there would be nothing. Real horror. Look at Swift's *A Modest Proposal*. Without the irony there's just the absolute horror of what happened to Ireland under British imperialism. The horror of genocide.'

What about his interest in the paranoid imagination? Is there a similar political dimension to that? 'What's paranoia for some people is reality for others,' he replies. 'There are things that happen to people who get involved in politics in this country. Phone tapping, mail tampering. These are facts of British daily life but they're never really brought into public discourse. So when you talk about it publicly, it comes out like paranoia.'

Conversation with Kelman keeps circling around the iniquities of the British state apparatus. Which makes it all the more surprising that he disclaims any intended political significance for his work. 'The stories are ends in themselves,' he insists.

At the same time, he is highly conscious of how his stories can take on a political colouring despite themselves. 'Although there is no intention to make statements or no intention to be polemical, by writing about your culture you can't help but be political. It's inextricably there. If you draw attention to the plight of people in our society, then not only are you being political but in a sense you're being subversive. By drawing attention to them you imply a cause and you imply also perhaps that there can be solutions. And I don't think society really wants cause or effect to be implied as a concern of social and economic policy.'

If the contents of Kelman's fictions – with their tramps, drifters, rogues and idlers – are political by chance, their style is so by design. As he admits. 'Formally I know that my work is extremely political because of the way that I use narrative. The way that it interferes with standard English literary form – that in itself is a very political act.'

What he is referring to is the refusal to distinguish linguistically between third and first person narration. Both are composed in the same slangy phonetic register, without recourse to the traditional voice of benign Eng Lit 'omniscience'. Kelman understands that language is least neutral when most transparent, that the rolling cadences of William Boyd or Julian Barnes represent a form of 'linguistic imperialism'.

'There is a whole clutch of contemporary mainstream English prose that is ultimately just boring and very old-fashioned. Its authors have never had to question the social values of the system; in that sense, they've never had to question the values of the language they operate in. Consequently, their work is full of shared suppositions – or presuppositions – and that's what makes it seem so cosy and so dull. They lose so much through never having questioned that; they lose the potential for genuine drama and mystery. Because of English Literature's endemic racism and elitism, they can never quite cope with the idea that people who are black or who speak with 'funny accents' can have an actual internal psychological existence.'

Kelman keeps harping on about the insularity of British contemporary fiction as if it's some kind of cultural backwater. Maybe he's got things the wrong way round. Certainly his interest in politics, psychology and language seems very traditional, very modernist. Nowadays we're taught by the prophets of postmodernism that cultural difference is something to be symbolically exploited rather than critically interrogated. It's almost as if the literary armature of modernism can only survive in those parts of the world least touched by the furious energies of late capitalism – in the post-colonial Third World, in the regions.

It's no surprise to learn that Kelman objected so vehemently to the City of Culture campaign. Not so much because it was a con trick played on his hometown (which it was – the staged festivities lost money overall and as a result the council is considering cutting social services and selling off public lands), but because of its attempt to redefine culture in terms of postmodern spectacle. 'It's fairly horrendous,' he says. 'What was presented as a celebration of culture has in fact proved to be an attack on culture. A lot of things will be closing down to pay for last year's losses.'

An additional reason for Kelman's suspicion of whirlwind image change is that he has come up the hard way. After leaving school at 15 he drifted through a succession of dead-end jobs in Glasgow, Manchester and the Channel Islands – factory labour, building site work, anything available. Got married, had a couple of kids. Went to Strathclyde University as a mature student in the Seventies to study English and Philosophy. Signed on the dole at odd times. As late as four years ago he was running round Glasgow in a transit van doing removal work in an effort to support his literary career.

Because, make no mistake, Kelman has been scribbling since the age of 21. 'For me, writing has always been Number One. Even when I was 22 and unemployed or when I was 25 and having to drive buses or 27 and working in a factory. Work was always a means to an end and the end was writing. It's an essential aspect of my life; it's just a way of being, a way of existing. That's what I do.'

Does he resent the hours spent in wage slavery? 'Work does dictate how much writing gets done,' he says. 'A lot of writing that should get done doesn't get done by people because of their having to work eight to ten hours a day for an employer at something they hate. It destroys their time; it destroys their energy.'

Recognition has been a long time coming for Kelman. His first collection of short stories was put out by an American independent publisher in 1973; it wasn't until the mid-Eighties that he landed a contract with Secker & Warburg. Meanwhile it's only in the last year that he's needed to get himself an agent.

The Booker nomination increased sales of his last novel, but it certainly hasn't made him a rich man. He still finds himself in the invidious position of memorialising a class and a culture which has been abandoned by capitalism. 'Not only abandoned, but attacked, victimised and occasionally criminalised. So often people who are at the sharp end of social and economic policy are then victimised; they aren't helped. Part of our system is that there is no such thing as a social policy or an economic policy that has social or economic effects. It is always the victims who are blamed.'

Kelman says he looks forward to living in a 'socialist Scotland' – an ambition shared by such politically motivated Glaswegian showbands as Deacon Blue and Hue And Cry. Is he appreciative of their efforts to smuggle politics into pop? 'To a certain extent. Although the most significant pop event of recent years was the decision made during punk to sing in English rather than American accents. There is no culture without the language of the culture.'

Whether in pop or in prose, it all comes down to a sense of responsibility towards the past. 'It's just pointless to jump back three generations and talk about the great blues players or something. That to me is irresponsible. People really have to look at things more seriously than that. There has to be a point when they realize that they should be taking account of what has happened. Not simply dismissing it as unfashionable.'

At which point, Kelman looks at his watch, slings back his pint and heads out into the night. He has a reading to give in a couple of minutes and he doesn't want to disappoint his audience.

drugs busts

You are in the Clerkenwell office of a trendy lifestyle magazine doing a drugs deal in the toilet. Money for Ecstasy. Your supplier is not reckoned to be the best journalist in town but he gets regular freelance commissions partly because editors find it useful to have him around. The office is still at the stage of being a chill-out space. Clubworld people drift in and out, promo records are spun on the decks, idle chat shifts into print. The magazine is full of illegitimate 'holes' (Gilles Deleuze and Felix Guattari). Years later you pass through the same space to find it an obstructive terrain of Mac clusters, work stations and editorial meetings. The only playground left is a miserable little fag-break zone and that's on its way out of the building. What happened to your supplier? He uses his drug connections to bounce past the style press and land himself a cushy number on Fleet Street.

TOBACCO CRAZE
i-D, 157, october 1996

The story of the burnt-out Westerner who heads off into the South American jungle to commune with native shamans, trip out on psychoactive plant concoctions and come back with a heady brew of stories has become a staple of post-hippie travel litera-ture. The interesting thing about Charles Nicholl's *The Creature in the Map* (Vintage) is that he demonstrates that the template for this particular transformational rite goes all the way back to Sir Walter Ralegh's quest to find El Dorado up the furthest reaches of the Orinoco river in 1595. Nicholl self-consciously organises his book as a stripping away of the layers of superstition and obfuscation surrounding Ralegh's journey and he is supremely adept at sifting the historical documentation (Ralegh's own report of his adventures, *The Discoverie of Guiana*; a parallel account written by minor crew member Francis Sparry; contemporary maps and engravings; Spanish stories of encounters with Ralegh's company) for shards of narrative insight. His own quest is to discover the reality behind the El Dorado myth and to this end he undertook a journey up the Orinoco in 1992, going beyond the point at which Ralegh turned back to take in the region's scattered community of gold-miners, hermits, Indians and lost visionaries. The irony is that he is never able to bring back anything more than his own cache of dreams to supplement those worked up by Ralegh. The two voyages circle each other without finding any points of contact beyond rumour, fantasy and coincidence. This could lead to comedy. Instead it results in an uncon-scious figuration of history as Nietzschean eternal return. If Nicholl is chasing Ralegh, then we soon understand that Ralegh is pursuing his own ghosts. He left for Guiana (now Venezuela) when he was an old man disgraced at court with little money and poor prospects. El Dorado was the name given to a fantastic City of Gold which was believed to exist in the jungles of South America. Nicholl makes clear that this was in part a refraction of Spanish tales of contact with the Incas but that it was also based on the quest narrative implicit in the romance tradition of Western alchemy. Ralegh was not a colonist. He had no intention of setting up a gold-mining town (or even, more practically, a tobacco plantation).

Instead, he expected a shower of gold to fall into his hands as a result of under-taking such an arduous journey in the first place. If the Indians he met on his travels offered him stories of how El Dorado was just around the next bend in the Orinoco, then he supplied them in return with visions of the English court as a poetic Arcadia inspired by Edmund Spenser's *The Faerie Queene*. He even handed out gold coins imprinted with Elizabeth's likeness to secure their vassalage. This suggests a point of departure never really taken up by Nicholl – the Indian transformation of imported Western commodities into hybrid new cargo cults. He does, nevertheless, end on a tantalising note. Everyone knows that Ralegh was responsible for popularising the tobacco craze in England. Less well known is that his 'Basalm of Guiana' was in use as a medicinal tincture up until the nineteenth century and that it may have contained South American plant additives now lost to historical view. Ralegh as the world's first psychedelic explorer? It's something to muse on.

MORAL PANICS
observer life, summer 1994 (killed)

Just as every moral panic has its folk devil, every subculture has its drug. Whether it's reefer-smoking jazz cats in the Thirties, acid-dropping freaks in the Sixties or pill-popping E-heads in the Nineties, those on the margins of society have always been vilified for their drug habits. The official line is that drugs are nasty, dangerous and addictive. That they have been made illegal as a matter of public safety. End of story. But in an age where the idea of harmful addiction has spread to take in everything from porn mags to video games, it's increasingly understood that drugs are more than just illegal plants or dodgy chemicals. They are instead controlled substances (either Class A or Class B, Schedule 1 or Schedule 2). Just like the shrink-wrapped, bar-coded commodities on sale in the local megastore, they are graded artefacts. The only difference is they don't come with obvious parental warning labels.

This new understanding goes beyond the old medical argument about legal drugs like alcohol and nicotine being more toxic than illegal drugs like heroin and cannabis. It even goes beyond the old sociological argument that what is illegal is often a misnomer for what is felt to be 'abnormal' or culturally different (the point at which herb-smoking Rastafarians lobby for recognition alongside other minority religions). It intersects instead with a semiotic argument which suggests that 'drugs' are part of a complex zoning procedure which controls the circulation of bodies and commodities across all sorts of borders.

Take the story of the criminalisation of opium. Opium and its derivatives like heroin and morphine were freely available from doctors and pharmacists – and even local grocery stores – up until the late nineteenth century. The habit of opium smoking had been introduced to the US in the 1840s by Chinese coolies brought to the West Coast to work in the gold mines and build the railways. With the economic downturn of the 1870s, whites began to compete for Chinese wages, the Hearst press invented the stereotype of the 'Yellow Peril' and the opium den became the object of horrified fascination. As a result, San Francisco banned opium smoking in 1875, Chinese immigration was stopped in 1882 and in 1909 the opium trade was suspended altogether.

These same tactics – objectification, vilification, legislation – have been used to scapegoat resented subcultures and social minorities ever since. It's the same story with black American jazz musicians and cannabis. Cannabis had been smoked by jazz players in New Orleans and Chicago as early as the 1920s. They found its intro-spective pleasures an inspiration. But it wasn't until 1937 that the federal govern-ment banned it. The reason? A Hooveresque bureaucrat called Harry J. Anslinger. Appointed boss of the newly created Federal Narcotics Bureau in 1930, he promptly set about securing his position by spreading entirely invented horror stories about the evil effects of 'marijuana'.

Mexican immigrants were blamed for introducing the drug into the US in the first place. But it was uppity jazz musicians who were targeted as the chief scapegoats, fingered for spreading the habit beyond the black ghettos into white districts. Of course, what really scared men like Anslinger were the kinds of cultural exchanges which were starting to occur between blacks and whites in the big Northern cities.

Banning marijuana and busting name musicians like Louis Armstrong was one way of trying to keep a lid on it.

It didn't work. By the 1940s and 1950s, jazz culture had reinvented itself. The big band combos of the swing era had given way to the more romantic scene of the bebop artists. Lester Young, Charlie Parker, Thelonius Monk, Billie Holiday – all saw themselves as isolated spiritual nomads beyond the pale of straight society. For many of them, this hipster control ethic found its corollary in the regular use of heroin, which typically leads to a sense of detachment and insulation. Charlie Parker reckoned he played horn better on junk, that he could follow the course of the groove more closely. Others were more attached to the closet rituals of scoring, fixing and shooting up.

Heroin use had been made illegal by the Harrison Narcotics Act of 1914. Again it was left to Anslinger to raise the stakes. Retooling his old scare campaigns with heroin rather than cannabis as the devil drug, he persuaded the government to pass tough anti-narcotics laws in 1951 and 1956 which increased the jail penalty for repeated heroin offences to forty years. Largely as a result of the climate of fear this produced, it became harder for hooked musicians to find regular work (especially in New York City) and many slipped into the comforting embrace of martyrdom. Charlie Parker died at the age of 35 in 1955. Billie Holiday was photographed and finger-printed by over-zealous cops on her death-bed in 1959. By the time of the rock boom of the late 1950s and early 1960s, Anslinger had retired from the Narcotics Bureau and was unable to drum up one of his trademark scares over amphetamine usage. The hypocrisies would have been obvious anyhow. Despite being banned in the late 1930s, amphetamine tablets were issued to British and US troops during the war to increase alertness and combat battle fatigue. The habit was brought back home by returning servicemen. The ban, however, stayed in place.

Endemic amphetamine usage is something which unites many of the subcultures of the post-war period, from the beats of the 1940s to the punks of the 1970s. For a beat like Neal Cassady, taking speed was a way of talking, driving and jiving at the same time, of keeping on the road of metaphysical affirmation and never coming off. For the Beatles in Hamburg, it was the boost they needed to keep them playing for nights on end and discover their identity as a band. For the Sex Pistols, the Banshees and the denizens of the 100 Club in 1976, it was a way of copping permanent attitude.

But it all started with ex-GIs hitting the road as truckers and spreading their amphetamine-charged goodwill across the rebel townships of the South.

Jerry Lee Lewis was tipped in Benzedrine capsules by an appreciative audience of truckers at one of his very first gigs. Johnny Cash got hooked on amphetamines after getting in with the roadies of the Grand Ole Opry and it took a full dose of religion to get him off. Hank Williams and the Everly Brothers were both addicted to speed. Elvis Presley was addicted to everything he could find in the Merck catalogue. Speed was the working drug that enabled a musician to make it through the night.

The downside of the drug is its jagged, nervy edge. But map this on to the jittery rhythms of urban life in the early 1960s and you have a portrait of a culture in crisis. The mod scene in London and the East Village boho scene in New York were both fuelled by speed. When The Who smashed up their equipment on stage it was more than a Dadaist prank, it was an inspired amphetamine jag (as was the stutter Pete Townshend forced Roger Daltrey to use on 'My Generation'). Similarly, the hectic exhibitionism of Andy Warhol's Factory scene – including the Velvet Underground's shrieking feedback – was largely the result of round-the-clock amphetamine (and later heroin) usage. If any drug were ever tailor-made for a subculture, however, then speed was for the mods. It fitted right in with the whole lifestyle. Being a mod was all about exchanging day for night and breaking the dull round of time into a succession of highly charged moments. It was about combining certain designated fetishes – Italian suits, Vespa scooters, soul music – to create a ritual microcosm of the everyday world. Mods weren't just smart, they were too smart. They took the dominant values of consumerdom and hyped them into what Tom Wolfe called a 'Noonday Underground', a concentrated space of posing, dancing and riding. Drinamyl, Dexedrine and Preludin were the brand names that held it all together.

Many sociologists like to think that the mods pulled a fast one on the straight world. The irony is that their hyper-commodified lifestyle in many ways paved the way for the yuppies of the 1980s. What Carnaby Street and speed were to the mods, Wall Street and coke were to the yuppies. Cocaine had always been drifting around on the margins of the jazz scene, but it wasn't until the early 1970s, when a white rock aristocracy snapped into media focus, that the drug came into vogue. Coke was the ideal drug for a lifestyle where partying was hard work. It was also expensive. For both these reasons it fitted right in with the high-profile status economy of the 1980s, where being a success was all about working hard, spending hard and looking hard.

Acid is a whole other story. In fact, it is a story which could almost belong in a Philip K. Dick science fiction novel. LSD (or to give it its full name, lysergic acid diethylamide-25) was first synthesised in 1943 by Albert Hoffman, a research chemist working in Switzerland, who put it on the market under the brand name Delysid as a psychiatric drug. One immediate buyer was the CIA, who (taking their lead from Nazi experiments with mescaline at Dachau) were interested in developing drugs which could be used as interrogation tools or even 'non-lethal weapons'.

One of the major ironies of the Sixties is that many of the acid evangelists of the counter-culture had their first taste of LSD on federally funded research programmes. Poet, guru and political radical Allen Ginsberg was first administered the drug at the Mental Research Institute in Palo Alto, California, in 1959. Prankster and cult novelist Ken Kesey was introduced to it a year later at the Veterans Hospital in Menlo Park, where he worked as a human guinea pig to subsidise his place on Stanford University's creative writing programme. Famed acid prophet Timothy Leary, meanwhile, first came into contact with LSD while experimenting with it as a psychology professor at Harvard University.

In the end, LSD was too good a secret to be kept in the hands of the government. Figures like Ginsberg, Kesey and Leary began to turn their friends on to its mind-altering properties and soon it was being manufactured by basement chemists all over the US. As the new drug began to slip from the control of the CIA into the hands of a radicalised hippie subculture, familiar scapegoat mechanisms came into play. The government was persuaded that LSD was a highly dangerous substance, the media and the medical authorities promptly fell into line and the drug was banned in 1966. Thereafter, the spectre of the psychotic drug-pushing hippie was often used as an excuse to crack down on student activism.

Not that someone like Timothy Leary was initially interested in politics. Owing to the largesse of an eccentric Wall Street millionaire, he was able to set up an experimental commune at Millbrook, a 64-room mansion in upstate New York, and it was here that he began to develop his acid religion. Essentially what he did was to programme the typical LSD trip with a philosophy that borrowed equally from Eastern mystical texts, pagan shamanic rituals, Freudian ego psychology and theories of genetic evolution. At Millbrook, tripping was all about meditating in front of a statue of the Buddha with Brahms on the stereo, trying to attain the white light of Nirvana. Lots of people bought the Leary package. The irony is that in attempting to programme an acid trip he was doing exactly the same as the CIA and Army scientists had done. Except whereas they were interested in pushing the drug as an anxiety-producing agent, he preferred to advertise it as a transcendental sacrament. Strictly speaking, LSD is neither 'psychotomimetic' nor 'psychedelic'. It is instead a mood amplifier. As Aldous Huxley put it, 'it makes you more of what you are'.

This is something understood above all by Ken Kesey. He had a set up to rival Leary's on the West Coast, except at his commune in La Honda there was no interest in psychology or mysticism. Dropping acid was all about partying and having a good time and it was at many of the raves – called Acid Tests – he organised that people varying from Hell's Angels to Grateful Dead fans were first introduced to the drug. When Kesey jumped on board a dayglo-painted bus in 1964 to turn on the rest of the country with his self-styled Merry Prankster buddies, he wasn't interested in being a prophet like Leary. He just wanted to fool around.

In many ways, Kesey anticipated the rave scene of the 1990s. When the trance beats of Deroit techno and Chicago house first began to percolate through to British clubs in 1988, they were immediately cut with Ecstasy on the dancefloor to generate a collective high that could go on all night. A type of MDMA first synthesised in 1914, Ecstasy is an amphetamine similar in molecular structure to mescaline. It produces a buzz which fades off at the edges into trippy empathy and was largely responsible for the popularity of the huge orbital raves staged outside the perimeter of the M25 at the turn of the 1980s.

It was the disturbance of traffic and Home Counties land values which prompted the government to crack down on E culture. Although old acid transcendentalists like Terence McKenna have attempted to graft a radical ideology on to the rave scene, it remained surprisingly apolitical and cynical up until very recently. It was only really the government's misleading anti-Ecstasy campaign of 1990, combined with its sponsoring of Puritanical legislation like the Criminal Justice Bill, which has persuaded many ravers to get a political education. Using the kind of scare tactics Harry J. Anslinger would have been proud of, the government has managed to bracket together ravers, New Age Travellers and a phantasmic underclass as a threat to public order. Drugs are scratched into the heady mix simply as extra spice.

All of which just goes to show that when it comes to the relationship between drugs and subcultures, it's generally the threat to public order which is uppermost in the minds of the authorities. As the liberal argument in favour of decriminalising cannabis gathers pace, and as the pathological model of consumer addiction increasingly starts to bite, 'drugs' will probably become less of an external threat and more of an internal problem. Less a fixed substance and more a free-floating category which can be pulled out of thin air to scapegoat any subculture for its habits (whether it's council estate kids watching 'video nasties' or 'dependent' single parents scoring benefit cheques). The drugs debate isn't over yet. Not by a long shot.

CELLULOID BINGE
new statesman & *society*, 6/269, 10 september 1993

High School Confidential is the kind of movie that David Lynch would love. Made in 1958 by the redoubtable Jack Arnold, it purports to show how the introduction of a simple stick of marijuana into a Middle American high school transforms the place into a teenage vice den. See that sweet-looking bobby soxer? She is really a dope fiend who would sell her soul for one more hit. And what about that black-clad hep cat? By night, he is a sinister pusher intent on the moral corruption of his classmates. Like I say, it's David Lynch without the irony. About the only surprise in this hysterical anti-drugs movie is that its protagonist – a finger-snapping delinquent who smokes dope in the principal's office and shakes hands with a flick-knife – is revealed to be an undercover narcotics cop.

Thirty-five years later, this would all be hilarious if it wasn't still pretty much gospel. 'Joint Ventures: Hollywood and Drugs', a season of twelve movies being screened at the National Film Theatre, is remarkable chiefly for the way it dramatises a consistent approach to the topic of drugs across a wide range of genres and periods. From D. W. Griffith's 1919 melodrama, *Broken Blossoms*, to the contemporary blaxploitation movie, *New Jack City*, from the 1957 problem picture, *A Hatful of Rain*, to the more recent cops-on-dope thriller, *Rush*, the myths remain the same.

The American writer Avital Ronell has argued that the whole idea of 'addiction' to 'drugs' is locked into a metaphysical fantasy of a pure or uncontaminated state of being which has no real purchase outside of Foucauldian regimes of normalisation. Which pretty much, of course, sums up the trajectory of the American Puritan experience: the gift of a Second Eden betrayed by the inevitable fall from grace. According to this mythic framework, 'drugs' (like 'Communism' before it) is merely the latest secular name for the old adversary. The 1916 film paired with the 1928 urban morality tale, *The Pace That Kills*, says it all. Its title is *The Devil's Needle*.

All the films in the season restage a Puritan psychodrama of sin and redemption with the accent falling heavily on punitive suffering. There are three big myths to contend with. The first is the myth of addiction as enslavement, of dope as both the price and reward of a Faustian pact. The 1936 propaganda flick, *Reefer Madness*, is the most obvious about this, what with its absurd claims that smoking marijuana leads to sexual frenzy and berserk violence, but *New Jack City* takes exactly the same line on the diabolical powers of crack cocaine. Suddenly, *High School Confidential* doesn't seem quite so camp.

The second big myth is the one which justifies, and even sanctifies, the life of the junkie. It suggests that coming off heroin is equivalent to the torments of the damned, that the withdrawal symptoms which punctuate the junkie's ritual progress are so many signs of martyred affliction. The culprits here are not hard to find. Not only is there Frank Sinatra climbing the wall in a locked hotel room as he kicks his habit in the 1955 problem picture, *The Man with the Golden Arm*, there is Don Murray screaming and twitching whenever he can't get a fix in *A Hatful of Rain* and Jason Patric chewing the carpet in *Rush*. The one thing you can say in mitigation of these episodes is that they coincide with the only instances of conventional 'bad acting' in each film.

Then there is the myth of the pusher as Mephistophelean dark angel, an evil seducer who corrupts the innocent with the offer of forbidden fruit. Often, this shades into racist stereotype. There is more than a hint of the Asiatic Jew in the characterisation of 'Snowy the Peddler' in *The Pace That Kills*. With his hook nose and black eyes, he slinks around the department stores and rooming houses of the film's Big City like the original snake in the grass. More often, the pusher is condemned, sometimes glorified, as a monster. Al Pacino as the vicious Cuban coke baron, Tony Montana, in Brian De Palma's *Scarface* is an appallingly charismatic figure. But Wesley Snipes' flash urban kingpin in *New Jack City* isn't far behind.

None of these films is willing to deal with the mechanics of supply and demand in the drugs business without resort to heavily moralised stereotypes. The pusher as the mythic author of natural depravity is as far as the analysis gets. On the rare occasions it goes any further, it stops at the North American border. In the doped-out Sixties biker movie, *Easy Rider*, Mexico is where Dennis Hopper and Peter Fonda pull off the coke deal which funds their version of the American Dream. Meanwhile, Al Pacino's Tony Montana tracks in from Cuba at the start of *Scarface*, before meeting his nemesis in the form of South American narco-assassins.What you would never know from any of these movies is that at the turn of the century cocaine and heroin were openly available in the drug stores of all the big industrial cities. They may not have been morally respectable, but they certainly weren't socially outlawed. A trip to a Chinese opium den in those days probably carried as much of a stigma as a visit to one of the smoke-filled nickelodeons which were springing up all over urban America in converted pawn shops and amusement arcades. All of which makes the appearance of the stereotypical opium den in *Broken Blossoms* and *The Pace that Kills* a skewed take on the class origins of the cinema.

Hollywood and drugs probably have more in common than is realised. Quite apart from the fact that the logistics of modern movie-making depend for their success upon a whole variety of different boosting agents, the finished product of any Hollywood deal has often found itself skirting the categories of psychopathological behaviour typically reserved for 'drugs'. Alcohol was banned in 1920, marijuana in 1937 – both as a result of the usual kind of myth-mongering Puritan hysteria. Hollywood should think itself lucky that the introduction of the Hays code in 1930 was as far as the mania for Prohibition went. Otherwise we might be more used to thinking of 'movies' as a controlled substance to rank with dope or junk.

VIAGRA OVERDOSE
i-D, 179, september 1998

Here is one possible vision of the future. You breeze into the Lifestyle Mall and begin to programme the evening ahead. You source the psychoactive stimulants from the organic produce mart, the audio environment from the media mart, the alcoholic relaxants from the drug mart and the sexual recreation effects from the biomedicine mart. This is one place where all the hype over the 'wonder-drug' Viagra seems to be leading – to a fully commodified lifeworld where the components of a multiply encoded sensorium can be combined into a self-assembled plug-in package.

It all began innocently enough. Ian Osterloh, a UK-based research scientist working for the multinational pharmaceutical corporation Pfizer was experimenting with manufacturing organic-based chemicals which could combat angina and hypertension by increasing blood-supply to the heart. Clinical trials showed that the compound sildenafil citrate had an unexpected side-effect. It increased blood-supply to the genital area and shut down the operation of an enzyme – phosphodiesterase – which generally inhibits the action of erectile tissue in both the penis and the vagina.

The compound was labelled Viagra (a name which manages to suggest energy, expenditure and aggression simultaneously) and marketed as an anti-impotence drug for men. Pfizer won a licence for its distribution from the US Food and Drug Administration on March 27 1998 and watched as its stock rose on Wall Street by 20 per cent in two months. Meanwhile American doctors wrote 300,000 prescriptions for Viagra in the first three weeks of its release. The drug is available in 25, 50 and 100 milligram dosages and is legally available in the US, Mexico, Brazil and Morocco at ten bucks a pop. The European Agency for the Evaluation of Medicinal Products is likely to pass it by September. Until then the drug is illegally available from Internet and mail-order sources (which are subject to sporadic surveillance by the Department of Health's Medicines Control Agency).

The National Health Service in the UK is poised for a potential crisis of demand. British general practitioners wrote 109,000 prescriptions for impotence last year at a total cost of £6 million. The Impotence Association estimates however that about ten per cent of the adult male population – or over 2 million men – suffer from impotence. If all these came forward for the drug the costs for the NHS could rise to £400 million a year. This is the main reason why Tessa Jowell, the Minister of State for Health, has said that the drug will be made available only to those with 'identified clinical need'.

Just what is Viagra's big attraction? Anti-impotence treatments have been available for some years now. The thing is that they have not been consumer-friendly. Caverject and Erecnos require users to inject themselves in the prostate gland with a hypodermic needle while pellets like MUSE have to be inserted into the tip of the penis. The big advantage of Viagra is that it is orally administered. It comes in the shape of a handy little diamond-shaped blue pill. And everyone understands pills.

This is part of the problem as far as many medical practitioners are concerned. They see Viagra being used not as a remedial medicine but as a recreational drug, not as a supplement but as a boost or an enhancer. This is something Pfizer understands. In a culture already conditioned to the use of mood-altering substances by brand-name commodities like Librium, Valium and Prozac, Viagra appears as one more psychosomatic chemical compound in the marketplace of designer affects – except now it delivers the experience of enhanced sexual pleasure which other drugs suppress.

It should be stated right at the outset that Viagra is not an aphrodisiac. Now that women as well as men are interested in obtaining the drug – with some women reportedly ordering it over the Internet under false male names – it needs to be emphasised that physical stimulation still needs to occur before the desired effects kick in an hour later. Even then there are a whole pile of side-effects – a drop in blood pressure, mild headaches, hot flushes, urinary tract infections, diarrhoea, a blue tint to vision – which need to be taken into account.

The most obvious danger is that inexperienced drug users will begin to take Viagra in combinations – like with nitrates – which are potentially lethal. Philip Hodson of the Impotence Association cautions: 'If Viagra is taken with poppers – the popular name for butyl nitrate which are legally on sale in sex shops in the UK and frequently taken by men and women – a lethal cocktail will be created. It creates a steep fall in blood pressure which is very dangerous because if there is not enough blood going to the heart it will stop – resulting in a massive heart attack.'

Meanwhile the social effects of Viagra use have barely been considered. Check the newsfeed. Item. Viagra Man's Comedown: Viagra Man Hospitalized With 36-Hour Erection. Item. Vice Girl Kills Viagra-Crazed Client Of 70. Item. Sex Attack By 89-Year-Old Viagra-Fuelled Man. Item. Tycoon, 70, On Viagra Leaves Wife. The tabloid media have certainly had fun sensationalising the Viagra story but at the same time they point to possible consequences for legal and health bodies, state bureaucracies, police agencies and sex industries alike.

Stripped of all the hype, the Viagra story begins to look more and more like a story of the baby boomer generation looking for the assisted means of prolonging their long summer of Sixties youth into the winter climate of a past-it millennium. All those old hippie studs who can't get it up any more are no longer willing to roll over and die like their fathers did before them. Instead they are forcing the creaking machinery of welfare capitalism to deliver them one last shot at prolonging their grip on the levers of power.

Late bulletin. Last year research by Rutgers University professor Barry Komisaruk and his colleague Barbara Whipple in New Jersey found that women with spinal cord injuries could still experience orgasm because the brain could receive sexual response signals from the cervix through an alternate pathway. The neuro-chemical which stimulates these signals was identified, synthesised and successfully lab-tested on rats. Last month Abbott Laboratories in Chicago confirmed that it was testing a compound called apomorphine which stimulates neuro-receptors associated with sexual arousal. This is what the post-boomer chemical generation really wants – sex delivered directly through a neurological rather than a physiological medium. Viagra still taps into a discourse of erectile tissue and cardiovascular response which feels a little quaint and nineteenth-century. For a generation hip to the neurochemical cycles of Ecstasy, Pfizer's phantasmic notion of a 'thrill pill' or an 'orgasm tab' has already been fully metabolised in the ambivalent shape of the 'love drug'. It just hasn't been made available on prescription. But the vision of the Lifestyle Mall may change all that.

It's possible to speculate that in the future sex may become more of an industry and less of a pleasure. In his seminal Seventies text *The History of Sexuality* Michel Foucault distinguished between an 'analytics of sexuality' which hooked up with nineteenth-century technologies of institutional hygiene, population control and mass social discipline and a 'symbolics of blood' which belonged to the more archaic legitimisation techniques of dynastic association and sovereign descent. In the post-modern era wires seem to have been crossed. While an 'analytics of blood' begins to take shape in the emergent techno-scientific practices of DNA fingerprinting, gene-splicing and human genome mapping, a 'symbolics of sexuality' can be seen getting itself together in the interlinked semiologies of fashion, cosmetics, media manufac-ture, drug synthesis and interface design.

The Ecstasy story has prepared the ground. In less than ten years MDMA went from being a dangerous substance and sign of transgression to becoming the plat-form for multiple forms of recreational subjectivity assemblage and industrial leisure management. One of the new careers that was briefly marked out in the bubble economy of Japan was the affect-stylist or designer of new kinds of emotions. In a culture where all the familiar human emotions have been stockpiled, dissected and theorised to death – and where Ecstasy casualties have the atrophied look of intro-nauts subject to the gravitational drag of massive internal accelerations – there is the sense in which new affects are increasingly desired as simple metabolic plug-ins.

New emotions inevitably mean shock emotions. The avant image labs of the haute-couture catwalks and conceptual photo media demonstrate that it is the fashion world which is leading the way in breaking old taboos to liberate the booty of transgressive affect. Not only is it arguable whether this kind of activity lightens the load of a taboo or whether – as Georges Bataille long ago argued – it actually increases its cultural weight, but it is debatable whether the thrill of the transgressive encounter – whether it's with bestiality, fist-fucking, sado-masochism, auto-fellation or castration – is anything that bears repeating. All pornography tends towards the state of being boring. What is actually desired is not the zoning or dezoning of new content but the modelling of new intensities.

This is what drugs are about. They attempt to give solid form to the abstract fields of a desire which is no longer a hydraulic power like the Freudian libido but some evanescent quasi-metaphysical substance. Something much like capital in its late phase as a transnational and perpetually circulating designation which has long since exceeded the old fetish of the gold standard. Drug lines and credit lines go together. The one exhausts the other (ask any addict/trafficker). The affect – the buzz, the high, the boost – is what grounds the circuit of exchange. It gets in the way like orgasm gets in the way when two human bodies come together. Simulate the experience of orgasm in drug-form and suddenly you have the ultimate commodity. Philip K. Dick called it Substance D. What are its other names? Instant Nirvana. Pure Transcendentalism. Final Solution.

blag artists

You are hanging out at a launch party for a beer company rebranding campaign which is putting together digital font design with aerosol art. The collision produces a 'shock of modernity' (Walter Benjamin) which resonates beyond the late industrial decay of King's Cross to spark an imaginative connection in your head. You are not yet immune to the crowded urban excitements of the media simulacrum. But increasingly the early evening round of private views, launches, promotions and openings tends to blur into one long substitution of signs. It is here that the back-culture of media careerism operates in a gestural economy of nods, tips and insider vibes. You remember the first time you talked your way into a nightclub how the passage was marked by a sense of no longer being a punter. 'Great work comes from the barbarians at the gates not from the courtiers in the salons.' (Ernesto Sabato)

CONFIDENCE TRICKSTER
i-D, 131, august 1994 (killed)

When Terence McKenna was in London recently, he spent an hour sitting cross-legged on the stage at Megatripolis, spinning a guru rap about the shamanic power of magic mushrooms, the millennial shift in human consciousness that was about to occur on a global scale and the 'strange attractor' at the end of time. It was entrancing stuff. But the whacked-out North American visionary only really came into his own with the question-and-answer session at the end. Prowling the stage with the mike like a predatory stand-up comedian, he looked every inch the post-modern tribal storyteller as he regaled his audience with tales from the far side of the druggie experience. By the end of the evening he was entertaining the crowd by reduplicating the elf babble he hears in his head after smoking the powerful hallucinogenic, DMT. He may be an old Californian pothead, but McKenna is also a consummate vaudeville performer. All his best qualities – his humour, optimism, intelligence and egotism – come together in his latest book, *True Hallucinations* (Rider), in which he tells the story of how he and his younger brother Dennis travelled to the Amazon Basin with some friends in 1971, got high on magic mushrooms and never really recovered. Written as an internal travelogue – an odyssey of the mind – which pastiches the conventions of the old colonial school of travel literature (check the subtitle: 'Being an Account of the Author's Extraordinary Adventures in the Devil's Paradise'), the book is simultaneously a scrupulous record of the drug-induced visions of Dennis, a romanticisation of contemporary shamanism, a collection of very funny dope tales and a sustained act of self-mythologisation. The story is simple but labyrinthine. Exiles from the post-Sixties landscape of the wrecked hippie dream, Terence and Dennis pack up their troubles and head south to search for the mythical shamanistic hallucinogen of the Witoto tribe, oo-koo-he. They never find it. Instead they are distracted by the profusion of magic mushrooms in La Chorrera, a small Amazonian Indian settlement in Colombia, and get completely out of their heads. McKenna's account of his brother's deeply weird trip is the heart of the book and, in many ways, the foundation text for his whole subsequent philosophy of psilocybin-fuelled evolutionary transcendence. Dennis didn't just get stoned. He was able to read Terence's thoughts, do perfect voice imitations of their parents (he even managed to speak to his mother on the cosmic telephone in 1953) and travel to the outer rim of the known universe in an act of magical flight. He became convinced that his trip had triggered a planetary revolution in consciousness and that Terence was the ambassador to his messiah. It took him weeks to come back down. McKenna is quite aware of the alternative paradigms available to characterise this experience – schizophrenia, ego inflation, craziness – and is always alert to the objections of the skeptical reader. It is what makes his book such a delight. That and the astonishing cast of minor grotesques – from John Brown, the 93-year-old son of a slave who witnessed the mass murder of the Amazonian Indians during the rubber boom, to Dr Karl Heintz, the ex-Nazi aristo turned Euro-industrialist who seems to have connections all over the place. But whereas Dennis eventually settled down to a regular job as a research pharmacologist in Silicon Valley, Terence never really became the career ethnobiologist he promised to be. He describes himself as 'in the absurd position of being either an unsung Newton or completely nuts'. You buy the book and decide.

REALITY HACKER #1
arena, 58, may 1996

The old federal highways are crumbling now. Like television, plastics and the Balance of Nuclear Power, they belong to another age. The weird thing is that the heroic myths they helped to sustain – from the outlaw wanderings of Jack Kerouac high on jazz, dope and visions of Nirvana to the acid-fuelled odysseys of Ken Kesey and his Merry Pranksters – just won't go away. They fade much less quickly in the public mind than does the pitted tarmac of Route 66 beneath the wheels of every fresh-faced college kid out to rehearse the epic songs of his ancestors.

The action has shifted to cyberspace. When US Vice-President Al Gore wanted to turn corporate investors on to the commercial potential of the Internet two years ago, he picked his metaphor advisedly. The Information Superhighway was something that every American CEO could understand. Gore's own father had helped to create the federal highway network when he was a Senator and the Detroit auto manufacturers and suburban real estate developers had cleaned up. Now their heirs – the telecom companies, datanet providers and Seattle software manufacturers – were poised to make a killing of their own.

There was just one problem. The heirs of Kerouac and Kesey had their own ideas about what the Internet was there for and it had little to do with turning a buck. Instead it was about escape, adventure and the rigours of staying up 96 hours straight on a diet of Jolt Cola and nachos. It was also about foraging for information, exploring the links of the datanets and – most importantly – hacking the system. The trick was to stay one step ahead of the telco engineers and not get caught.

Simple stuff when the Internet was in its infancy back in the Eighties and the dominant user culture was one of open access, shareware and freedom of information. Harder to pull off when – as has been increasingly the case since Operation Sundevil, the Secret Service hacker crackdown of 1990 – the federal government begins to take an interest in policing the Internet and supposedly making it safe for democracy. Harder still when the telcos begin to hire ex-hackers as their datacops and the old tricks don't work so well anymore.

Which is where Kevin Mitnick and Tsutomu Shimomura enter the picture. The Tsutomu and Kevin (it's all first names in cyberspace) hacking duel has already become one of the great myths of the Information Age, something to rack up there against Pat Garrett and Billy the Kid or Eliot Ness and Al Capone. Three books have been published so far in the US and are gradually making their way into the UK. Take your pick between *Takedown* (Secker & Warburg) by Tsutomu Shimomura with John Markoff, John Littman's *The Fugitive Game* (Little, Brown) and Jeff Goodell's *The Cyberthief and the Samurai* (Dell). *Takedown* is pro-Tsutomu (as you might expect), *The Fugitive Game* pro-Kevin (more or less) and the Goodell book somewhere in the middle. If that's not enough, *Catching Kevin* is in turnaround somewhere in Hollywood and there's a video game in the pipeline.

That's a lot of media action for one hacking bust. But then Kevin is something of a folk hero in the great plains of cyberspace, a Jesse James, Jack Kerouac and Gary Gilmore all rolled into one. His cuttings file is almost as long as his arrest record and when the FBI gained entry to his apartment at 1:45 AM on February 15 last year in Raleigh, North Carolina, they were conscious that they had a celebrity on their hands. Tsutomu, if no one else, had made sure of that. He had been tracking Kevin since his own system in San Diego had been hacked the previous Christmas and was duly on hand for the arrest.

It seemed like a wrap. This was the sixth time Kevin had been busted, but the first time he'd had the grace to acknowledge the status of his chief opponent. When he'd been arrested in 1987 for hacking the Santa Cruz Operation, a multi-million dollar UNIX operating system vendor, the young sys op who'd been instrumental in tracking him down congratulated him on his success in eluding detection for so long. 'Well played, well met.' Kevin ignored him. In the court-house at Raleigh it was different. Dragged before the judge in leg-irons and prison greys for his bail-hearing, he paused before Tsutomu – dressed in ski-bum T-shirt, cotton khakis and Birkenstock sandals with Oakley shades propped on top of his flowing locks – and said: 'Tsutomu, I respect your skills.'

This time, it was his anatagonist's turn to play it cool. Or as Tsutomu puts it in his book: 'There didn't seem much to say. In our contest he had clearly lost.' That didn't stop him from saying plenty to the assembled press, however. All about the new courtesy ethic which now prevailed in cyberspace. Kevin had apparently hacked into Tsutomu's home computer, left his private correspondence lying around on the Internet and 'gentlemen don't read each other's email.' As a National Security Agency consultant, top-flight programmer and computer security expert (not to mention noble citizen of Japan), he had felt obliged to hunt down his barbarian persecutor as 'a matter of honour.'

Kevin, meanwhile, couldn't say much even if he wanted to. The federal authorities were restricting his telephone access and definitely keeping him away from anything resembling a computer. They'd heard the stories. Like how he'd disconnected the phone of one of his probation officers and tampered with the credit ratings of a judge. How he'd released a phoney memo from the Security Pacific National Bank warning of anticipated losses of $400 million after they'd turned him down for a job. How he'd hacked into the North American Air Defense Command computer (just like the kid in the movie *War Games*) and had literally had the ICBM launch codes at his fingertips. Even how he'd learned how to send bogus commands to the eight unmanned interplanetary Explorer spacecraft controlled by NASA's Jet Propulsion Laboratory.

There was only one problem with all this. The stories were all denied by Kevin himself. It didn't matter. They were by now a part of the Kevin myth – 'Darkside Hacker', 'the John Dillinger of the computer underground' – which had been steadily accumulating since his first arrest in 1981. Kevin didn't exactly help matters in this regard. His favoured Internet handles included 'Condor' and 'Marty' – both borrowed from Robert Redford movies (*Three Days of the Condor* and *Sneakers*) in which the Golden-Haired One plays romantic cyber-sleuths – as well as 'Yoda' and 'James Bond'. Kevin, it seemed, didn't mind diving through the dumpsters of popular culture in order to enhance his own status.

Which only leaves one question. Just who is Kevin Mitnick and how did he become America's Most Wanted in cyberspace?

It's a tough one to answer. Let's start with some of the Kevin myths which he doesn't want to deny. Like how he knows a thousand and one ways to disguise himself, which is why his arrest mugshots show his weight fluctuating rapidly within a matter of months. How he has an actor's talent for manipulating his voice and is adept at 'social engineering' technical secrets from unwitting phone company employees by posing as one of their guys in the field. How he has a photographic memory which gives him an encyclopaedic knowledge of the telcos' computerised control switches. How he is able to cover his tracks as he lights out for the territories of cyberspace by skipping from one long-haul carrier to another leaving only a trail of false credit card numbers behind him.

And like how he has eluded the attempts of the authorities to pin him down more often than he has been caught. This is, perhaps, the real kernel of the Kevin myth. It's the darkside hacker as a combination of Houdini and Phantomas, leaving his digital fingerprints all over the scene of the crime to taunt his pursuers but dematerialising at the last minute before they close in for the kill. Or as a string of voice-mail had it on Tsutomu's machine mere days after he's been hacked: 'Hey, boss, my kung fu is really good. Your technique will be defeated. Your technique is no good.'

Snapshot of a typical Kevin arrest scene: a bare motel room just off a highway development strip somewhere in Seattle or Denver or Sacramento, Fat Burger cartons and Red Hot Chili Pepper CDs littering the floor, a Toshiba laptop propped open on the kitchen table with the modem still winking, a posse of state-troopers and FBI agents inside the splintered door with their guns drawn, their mouths open and their cover blown.

It all fits with the story of how Kevin liked to work with two computers. One for hacking his way round the Internet, grabbing source code from the operating system vendors and cellular phone companies and stashing it in phoney accounts. The other for running a check on whether the FBI had a warrant out on him and how far away they were likely to be. One of his favourite escape tricks was to manipulate the call-forwarding device on the telco computers so that any wiretap led only to a dead end. It would almost be funny if it weren't for the fact that one of the random numbers attached to the end of a false Kevin trail belonged to a Middle Eastern immigrant in Santa Monica, who was watching TV in his underwear when the FBI burst into his apartment in 1988.

So much for Kevin the Merry Prankster of the datanets. There are other Kevins. Like Kevin the 'serial offender' of FBI lore. Or Kevin the 'computer addict' as his attorney, in a novel line of defence, managed to persuade a US District Judge that he was after his arrest in 1988 for grabbing hold of Digital Equipment Corporation proprietary software. There's also Kevin the victim of a 'culture of complaint', brought up by his Jewish mother in the tractlands of the San Fernando Valley after his father split when he was three.

Most intriguing of all, perhaps, is Kevin the 'techno-nomad', a kid who learned his hacking skills by punching out his own codes on discarded LA bus transfers before reinventing himself as a ham radio freak and making the move into cyber-space. But the Kevin who appears in *Takedown* is none of these things. Instead he's a 'grifter', a 'con artist', a 'thief' and, just to make sure everyone gets it, a 'bad guy'. He doesn't even qualify for the dubious 'hacker' sobriquet, which Tsutomu wants to reclaim on behalf of elite programmers like himself and the guys who founded Apple Computer. The thing about Kevin is that he doesn't know how to code, he's computer illiterate, a 'cracker' (the implied redneck slur is perhaps merited given that the voicemail on Tsutomu's machine contains ugly references to 'Japboy'). He doesn't write software himself. He just takes other people's.

So how can he expect to stand a chance against Tsutomu when the cyber-samurai has him in his sights? One thing you can say about Tsutomu is that he tells a good tale. His ghost-writer Markoff, who had done the job of hyping Kevin as a dangerous computer terrorist in the pages of the *New York Times*, landed a $750,000 publishing deal with Walt Disney within a week of the Raleigh bust (at which he was present). Their story is the Authorized Version of the Catching of Kevin and, even if it's full of holes, it deserves a fair hearing.

Let's go back to Christmas Day 1994 when an unauthorised intruder gained access to Tsutomu's home computer system in San Diego by masquerading as a friendly caller. The trick, known as 'Internet Protocol spoofing', took advantage of a weakness in the transmission procedures of the Internet, which were concerned merely with clarifying – rather than actually verifying – who was on the line. Tsutomu was able to spot the intrusion because the log files on his system were shorter than they should have been given the amount of time his system had been up and running over Christmas. Someone, obviously, had been trying to mask the signs of their presence.

Tsutomu froze the information on his computer, transferred it all to read-only files and began to write a series of programmes designed to retrieve the hidden data and reconstruct the actual sequence of key-strokes which had led to the break-in. It was the equivalent of sealing the crime scene and dusting it for prints. The results of this new type of forensic analysis yielded the fact that a whole bunch of Tsutomu's private correspondence – as well as a piece of diagnostic software that he had reverse-engineered from the Oki 900 cell phone with the aid of a friend – had been copied and taken away. It was a brilliant piece of deduction and Tsutomu duly reported his findings to the Computer Emergency Response Team, a government-funded organisation designed to alert users to possible security flaws in their systems. There things might have rested had Tsutomu not received a call drawing his attention to the fact that his files had been stashed in a series of illicit accounts on the Well a mere 12 hours after being seized. Now it was getting personal. Tsutomu duly drove down to the Well's head-quarters in San Francisco for a conference of war with its managers and the FBI.

The Whole Earth 'Lectronic Link is one of the more notorious virtual communities in cyberspace, an alternative bulletin board system, conference centre and all-purpose boho hang-out set up by ex-Merry Prankster Stewart Brand in the Bay Area. In 1994 it had been bought out by one of its principal investors, Bruce Katz, who was determined to upgrade its computer systems, strengthen its interfaces and turn it into a profit-making venture. He was disturbed that an intruder had been able to hack into the 'root account' of the system, take it over and effectively use it as an electronic storage locker where he could hide the tools of his trade – password-grabbing devices and cloaking programmes – as well as any contraband information he had managed to find. That was why, over the protests of some of his more libertarian-minded colleagues, he had called in the FBI.

This is where the dragnet began to close in around Kevin. The feds already had suspicions that the uber-hacker was interested in amassing copies of cell phone source code and had reason to believe that Motorola, Novatel, Nokia and Qualcomm had all been hit. The Oki hack on Tsutomu's system fitted the pattern. They were entertaining paranoid fantasies of how he might sell the software on to the black markets of East Asia. But that had never been Kevin's game. He was only interested in the power of information for its own sake. One thing Tsutomu did learn from his access to FBI files was that 'Marty' was one of Kevin's favoured aliases. It duly appeared on the Well as the tag for one of the illicit accounts.

With a cursory glance at what exactly US electronic privacy legislation allowed them to get away with, Tsutomu helped the Well to set up a bunch of monitoring software on their system. Using one of the tricks of the intelligence trade – 'traffic analysis' – he was able to generate a list of the intruder's comings and goings. It soon became obvious that his nemesis was logging into the Well from Netcom, one of the largest Internet service providers in the US. His next task was to travel to San Jose and conduct the same kind of surveillance at Netcom as he had at the Well.

This was where things began to get more difficult. As Tsutomu puts it: 'Dealing with the Well had been like standing at a street corner on Main Street in a small midwestern town and intercepting all the red Fords or all the cars with California licence plates as they went by and photographing the driver of each one. Netcom, in contrast, would be like coming to Los Angeles and doing the same thing on the Santa Monica freeway.' He managed to pull it off, though. Isolating a Netcom account which tallied with the log-in times of the intruder at the Well, he was able to discover that it had been accessed by one of the 51 local modem dial-up lines which the Internet service provider provided around the US.

The calls were coming in from Raleigh, North Carolina. From here it was a short step for Tsutomu to chivy the FBI into initiating a trap-and-trace on that particular line. In the meantime, he was able to monitor the target's real-time exchanges with an Israeli contact over the Internet Relay Chat protocol. Signs began to emerge that Kevin was indeed their man. When asked for his nickname, the intruder duly typed in 'Marty'. Furthermore, he explicitly identified himself as the subject of a recent Kevin scare story in the *New York Times*. He was giving himself away.

From here it was a short step to his eventual capture. The FBI traced Kevin to a number which belonged to a phone company recently acquired by Sprint Cellular. The only problem was that the number led nowhere. Kevin had hacked the switch. This is where Tsutomu's intelligence skills came in handy again. By forgetting about actual telephone numbers and analysing the pattern of the calls made by Kevin between Sprint and Netcom, he was able to narrow them down to one particular cell site in Raleigh. An FBI radio-direction finding team – in combination with a crew of Sprint technicians kitted out with a Cellscope 2000 radio transceiver and Tsutomu working with his own Oki detection gear – was soon able to track him down.

Tsutomu had got his man. End of story. Except as Littman points out in his own account of the affair, the Japanese cyber-sleuth has perhaps been a little economical with the truth. There is no evidence, for example, that Kevin was responsible for the taunting voicemail left on his machine. No evidence that he performed the initial hack on his home system. No evidence that he was really that hard to catch. At the same time, there is plenty of evidence to suggest that Tsutomu's home system had already been hacked once before in the summer of 1994. That the software that was stolen at Christmas was not that valuable. That he could have immunised his system against attack if he had really wanted to and had actually set up a 'bait machine'. Furthermore, the FBI used a collection of blank search warrants (which were filled in later) as the authorisation for busting into Kevin's apartment.

It seems that Tsutomu came as close as his adversary to hacking the Internet in order to pin him down (he bears an uncanny resemblance to a cellular phone hacker described by Markoff in a 1993 *Wired* magazine story). It's just that he knew how to hack the media as well.

It's all ended on a bit of a false note. Kevin was able to plea-bargain down the charges he was facing in Raleigh to one count of cellular phone fraud and is now in an LA jail facing further charges. Meanwhile, the FBI have been made to look like heroes, Internet service-providers like Netcom and phone companies like Sprint have an excuse to lobby for the tightening of electronic security legislation, the dangers of digital data theft have been gift-wrapped in a neat package for the media and Tsutomu has become a minor celebrity.

The story of the Cyberthief and the Samurai has diverted attention from what is really at stake in cyberspace now – issues of corporate power, public access and profit motivation. It's like the last scene from some mythical Peckinpah movie devoted to the closing of the digital frontier. The Information Superhighway is being built over the old trackways of the Internet. Federal agents, corporate bagmen and suburban homesteaders are moving in. There's no place anymore for the old breed of electronic outlaws. Either, like Tsutomu, they get with the programme. Or, like Kevin, they get closed down.

REALITY HACKER #2
i-D, 167, august 1997

The Critical Art Ensemble are a crew of North American activists interested in rede-signing techniques of political resistance and subversion to employ in a symbolic landscape dominated by nomadic capital and viral information. They are New Media Pranksters. *Electronic Civil Disobedience* (Autonomedia) is a collection of recent essays which updates the recommendations – data hostage taking, blocking infor-mation access, electronic trespass – of their earlier book *The Electronic Distur-bance* and spirals off into productive new directions. CEA take a Deleuzian view of power/knowledge relations in the late twentieth century. Now that assembly lines and production plants can be shifted around the world at the touch of a button, it makes no sense for radicals to persist in thinking of the physical domain – the street, the factory, the fortress – as the site of contestation. The action has shifted into cyberspace. The CAE reckon that alliances between fit young hackers and seasoned old activists should be formed in order to deal with the spectre of tyranny. They are anarchists flying the flag in the virtual domain. The best example they give of their practices is designed to take place in a site of 'extreme consumption' like a theme park or a shopping mall. An activist sits down at an exit and begins to play with some toy cars; a crowd gathers and speculates about whether he is a madman, a Vietnam veteran or a simpleton; soon the security forces arrive and make it clear that unless the activist unblocks the exit then he will be arrested; the activists packs up and leaves. The point of this 'invisible theatre' is to raise consciousness about the levels of subliminal policing which occur in most public domains. This is something the Situationsists and Yippies were doing back in the 1960s and to a certain extent the CAE are simply retooling tried and trusted techniques. They are at their most radical, however, when their theories drift into the realm of the anthropological and they begin to identify the irrational acts of expenditure which fuel the rational econo-mies of the West. They see the road traffic accident statistics as an index of the hidden sacrifices needed to keep the consumer society going (the artist Gregory Ulmer proposed that the names of those killed on the roads should be added to those on the Vietnam memorial but was turned down). They see technology reaching its moment of transcendental purity in the state defined by its uselessness (so that nuclear tech is the most sacrosanct of all). They see how the totems of everyday life can double as 'abject objects' which carry subliminal reminders of death and sacri-fice (automatic garage-door openers, guns, spectator sports). They see the 'myth of addiction' as an ideology designed to train consumers into becoming self-policing (so that the addict in rehab pays for his own incarceration). They see, in short, that the developed economies of the West are just as 'primitive' as those studied in the Amazon rainforest or the Siberian steppes. It's something to bear in mind.

AVANT BARDIST
i-D, 169, october 1997

Stewart Home is probably best known for his sheer nerve. He's the man who self-consciously positioned himself at the end of twentieth-century avant-gardism by crashing the Neoist movement in 1982, rewriting their post-punk manifestos to take account of situationism and then quitting while he was ahead of the game. He's the man who tracked the surrealists and their interest in the pulp detective novels of the *Phantomas* series by recycling tropes borrowed from Richard Allen's 1970s bootboy fiction into radical conceptual novels which subvert received ideas of sex, politics and violence. He's the man who appropriated the idea of an Art Strike in 1990 and made it his own by refusing to write anything for three years after the publication of his first two novels, *Pure Mania* and *Defiant Pose*. Home takes himself seriously. So why do the literary establishment insist on seeing him as a joke? Probably because his brand of Proletarian Postmodernism is a little too sophisticated for their tastes (Home is that rare thing – a white male punk who refuses to be patronised as a Working Class Hero). All of which is by way of introducing *Come Before Christ and Murder Love* (Serpent's Tail).

Home's latest novel marks a change of approach from his earlier work. The devices patented in *No Pity* and *Red London* – detournement, appropriation, repetition – are used here to investigate the discourse of 'magick' as an agent of subjective transformation. Home understands very clearly the elective affinities which exist between the occult (with its secret societies, ritual activity and fetish of the will) and espionage (with its secret identities, simulated actions and myth of the conspiracy) and to some extent *Come Before Christ* reads like a John Le Carré thriller deconstructed by a Stirnerite speed freak. The narrator skids from one identity to another as he attempts to discover whether he is really an agent of the British secret state, a member of the South London Antiquarian Society or the head of the Lodge of the Black Veil and White Light. He jumps around the ley-lines of London pursued by various different women (who are all either avatars of the same goddess or agents of the same power), pausing only to engage in acts of ritual sex and compulsive eating (the elimination and ingestion of sacred matter from the body are the novel's crucial symbolic actions) while offering a feverish commentary on his own thought processes ('my forgetting of everything I knew … was simultaneously an act of remembrance'). The delayed climax which Home obsessively returns to is that moment of ritual human sacrifice which according to Rene Girard's theory of the scapegoat effectively offers a foundational myth for society. The fact that *Come Before Christ* is interrupted by successive acts of mimetic violence suggests that this myth of functional sacrifice is no longer plausible. All that's left is the nihilistic drift of desire. The novel's litany of sardonic jokes, cartoon splatter, tedious antiquarianism and downmarket brand names carries faint echoes of Brett Easton Ellis's *American Psycho*. There's the same self-cancelling irony and the same blank provocation. *Come Before Christ* is a dazzling rhetorical performance from which the author himself has vanished. Which is no mean trick when you think about it.

conspiracy altars

You are pitching the idea of a story on body-piercing to the upwardly socially mobile editor of a fashionable men's magazine. You give it a pop anthropological spin and say it's about the return of the sacred in everyday life. Your editor doesn't buy it. To him it's all about self-mutilation. You censor the idea of a tattoo story. Later you are invited to attend a panel discussion at London's Institute of Contemporary Arts on the connoisseurship proper to postmodern culture. It has been organised by an officious middle youth operator who co-edits an influential arts & ents magazine. He comments derisively on the habit socially excluded people have of assuming that the culture industry is run by a series of interlocking cabals. You and your editor are crammed into the room with a number of other Groucho club veterans all eager for a piece of the new media action. 'For a conspiracy to occur it's only necessary for significant people to think the same way.' (Gore Vidal)

DIANAGATE
i-D, 176, june 1998

When the Mercedes S-280 bearing Diana Princess of Wales crashed into the thir-teenth pillar of Paris' Alma Tunnel on 31 August 1997 it was 12:25 AM. Reuters issued a news bulletin which hit the Web at 6:40 AM. Within 13 minutes a discus-sion board went up in Australia called 'The First Diana Conspiracy Site'. One hun-dred days later and there were more than 31,000 Diana sites on the Web, from www.mcn.org/b/poisonfrog/diana to alt.conspiracy.diana. The conspiracy theories have been busily proliferating ever since. The death of Diana has become a postmod-ern version of the Kennedy assassination, our very own shrine to the dreadful myster-ies of the cover-up, a symbolic black hole through which occult mythologies begin to leak, a trepanation of consensus reality. The Egyptian population believe that British folks are deluded if they cannot see that Diana was murdered by MI6. The reason? The likelihood of her consort Emad 'Dodi' Fayed becoming a step-father to the heir to the English throne represented an Islamic threat to the Crown. So far, so plausible. Other theories – the ones which drop the Vatican, the IRA, Mossad or BMW into the frame – are less bound by reason (perhaps the most poetic conspiracy theory is the one which has Diana killed by agents of the arms industry in revenge for her high-profile campaign against anti-personnel landmines). They begin to conjure the signs of conspiracy on the hallowed ground of the media simulacrum, untainted by evidence, causality or history. They become pure events structured only by the karma of synchronicity. Thus it is imagined that the Merc driver Henri Paul had been brainwashed so as to respond to last-minute kill orders. That bodyguard Trevor Rees-Jones was an MI6 agent who was issued special protective head gear to survive his assassination mission. That the Merc had been bombed. That its tyres had been shot out. That the mysterious 'Fiat Uno' seen by on-the-spot witnesses colliding with the Merc was a mobile assassination platform. That it was a rescue vehicle which picked the lovers up after they had staged their own deaths. That it was a UFO. It is also imagined that Diana was pregnant. All of these phantasms are drawn irresistibly to the scene of the crash like the paparazzi who arrived within seconds of the event to photograph the princess in her death agony.

So what really happened? The official story is that Henri Paul had ingested a vicious cocktail of antidepressants and alcohol which impaired his driving judgement on the dangerous approach to the Alma Tunnel. Fine. Except that still leaves unan-swered questions. Like why it took medical rescuers one hour and forty minutes to get Diana to Pitie-Salpetriere hospital when the journey normally takes ten minutes. Like why roadside surveillance footage of the Merc's route has not been released. Like why the results of the autopsy conducted on Diana's body by Crown coroner John Burton remain secret. Thomas Sancton and Scott MacLeod offer the most coherent account of events so far in *Death of a Princess* (Weidenfeld & Nicolson). They come to no definite conclusions. But they do point out that there is a straight line route from the Place de l'Alma to the British Embassy on the rue du Faubourg St Honore. Leylineologists take note.

ALIENZ R US
i-D, 167, august 1997

Howard Menger was a US Army veteran who claimed to have been an alien in a previous life and to have been contacted by 'space people' since he was a child in the 1930s. He even said that he had ridden UFOs to most of the planets in the solar system. Come the 1960s, Menger denied his alien pedigree and said that the CIA had been using him to test public reaction to the possibility of extraterrestrial encounters. Later he recanted the CIA story and began to preach a message of 'love and understanding'. This is just one of the stories racked up by Jim Marrs in *Alien Agenda* (HarperCollins), a collation of twentieth-century UFO mythology which is 'not really a book about UFOs' but 'a book about mind-set'. What this means is that Marrs does not attempt to untangle in Mengers's story the weird mix of Hindu reincarnation beliefs, messianic megalomania, shamanic flight programmes, conspiracy theory and Christian fundamentalism. Instead he simply documents it. Marrs is a conspiracy theorist whose last book, *Crossfire*, was used as the basis for Oliver Stone's *JFK* and he is on home turf when reporting on the international secret societies and US military organizations which have been shadow players in post-WWII political history. He is more obviously on alien territory when detailing trips to Alpha Centauri. What Marrs makes clear is that the UFO meme is the master narrative of post-industrial folk culture – it attempts to give a mythic continuity to the fragmented timeline of postmodern history. Not only do stories of the 'greys' replicate earlier tales of little green men, woodland elves and Biblical angels, but they articulate fears of abduction and seizure by shadowy authority figures (Debbie Tomey's memories of being subject to gynaecological studies on board a UFO in 1983 coincide with a medical history which includes gall bladder and appendix removal); not only do stories of alien contact mythify the incomprehensible reality of twentieth-century technology from Nazi buzz bombs to NASA rockets but they resignify History as one long cover-up (the USA's International Telephone & Telegraph Corp and the Rockefeller-owned Standard Oil supplied Nazi Germany with artillery fuses and gasoline respectively during WWII); not only do stories of cattle mutilations and crop circles attempt to reinsert the Country back into media discourses dominated by the paradigm of the City, but they put into question the matter of land ownership (the US Air Force conducted an illegal land seizure in 1984 in order to extend the size of its 'Area 51' or 'Dreamland' base at Groom Lake, Nevada). The cultural historian Fredric Jameson noted long ago that conspiracy theory offers a degraded window on to the deep machinations of late capital and *Alien Agenda* has certainly collected enough material to support this view. Marrs himself is neither a proselytiser nor a sceptic; he simply presents the case histories. What needs to be done is to re-theorise conspiracy theory itself as the devotional fetish of displaced patriarchs who no longer find themselves at the centre of the historical action. But that would take a whole other book.

NEW WORLD DISORDER
i-D, 92, may 1991

When Robert Anton Wilson was in town at the height of the Gulf War, he had just the kind of audience he deserved. Born-again hippies, cyberpunks and bug-eyed paranoiacs. They had assembled in a shabby Camden theatre, like a congregation of the deviant, eager to tune into the latest public broadcast from the guru of alternative American satire.

He didn't let them down. Recycling the best bits from the stream of books he has authored over the last 15 years, he treated them to a stand-up dissertation on everything from pop theology ('Eastern mystics talk about Yin and Yang, I prefer my own theory of the Hodge and the Podge') to the hidden depths of quantum mechanics ('the science of the Definite Maybe').

But the loudest cheers of the evening were reserved for his musings on conspiracy theory. Hardly surprising. Wilson is something of a reluctant expert on this subject. His first novel, *Illuminatus!* (co-authored with Robert Shea), is a playful and exhaustively researched fable which reduces the spectacle of human history to an occult artefact, residue of a secret struggle between rival cosmic factions. It all adds up to a skilful dissection of the paranoid mindset. Which hasn't stopped some poor deluded souls from taking it seriously.

The fact that they all seemed to be in the back row at Camden didn't spoil Wilson's fun. He explained how, back home in California, he'd been monitoring the switchboard buzz of talk radio and had picked up the craziest Gulf War stories. Every voice on the line had a different theory about what was really going down in the Gulf. Operation Desert Storm was more than a military campaign for these phone-in conspiracy freaks, it was a real-life whodunnit. And only they had the answers. Lots of answers. The following is just a sample:

The Skull and Bones Theory – George Bush dunnit. He was a member of the occult secret society, Skull and Bones, when he was at Yale. So were most of the American ruling elite. According to legend, Skull and Bones displays the skulls of Geronimo and the Confederate General, Robert E. Lee, in its crypt. Bush declared Saddam to be Public Enemy Number One because he wanted to enlarge the collection and impress his friends.

The Favourite Son Theory – George Bush, Jr dunnit. The President's son owns a group of oil wells in Bahrain. When Saddam invaded Kuwait, he felt threatened and got his pa to send in the troops.

The 'Rollover' Theory – The El Sabbah family dunnit. They have over $200 billion invested in the Western banking system. When Saddam Hussein invaded their Kuwait fiefdom, they mailed Washington a video of *Rollover*, the Seventies disaster movie about a stock market crash engineered by a conspiracy of Arab oil sheikhs. That was enough to do the trick.

The Oil Theory – The CIA dunnit. They sponsored Saddam throughout the Iran/ Iraq war, but found him increasingly difficult to manage once he had come out on top. They therefore secretly encouraged him to invade Kuwait knowing that it would provide the perfect excuse for direct American intervention in the oil economy of the Middle East. It's no accident that Bush is an ex-CIA man.

The Vatican Theory – The Pope dunnit. He was the only world leader to condemn the Americans for going to war. Therefore he was backing the other side. If you think about it hard enough, he was ultimately supporting the cause of Islamic fundamentalism. And that's because for thousands of years Islam has been a secret sub-ministry of the Catholic church.

The Alpha Centauri Theory – Aliens dunnit. Beings from another galaxy have been secretly running the American government ever since the Fifties. Now the Cold War is over and the risk of nuclear annihilation reduced, they are planning to take over the world. Trashing Iraq is just the start. Anyplace could be next.

Whodunnit? Anybody except Saddam. That would be too obvious. What all these narratives have in common is an attachment to plot at the expense of plausibility. Effects are taken for causes, causes for effects, motives are back-dated, actions brought forward. Events signify only if they can be twisted into proof of the Plot. For the conspiracy theorist knows that there is a dark cabal of ministers secretly shaping human affairs according to its own evil lights. He is essentially an adept in the art of exegesis, a semiotic devout who reads coincidences as coded signs, accidents as secret marks of intent. Nothing is random, everything is preordained. The world is a gnostic text authored by a hidden hand.

But whose exactly? Candidates in the past have included the Masons, the Catholics, the Jews and the Communists. More recent scapegoats range from international syndicates like the Trilateral Commission, the Bilderburg Group and the Mafia to secret intelligence networks like the KGB, the CIA, Mossad and MI5. Even to aliens from Alpha Centauri. But no matter who the target, the result is the same. History is telescoped into fiction, reality invaded by fantasy.

Wilson is particularly trenchant on this score. He reckons that conspiracy theory is 'history for amateurs'. Fascinating because so utterly fantastic. 'It all depends on how imaginative you are, how much you're willing to be governed by the rules which control scientific or legal argument. Most conspiracy buffs aren't even limited by legal argument, which is a lot looser than scientific argument. They'll go on speculating endlessly.'

Conspiracy theory is indeed an exercise in infinite interpretation. The Plot it seeks to decipher has as its end the perpetually deferred moment of Total World Domination. In the meantime, events proliferate, signs spiral in on themselves and the conspiracy buff finds himself exhausted by the task of constantly changing his story to keep pace with the stream of new evidence. Perhaps that's one reason why conspiracy theory is often an anonymous, free-floating enterprise, a collective hermeneutic labour. Stories are swapped on computer bulletin boards, updated and revised, faxed randomly across the globe, to return to the sender in altered shape.

A wonderful irony. The practice which starts out wanting to expose the hidden agency responsible for plotting the course of world history ends up itself opaque, globally dispersed and seemingly authorless. But perhaps that's appropriate. Conspiracy theory has grown increasingly popular as a way of explaining how the world works ever since the assassination of President Kennedy during a Dallas motorcade thirty years ago. For good reason. When the official body appointed to investigate the murder turned in a report which fingered a lone gunman, Lee Harvey Oswald, for the crime, its manipulation of testimony and mishandling of evidence were transparent.

The Warren Commission was involved in an obvious cover-up. Its most notorious conclusion was dubbed by its critics the Magic Bullet theory. A fully intact bullet produced by the Commission was deemed to have entered Kennedy's back, exited his neck, swerved in mid-air, struck another politician travelling in the motorcade, again in the back, before emerging from his chest and going on to pierce his wrist and bury itself in his thigh. It was supposedly discovered on a stretcher at the Dallas hospital where the injured were treated.

This gravity-defying flight path is emblematic of the torturous narrative trajectory of the Warren Commission report, which produces its fully intact lone gunman from a complex body of knowledge which stretches to 26 volumes. So what was the real story? Conspiracy theory was soon draughted in to reconstruct an alternative version of events and fill the aching void at the heart of the assassination.

The death of Kennedy is the primal scene of postmodern conspiracy neurosis. Nowadays, no public scandal or political crisis is complete without the accusation of cover-up. The evaporation of trust in elected officials, combined with increasing scepticism of statistics, press releases, adverts and news media have all played their part in popularizing conspiracy theory as the layman's guide to politics. The post-Kennedy roster of intrigue is almost endless. Think of the assassinations of Robert Kennedy and Martin Luther King, Henry Kissinger and the bombing of Cambodia, Nixon and the bugging of Democratic Party headquarters in Watergate, Reagan and the arms-for-hostages and guns-for-drugs deals of Iran/Contra, Bush and the invasions of Panama and Iraq.

And that's just the States. In Japan there was the Lockheed scandal, an episode of bribery and corruption reputedly involving the CIA. In Australia, the mysterious collapse of Gough Whitman's Labour government. Meanwhile in Europe there was the sudden death of Pope John Paul I and its coincidence with the Vatican bank scandal, the assassination attempt on John Paul II, terrorist bombings by fascist para-military groups designed to look like the work of the Red Brigades. Closer to home there was the imprisonment of the Guildford Four and the Birmingham Six, dirty tricks in Northern Ireland, MI5 plots against Harold Wilson. It's no wonder that some feverish commentators supposed Margaret Thatcher was deposed by an inner oligarchy of the Tory Party known only as the Men in Grey Suits.

The problem with conspiracy theory is that it is always prone to make a melodrama out of a crisis. Which is also its attraction. It's unsurprising that Wilson should have hauled in his catch of Gulf War stories from the tribal deep of talk radio, a natural medium for the spread of gossip and malicious rumour. Is it too much to think of conspiracy theory as a form of spontaneous folk art? Wilson is prepared to incline mischievously in that direction. 'Conspiracy theorists as a group are unduly modest. They don't realise what great artists they are. At least they remind us reality is nothing like what the media tell us. Things are a lot weirder and more complicated.'

Take the *Gemstone File*. A perfect example of conspiracy theory as poetic *samizdat*, this unauthored sheaf of documents has been drifting across the global underground since the Seventies. Its solution to the riddle of the Kennedy assassination is astonishing. Aristotle Onassis dunnit. That's why he got to marry Kennedy's widow (it's a Mafia thing). But that's not all the wily old Greek tycoon did. He also kidnapped American billionaire Howard Hughes, put his double in his place and pumped him full of drugs so nobody would notice the swap, took control of the Mafia's rackets, ran the American elections and generally came on like the Master of the Universe. Perhaps he was the chief alien from Alpha Centauri. No matter. What's interesting about the *Gemstone File* is that buried in the dross is a lot of hard fact. It has become a polymorphous disinformation vector, continually remodified, reprinted and redistributed.

At which point an alternative explanation suggests itself. Maybe conspiracy theory is a subversive phenomenon, a bulletin from the collective political unconscious. Like its close relatives, the urban legend and the sick joke, it almost seems to be a species of civil defence against media fall-out. Perhaps the growth of conspiracy theory is an information immune system developed by the body politic, a means of deterring the viral incursions of corporate databases and computerised sign systems. If this were the case, then the more implausible the conspiracy theory the better. What better way of combating the spread of hyperreal static than by simulating its effects in advance? This would be a new form of popular resistance. No longer counter-intelligence, but counter-imbecility.

Would it were so. It's a neat theory, but ultimately nothing more than another conspiracy theory – the most seductive of them all because the one which is multiplied to the nth power. If conspiracy theory has any political value, it is not as a shot of remedial nonsense but as a form of cognitive shorthand. It puts together the pieces of a complicated puzzle like Iran/Contra in a way which provides an idea of the Big Picture even though there are still some bits missing or left over. It is not afraid to make informed guesses or intuitive connections. Wilson admits this when pressed. 'Ever since Jimmy Carter was elected, the Senate Intelligence Committee is supposed to be informed about what the CIA is doing. As a result, they finance operations by getting involved in all sorts of illegal activities, which include drug dealing, gun running and the looting of the Savings and Loans industry, it looks like. The strength of conspiracy theory is that it recognises there is a lot of cover-up going on.'

The difficulties start when it becomes possible to put together the pieces of a puzzle and come up with more than one picture. Take the Kennedy assassination. No self-respecting conspiracy buff is content with the lone gunman theory. But the likelihood that Oswald was himself 'put together' (in the jargon) by one intelligence agency or another only adds to the confusion. Here was a Marine who defected to the Soviet Union and then came back to the States without a hitch, an activist who was a simultaneous member of pro and anti-Castro organisations in New Orleans. The CIA kept a secret file on Oswald, but just because it lists him as a subversive doesn't mean it couldn't have been part of his cover as an operative.

In the shadowland of intelligence-gathering, information merges with disinformation, simulation slides into dissimulation. It might as well be a parallel universe, a happy hunting ground for secret agents. No wonder they call themselves spooks. Was Oswald attempting to infiltrate Communist Cuba for the CIA or was he penetrating anti-Castro organisations on behalf of Cuban agents? Or was he being cultivated as a multi-purpose fall guy by a network of intelligence operatives and Cuban exiles? His paper trail stretches from Dallas to New Orleans to Mexico City to Minsk.

When the cover-up begins before the crime, the conspiracy theorists don't stand a chance. They've been second-guessed by experts. It's therefore no surprise to find that they all shoot off at such different tangents. Who killed Kennedy? Castro dunnit, the Cuban exiles dunnit, the CIA dunnit, the Mafia dunnit. They all had motive, means and opportunity. It's almost enough to make you believe that maybe the Warren Commission was right and Oswald dunnit all by himself.

Since then there have been further official investigations into the matter, but they hardly clarify things. In 1979 the House Assassinations Committee concluded on the basis of new acoustic evidence that there was a second gunman in Dallas and that Kennedy 'was probably assassinated as a result of a conspiracy'. Buff euphoria was brief. Three years later the National Academy of Sciences re-examined the evidence and condemned the Committee's findings.

That hasn't deterred the conspiracy theorists. Over the last few years, most conspicuously in 1988 on the twenty-fifth anniversary of the case, a new breed of hi-tech audio-visual aid buff has emerged. The contrast with the older paper-chasing types couldn't be more explicit. The new guys are obsessed not with the elevated mysteries of the intelligence services but with the on-the-ground details of the assassination itself. They pore over old tourist polaroids and movie footage, especially the Bronson and Zapruder films, looking for signs of secret gunmen and raised rifle barrels. They blow up details, computer-enhance obscure shadows, stare deep into the grainy abyss and bring back images only they can see: Black Dog Man, Badge Man, the Babushka Lady, Umbrella Man.

This is getting very close to the surreal account of the Kennedy assassination in *Illuminatus!*, where legions of snipers and other mysterious characters are literally stepping on each other's toes to take a shot at the President. Even with all the latest technology at his disposal, the conspiracy buff can't resist the lure of the ob-scene, of the figure behind the mirror. Which is probably why Robin Ramsay insists on making the distinction between conspiracy theory and something he calls conspiracy research. 'Conspiracy theory tends to take complicated situations and make them simple. Everything boils down to the Jews, the Masons, whatever; it's fundamentally a reductionist process. Whereas conspiracy research tends to take extant, received versions of events and by digging a little deeper make them very much more complicated than they were to begin with. The two things work in different directions entirely.'

Ramsay should know. Along with his working partner Stephen Dorril, he started out as a Kennedy assassination buff and has slowly evolved into an alternative historian of the political scene. Together the pair of them publish *Lobster*. An investigative newsletter which comes out two or three times a year, it wields an influence disproportionate to its tiny circulation and is read by researchers, politicians and spooks across the world.

Lobster broke the Colin Wallace story in its first issue back in 1983, publicising details of the secret Shoot to Kill policy in Northern Ireland before any national newspaper. Since then, the Hull-based magazine has consistently enjoyed taking apart the intricate political machinery of the British secret state. Past stories have been headlined 'A Who's Who of British spooks', 'Falklands conspiracy theories', 'Wilson, MI5 and the rise of Thatcher', 'Overthrowing Gough Whitlam', 'the London CIA station', 'the CIA and the British Unions'. Meanwhile the latest issue reports the death-bed confession of an ex-Dallas cop who claims to have been the second gunman in the Kennedy assassination. There's nothing sensationalist about any of this. *Lobster* is not a scandal sheet. Mostly, it consists of sober columns of facts and figures. All the information it carries is publicly available in various obscure research papers. In many ways Ramsay and Dorril are simply providing a news-clipping service. Except the news they are interested in is the hushed whisper emanating from the corridors of power.

Ramsay feels that he is delivering the dirt on the rotten business of political history. And that this is something few others are prepared to do. 'There are two received versions of history,' he says. 'There's the orthodox liberal-democratic version and there's the Marxist version, neither of which I think are satisfactory. The liberal-democratic version doesn't deal with the state at all. It tends to talk about Parliament and Ministries of this and that rather than GCHQ, MI5, MI6 and Army intelligence. What characterises all these institutions is that they're secret, as indeed is the entire British state. Meanwhile the problem with the Marxist version is that it talks about the ruling capitalist oligarchy but never tells us who's in it. Nobody ever wants to do the detailed work and find out who the bastards are.'

The latest issue of *Lobster* also features an essay by Peter Dale Scott on the involvement of the U.S. government in what the CIA has itself called 'one of the worst mass murders of the twentieth century' in Indonesia during 1965. Scott's method is exemplary. His footnotes take up as much space as his main text. Every document is sifted, every claim balanced. This is light years away from something like the *Gemstone File*. Scott has published a number of books on American intelligence. Watergate and Iran/Contra have received his patient attention. His upcoming book, *Cocaine Politics*, documents the involvement of the CIA in drug-trafficking and gun-running in Central America, while his unpublished manuscript, 'The Dallas Conspiracy', contains some intriguing hints about who was responsible for the Kennedy assassination. A mild-mannered English professor at Berkeley by day, by night he is the acknowledged dean of conspiracy research. Or the science of 'parapolitics' as he prefers to call it. The mock definition he gives the term in his book, *The War Conspiracy*, is worth quoting in full:

'PARAPOLITICS n. 1 – a system or practice of politics in which accountability is consciously diminished. 2 – generally, covert politics; the conduct of public affairs not by rational debate and responsible decision-making, but by indirection, collusion and deceit, cf. CONSPIRACY. 3 – the political exploitation of irresponsible agencies or power structures such as intelligence agencies.'

Scott claims wearily to have grown tired of the Kennedy assassination, to have become irritated with the buffs who read volumes into his every sentence and disappointed with the mainstream historians who routinely ignore his work. Yet even as he says all this, he admits that he is in the process of examining a draught of National Security Action Memorandum no. 273, the policy document which made the commitment to win in Vietnam and reversed Kennedy's NSAM no. 263 two days after he was killed.

This scrupulous quoting of serial numbers is typical of Scott's method. But why is he back loitering in an obscure by-way of the Kennedy assassination trail? It seems that he can't let the matter rest, even though it sickens him. He is faintly reminiscent of the mournful assassinologist in Don DeLillo's fictional solution to the Kennedy case, *Libra*: a figure both appalled and fascinated by 'the endless fact-rubble of the investigations.'

He is aware this is a response not shared by the majority of his fellow citizens. 'Most Americans think something big and awful happened on that day but the same people think we're never going to know what it was. And a good many of them, perhaps more than half, think that's just as well. They'd rather not know.'

This pathological disavowal syndrome is linked in Scott's view to the enormous media appetite for conspiracy theory, which saturates the public with an overdose of scandal in order to inoculate it against the much less virulent strains of the truth. Scott doesn't point the finger, but it's not hard to find examples of what he means.

Think of *Air America* and its cynical vision of cowboy spooks running wild in South East Asia, *The Godfather III* and its interpolation of the Vatican bank scandal into the Corleone family saga or Oliver Stone's mixing of queer culture with the Kennedy assassination in *JFK*. Closer to home, take Ken Loach's *Hidden Agenda*, which stirs the Shoot to Kill policy, the MI5 plots against Wilson and the Thatcherite accession into a heady brew of conspiratorial intrigue.

'It's what the French call "intoxication",' says Scott. 'You take a good story and poison it with bad stuff so it isn't a good story anymore. People's mass entertainment is built on much more fascinating, but unfortunately false, views of recent political history than the dreary truth. Every sensitive area has been anticipated by faction, that terrible amalgam of truth and falsehood which creates an environment where you can't tell what is true anymore. And I don't think this totally coincidental.'

The wider conclusion to be drawn from Scott's remarks is that conspiracy theory, in seeking to expose the secret workings of American imperial power, unwittingly serves its interests by reproducing it as a spectacle, a 'covert spectacle'. Even in its most respectable guise as a form of cognitive shorthand, conspiracy theory mythologises power in the very attempt to demystify it.

In that sense, conspiracy theory is identical in its effects, though opposite in its assumptions, to the cock-up theory of history. Where the first is essentially paranoid, always on the look-out for the secret figure in the ground of events, the second is schizophrenic, quite content to skim the surface of history and idly celebrate its randomness. The conspiracy theorist suffers from a nagging repetition compulsion, he always wants to return to the scene of the crime and reconstruct events. His opposite number suffers from a psychotic indifference. Who cares whodunnit? Shit happens. Power in its postmodern phase seems to collapse the traditional distinction between covert action and public spectacle, secret plot and symbolic message. This was so as far back as the Fifties, when the CIA toppled nationalist regimes in Guatemala and Iran and publicised its feats in the *Saturday Evening Post*. The warning to other Third World countries was clear.

It's the same story today. Except that as a result of steady economic decline and perceived political weakness, the US is increasingly manufacturing covert spectacle for domestic consumption too. The Grenada invasion, the Libyan bombing, the Panama invasion, the Gulf War – all functioned as symbolic recovery efforts. As the cultural commentator Michael Rogin notes, such episodes 'transform the political relation between rulers and citizens from accountability to entertainment'. Power becomes a special effect. Literally so in the case of the Gulf War, with its endless video footage of smart missiles homing bloodlessly in on their designated targets. Meanwhile a countless number of Iraqis who were unfortunate enough not to be members of the paying audience are even now being bulldozed into the ground.

It doesn't pay to get too paranoid. The last word on this depressing subject better go to Robert Anton Wilson. 'Have you heard the one about the Texas oil-man? A Texas oil-man starts a rumour that they've found oil in hell. So everybody goes off to hell to drill for oil and he's laughing his head off. After the last one has left, though, he suddenly thinks, "Gee, there might be some truth in it." And so he goes to hell too.' George Bush, of course, is a Texas oil-man. What a coincidence.

ORGANISED CRIME
i-D, 114, march 1993

The crusade against the Red Menace, which lasted from 1917–1989, has meant that the history of the Western security services has, up until very recently, been a clas-sified matter. The paper trails stretching from one secret agency to another entwine themselves around episodes as diverse as Prohibition and the Kennedy assassina-tion but do little more than wink mischievously at the puzzled historian. When the history of the twentieth century comes to be written, it will have to rely upon more informal sources than the official record: rumour, innuendo and conspiracy theory. The English investigative journalist Anthony Summers has already written a meticu-lously researched book on the Kennedy assassination. He has also written a muck-raking biog of Marilyn Monroe. His new book, *Official and Confidential: The Secret Life of J. Edgar Hoover* (Gollancz), falls uneasily between these two domains. It is scrupulous and sensationalist at the same time. Hoover, who was Director of the FBI from 1924 until his death in 1972, gets the full treatment. We hear that as a young lawyer working in Washington, he was rumoured to be a black man 'passing' as white; we learn of his excessive devotion to his mother; we learn lots about his alleged homosexuality, including stories that he enjoyed dressing up in stockings and suspenders before getting tossed off by young boys.

Summers sees Hoover's private guilt and confusion as the source of his petty public despotism. He refused to permit blacks to join the Bureau, even at the height of the civil rights struggle; sidelined women into performing menial office duties; and fulminated against the corruption of an idealised America by Communism. If Hoover had merely been some authoritarian hangover from the Victorian era, Sum-mers' documentation of his hypocrisy and egomania would have been entertaining but trifling. The fact that Hoover was also one of the most powerful men in America this century means that much of the material Summers has uncovered is too big to fit inside the narrative strait-jacket of biography. It simply hovers tantalisingly in the background, suggesting all sorts of alternative interpretations of recent American history. The source of Hoover's power lay in his confidential files. Over the years, he built up a spy network of agents and ex-agents who would snoop not only on petty criminals but also on politicians, judges, and media and corporate executives. What-ever dirt they collected would be relayed back to the Director, who would always let his victims know that their secret would be safe with him. Hoover got his way for so long because he was an expert at the art of blackmail (Summers suggests that, of all the Presidents he served, only Truman escaped his attention).

The irony is that Hoover was probably being blackmailed himself by mafia boss Meyer Lansky, who may have had photographs of him in sexually compromising positions with his long-time associate Clyde Tolson. For this reason, Hoover always publicly refused to acknowledge the existence of organised crime. Summers suggests he was in their pocket and enjoyed it that way. The implication of all this is that 'crime' is simply a discourse which codes a tremendous amount of human activity – sexual, political, commercial – we are still inclined to moralise. Summers reports that Hoover never really believed in the Red Menace; it was just a convenient cover story which justified the collection of all sorts of information. In the same way, we shouldn't believe in any account of Hoover which pretends to judge him. It is too early for that. For the moment, he is more useful as a device for mapping the tangled web of political corruption in twentieth-century America.

KENNEDY ASSASSINATION
i-D, 131, august 1994

What exactly happened to America in the Sixties? J. G. Ballard claims that the assassination of John F Kennedy in 1963 was the media event that kick-started the image bombs – Vietnam, Altamont, riots, protest marches, rock'n'roll – of the decade to come. He sees the events in Dallas – an imperial president executed at a public crossroads – as a sacrificial act responsible for releasing ragged pulses of Dionysiac energy through the social fabric. Other more commemorative souls prefer to tour the scene of the crime and fetishise the relics – the bullet casings, bone fragments, chipped kerbstones – left behind. Some weave these fragments into elaborate paranoid fantasies which see the noble young leader cut down in his prime by an assorted band of mafia hit men, CIA renegades and Cuban exiles hiding in the shadows of Dealey Plaza. Others still prefer to pick apart the biographies of the handful of leading players involved in this political drama. Lee Harvey Oswald, the ex-Marine, American defector, paranoid egotist and putative assassin. Jack Ruby, the sleazy club-owner who shot Oswald in a supposed fit of patriotic anger. Guy Banister, David Ferrie, J. D. Tippett, E. Howard Hunt. The list goes on.

Three decades later and everyone is sick of conspiracy theories. Especially after the ballistic overkill of Oliver Stone's *JFK*, which threw every conspiracy theory it could think of into the Dallas mix in the hope that something would stick. By the time of the thirtieth anniversary of the conspiracy things had turned full circle and Gerald Posner was able to publish *Case Closed*, in which he argued that, hey, the Warren Commission appointed by President Johnson to investigate the assassination was right after all. Oswald really did act alone and all the coincidences which had accumulated over the years were just that – coincidences. Peter Dale Scott is having none of this. Drawing on two manuscripts – 'The Dallas Conspiracy' and 'Beyond Conspiracy' – which have been much cited in the assassination debate but never before published, his *Deep Politics and the Death of JFK* makes it clear that what really happened to America in the Sixties was something equivalent to a Second Civil War. He starts out from the same questionable premise as Stone does in his movie – that shortly before his death Kennedy was planning to wind down the Vietnam War but was opposed by a cartel of business interests eager to plunder South East Asia. But from there he moves on to probe the deep structure of American political life in a way that is almost Foucauldian in its cool patience and passionless exactitude. Scott takes it for granted that the American political system is a racket, an informal understanding between government and organised crime for the division of the spoils of the drug trade. The amazing thing is that he is pretty much able to document it. Scott doesn't do anything as banal as tell you who killed Kennedy. What he does do is tell you that Oswald was working for the FBI. That the FBI was in the pocket of organised crime. That organised crime had links to the Dallas police. That many of the Dallas police were members of the US Army Reserve. That an army reserve officer was responsible for the choice of Kennedy's motorcade route. He tells you how the system works. And for that his book – published last year but only available in the UK now on import – is invaluable.

flesh wounds

You are hunched over your Amstrad in one of the run-down bedrooms of a Brixton flatshare rushing to beat the magazine copy deadline. A motorcycle courier hovers at your shoulder as an editorial warning sign more compelling than any waiting fax feed. You have placed yourself in this servile position as a result of pursuing an 'avoidance lifestyle' (Murray Bookchin) which has taken you from a student grant to the dole to a low-wage economy of freelance journalism commissions. The time and energy you free up is uselessly spent. Somehow you're drifting along with the death drive. One way of turning things round is to process your surplus subjectivity through the lifestyle designations of a newspaper ego column. But you lack the wit to defraud yourself. Instead you write your way out the hard way with a quarter of a million words of occulted bad faith.

SEX INDUSTRY
i-D, 170, november 1997

Porn is cool right now. Academics are beginning to sniff around porn films sizing up a new territory where all the old theories of gender politics and the visual grammar of power spring back into life. Entrepreneurs understand how porn has reached a moment of archival self-consciousness which allows its past to be aesthetically recommodified. Artists see how the semiography of porn offers up rich source material for appropriation and recoding. Everyone has been taught to love porn. That's why a book like Anthony Petkovich's *The X Factory: Inside the American Hardcore Film Industry* (Headpress) is so valuable. Not only does it rack up the emergent star system of a new Hollywood Babylon – with interviews with porn auteurs like Gregory ('Salvador Dali of Porn') Dark, John Leslie, Patrick Collins and Bruce ('Godfather of Porn') Seven and sketches of porn divas like Stephanie ('Too Good For Porno?') Swift, Nici ('Nice'N'Sleazy') Sterling, Christi Lake, Nyrobi Knights, Star Chandler and Nina Cherry – but it also delivers the hard empirical data on what it's like to work in the sex industry. The most striking thing is that the rhetoric of post-feminist self-empowerment (or 'girl power') seems to have become the official discourse of the new porn economy. Women do not do it to get paid, they do it to get laid; they are no longer sex objects in a system of exploitation but sex subjects in a game of manipulation – that's the new postmodern orthodoxy. But is this really so new and transgressive? Radical feminist and anti-porn campaigner Andrea Dworkin argued as long ago as the 1970s that the image-repertoire of porn was based on a metaphysical formula which insisted that all women were whores who would do it for nothing on principle. The postfeminist supersession of Dworkin seems to be nothing more than a self-conscious appropriation of her mapping of the Sexual Unconscious which turns it into a Baudrillardian manual of seduction. Petkovich's sleazoid tour of the porn industry does nothing to disabuse his subjects of their illusions because he's basically too busy getting off on it all. Despite the intensity of his misogyny and homophobia, however, the grim facts of the business do creep into his text. The book's final chapter, 'No Escape from LA', is particularly gruelling. A report from the set of John T Bone's fuck-fest *World's Biggest Gang Bang 2*, starring Jasmin St Clair, it's a detailed account of the attempt by the porn star Jasmin St Clair to beat the record set by Annabel Chong in 1995 when she was penetrated by 251 men ('she took cock in mouth, cunt, ass'). St Clair manages to get up to 300 but Petkovich feels cheated because unlike her predecessor she insists on the implementation of basic health and safety regulations (HIV tests, condoms, filed nails), protects herself with a series of prohibitions (no kissing, no sodomy, no eating cunt) and makes no attempt to disguise her pain ('I feel I have a rope burning my crotch'). It seems that degradation is the reality of pornography once all the cute ironies have been stripped away. So what else is new?

SLAVE TRADE
i-D, 123, december 1993

Paul Gilroy has been in the forefront of recent attempts to understand what it means to be black and British. *Black Atlantic* (Verso) sees him attempting to systematise the problem by placing it in the context of the wider history of the slave trade. For Gilroy, history does not conveniently stop at national borders. The history of modernity has been a history of mobility, trade and international cultural exchange which radically calls into question the idea of fixed national identity. The concept of 'diaspora', or forced dispersal, is the starting point for any genuinely trans-national attempt to theorise black identity. Gilroy patiently documents how the slave trade, far from being some late survival of pre-modern mercantile capitalism, was the founding moment of modernity, the point of rupture which made multinational capitalism possible. By drawing extensively on the writings of such black American moderns as W. E. B. Du Bois and Richard Wright, he is able to demonstrate that the 'double consciousness' which we think of as characteristically modern was something which the ex-slave populations of the eighteenth and nineteenth centuries had to contend with first. Before Kafka or Kierkegaard, in other words, there was the experience of thinking of oneself as a free man and being treated like a slave. The dominant response to this kind of skewed perspective has been to invent an empowering new mythology of black Africa as the fount of all civilisation. Gilroy is harsh on this brand of Afrocentrism, seeing it as a form of 'ethnic absolutism' which reduplicates the worst aspects of nineteenth-century racism. At the same time, he is equally severe on the postmodernists who want to collapse all signs of cultural difference into some dehistoricised field of play. For Gilroy, history and hybridity go together. His theory of the 'black Atlantic' as the preferred mythic homeland emphasises discontinuity, marginality and exile as the determining features of global black identity. His privileged thematic device for recovering a true memory of what it means to be black is the ship – first the slave ship and then those merchant ships which allowed the peoples of America, Africa, Europe and the Caribbean to trade and communicate with one another. The second mnemonic device he isolates is the gramophone record, a cultural artefact whose transit across the Atlantic transcoded deep memories of oppression, liberation and struggle. Gilroy is particularly good on music and his chapter on the trans-culturalism of everyone from the Jungle Brothers to Jazzie B (in which he takes a pop at Nelson George) is well worth reading. For more practical criticism of this sort, flick through the bits and pieces in *Small Acts* (Serpent's Tail). A round-up of Gilroy's journalistic output over the last few years, it includes valuable pieces on Frank Bruno (for) and Spike Lee (against) as well as sparky interviews with Toni Morrison and Isaac Julien. The best piece here is an extended essay on the cultural significance of black record sleeve art (tracing, among other things, the shift from a Biblical iconography of chains and bondage to a sci-fi interest in Nile Valley spaceships). Both books are well worth forking out for.

STRUCTURAL UNEMPLOYMENT
sight and sound, 3/4, april 1993

The vampire, the werewolf, the Frankenstein monster, the Egyptian mummy, even the stalk-and-slash killer – these fabulous creatures of the cinema have all had their critical apologists, their chroniclers and mythologists. But what of the humble zombie? Tom Savini's remake of George Romero's seminal 1968 horror film, *Night of the Living Dead,* offers a chance to expand upon this question. Like the vampire or the mummy, the zombie has returned from the other side of the grave. But it lacks the singular magnificence of a Dracula or a King Tut. Zombies always hunt in packs. They are blood-thirsty automatons who add to their numbers by feeding on human flesh. Individually, they are slow, stumbling and weak. Collectively, they are a rampaging mob of clawing hands and gnashing teeth.

'Zombies are the real lower-class citizens of the monster world and that's why I like them,' Romero has said. But what did they represent outside the 'monster world' of cinema. What was their larger political significance? The flesh-eating ghouls of *Night of the Living Dead* were an obvious symptom of social disorder. Romero himself was always anxious to play down their allegorical significance, but that didn't stop critics from trying to pin something on them. The packs of zombies – shambling, entranced, menacing – were variously interpreted as Nixon's 'silent majority' risen from their condos or as the returning waves of corpses from Vietnam.

Both judgements now look partial. If these useless bodies represent anything it is the structural unemployment which has been the legacy of our transition from a Fordist to a post-Fordist political economy, from a uniform to a two-tier society. Romero's zombies stand in for those workers and consumers who, since the flash-point year of 1968 – when the crisis in the old Fordist system first blew up – have been thrown on the scrap-heap. Economically extinct, socially displaced, they return to devour those who have survived them. Less the lower-class citizens of the monster world and more the disenfranchised under-class of the material world, they are a projection of postmodern capitalism's worst anxieties about itself.

Marx famously described nineteenth-century monopoly capitalism in gothic terms, as a vampiric process whereby capital – or 'dead labour' – sucked the vital juices from labour. The metaphor could do with up-dating. Capital in its late twentieth-century guise is 'undead labour' which survives by consuming the empty husks of dead labour. It is mining communities turned into theme parks, industrial warehouses turned into electronic offices, Victorian hospitals turned into luxury apartment blocks. It is the misery of unemployment turned into a prime-time moral panic. Romero's zombies are a figure of surplus human capacity processed through the system as grotesque 'social waste'. In other words, they indicate a hysterical class fantasy. The big fear of *Night of the Living Dead* is not only that the zombies are rapacious, but that they are unstoppable. Shoot them in the chest and there is the barest recoil before they keep on coming. Shoot them in the head and they go down, but not before another one has taken their place.

This unconscious sense of unemployment as social plague is particularly prevalent in today's recessionary climate. Not that Savini, who worked as the special effects artist on Romero's two sequels to *Night of the Living Dead,* is too interested in the political sub-text of his remake. Apart from shooting in colour, he sticks very close to the original film. The set-up is the same: a group of squabbling survivors take refuge from their zombie persecutors in a remote farmhouse and try to make it through the night. The only changes are minor. The events of the siege narrative are reshuffled (there seems to be an awful lot more banging and hammering), some of the characters are rejigged (the heroine is no longer a gibbering wreck but the usual post-*Aliens* survivalist babe) and the irony of the ending is changed (so that it's someone else who gets shot).

Savini doesn't come close to expanding upon the role of the zombie in the Nineties (his film was made in 1990). Romero, by contrast, really shook things up. He completely reinvented the zombie mythology he inherited from the voodoo movies of the Thirties and early Forties. *White Zombie, Revolt of the Zombies, King of the Zombies, Revenge of the Zombies, Voodoo Man*: these gothic shockers used the same formula. Typically, Bela Lugosi would be the evil sorceror who ran a Caribbean sugar plantation, while the zombies would be the workforce of resurrected corpses he controlled with his 'devil doll'. Shuffling, blank-eyed, anonymous, they provided what James B. Twitchell has called some of the 'most concussive images' in film history. He goes on: 'If the audience of the Depression thought the blank stares of the bread-liners were unsettling, these images make them seem tame. It is not death that is macabre; it is living death.'

Romero went on to give the imagery an extra bite. He is almost entirely responsible for the familiar incarnation of the zombie as ghoulish cannibal. Or, as Kim Newman puts it: 'The most obvious and immediate effect of the success of *Night of the Living Dead* was a sudden epidemic of inferior flesh-eating zombie films.' These include Ted V. Mikels' *Astro-Zombies* (1969) starring John Carradine; Bob Clark's *Children Shouldn't Play with Dead Things* (1972), a teens-in-jeopardy horror spoof, and his *Dead of Night* (1974), a return-from-Vietnam cartoon allegory; *Vengeance of the Zombies* (1972), and *Brackula: Terror of the Living Dead* (1972), baroque *Living Dead* retreads starring Spain's horror superstar, Paul Naschy; Armando De Ossorio's Spanish/Portugese *Blind Dead* trilogy – *Tombs of the Blind Dead* (1972), *Return of the Evil Dead* (1973), and *Night of the Seagulls* (1975) – all of which use slow motion to enhance the eeriness of their resurrected Templar knights galloping sightlessly through the night in search of victims; the blaxploitation horror movie *Sugar Hill* (1973), starring Marki Bey as a voodoo priestess who raises hit-men from the dead to take on the mafia; *The Child* (1977), which is *The Omen* plus cannibal ghouls; Ken Wiederhorn's *Shock Waves* (1979), starring Peter Cushing as the leader of a Nazi zombie army; Fred Olen Ray's *The Alien Dead* (1979), which features Buster Crabbe battling zombie Florida tourists; and Jean Rollin's *Zombies' Lake* (1981) and Jesus Franco's *Oasis of the Zombies* (1981), both rip-offs of *Shock Waves*. Meanwhile, the post-punk black farce of Dan O'Bannon's *Return of the Living Dead* (1985) gave rise to camp genre-benders like *Hard Rock Zombies* (1985), *Raiders of the Living Dead* (1987), *The Video Dead* (1987) and *Chopper Chicks in Zombietown* (1992).

As if that were not enough, there is the Italian cycle of zombie movies. These include Jorge Grau's *The Living Dead at the Manchester Morgue* (1974), first of the Italian splatter-zombie movies, shot in Yorkshire with an international crew and cast and considered a rare treat by horror fans; Lucio Fulci's *Dawn of the Dead* cash-in, *Zombie Flesh Eaters* (1977), a return-of-the-repressed take on post-colonial zombie 'contagion' with especially putrid special effects; Fulci's less successful gothic horror movies, *City of the Living Dead* (1977) and *The Beyond* (1981), which feature ghostly zombies-from-hell scenarios. The list of cheap porno-zombie-splatter movies goes on. There is Marino Girolami's *Zombie Holocaust* (1980), Bruno Mattei's *Zombie Creeping Flesh* (1980), Andrea Bianchi's *Zombi 3* (1980), as well as Aristide Massaccesi's zombie trilogy – *Island of the Zombies* (1980), *The Anthropophagous Beast* (1981), and *Absurd* (1981).

Romero gave the zombie a new lease of cinematic life by making it resonate with the implication of social plague. But he was not the first to bring it back home. The spate of science-fiction monster movies which appeared in the Fifties used the glassy-eyed trance of zombiedom as an image of alienation. In movies like Don Siegel's *Invasion of the Body Snatchers* and Gene Fowler's *I Married a Monster from Outer Space*, aliens take over the bodies of innocent smalltown consumers in preparation for a mass invasion. What gives them away to the vigilant observer is not so much their lack of animation as their trivial deviations from the social norm (working late in the basement, failing to turn on the car headlights). These are films whose political unconscious has less to do with the Red Menace or McCarthyism than with the social conformism demanded by Fordist economic integration. The anxiety they express is not that some Americans might be secretly different but that all Americans might be obscurely the same, serial instances of such contemporary stereotypes as William H. Whyte's Organization Man or Herbert Marcuse's One-Dimensional Man.

Romero's zombies are literally different. No longer representative of the faceless masses of Fordism, they instead refer to the hollowing out of this constituency by a post-Fordist organization of labour. Once released from the vampiric embrace of capital, the Organization Man becomes little more than a vagrant in a suit – just like the first zombie to pop up in *Night of the Living Dead*. After that, anyone is game. The point about Romero's film compared to Siegel's is that his zombies, far from being anonymous, are heterogeneous. They are lean, fat, old, young, male, female; they are dressed in suits, jeans, pyjamas, slips, nightgowns and, in one case, nothing at all; they are rural, metropolitan, suburban. The implication – one that has become more transparent to more people since 1968 – is that nobody is immune from the social restructuring of post-Fordism. Everybody's job is potentially at risk.

This is especially apparent in Romero's two successor movies to *Night of the Living Dead*. In *Dawn of the Dead*, which restages the siege narrative of the original film inside a shopping mall, and *Day of the Dead*, which shifts the scenario underground into a military bunker, the social typology of the zombies is absurdly specific. In *Dawn of the Dead* alone there is a nun, an air force general, a Hare Krishna disciple, a softball player, an insurance salesman, and a clutch of highly individuated grotesques. Because the film is set in a shopping mall, critics have been tempted to view its zombies as parodic consumers. Romero has suggested as much himself. But *Dawn of the Dead* is not a satire on the Fordist consumer society, however much it thinks it is. It is a film unaware of its real political significance.

If the methodology of Fredric Jameson is adopted and the film is treated as a 'dream-text' with a political unconscious buried beneath a layer of critical defence-mechanisms, then it is possible to see that the zombie is a figure of an expanding post-Fordist under-class filtered through a bourgeois imaginary of disgust. Exiles from the shrinking borders of that part of society which still works, Romero's zombies are seen as moaners, idlers, scavengers, dummies. They are presented as the scum of the earth. Raw, blown apart, exposed, they have been completely desubjectified (they do not even qualify for a point-of-view shot). The survivalists of *Dawn of the Dead* are permitted their cameos of consumer boredom (playing poker with thousands of useless dollars, getting dressed up with no place to go). The zombies are permitted only to wander. If they get in the way, they are run over, shot, sideswiped or otherwise pulped. All very ironic given that the only material difference between the two classes of bodies is that, in Paul Virilio's terms, they are 'metabolic vehicles' that move at different speeds. The zombies want to consume as much as their human counter-parts. It's just that they've forgotten how. Unlike the somnambulistic zombies of *Invasion of the Body Snatchers*, the zombies of *Dawn of the Dead* are juddery and inept. They bump into each other, fall over, stumble up the escalators, knock over display cabinets and crush goods under-foot. The confusion is all very comical, but it is not a satire on mindless consumerism. It is an oblique commentary on precisely the loss of those smooth reflexes which sustain the Fordist economy. The zombies are victims of a selective abandonment of the 'metabolic vehicle' of the masses by postmodern capitalism. They are demobilised Organization Men.

Day of the Dead* is a more traditional film than either *Night of the Living Dead* or *Dawn of the Dead*. Its location – an underground military base – is presented as the microcosm of a familiar dystopian society rather than, as in the previous films, a social terrain which it is the purpose of the 'action' to dispute. The zombies are a poor lot as well. Having been reabsorbed into a conventional military machine by the leaders of the base, they don't signify much more than the proletariat in chains. Certainly, it's no surprise to see Frankenstein's monster dragged out of the myth pool during the course of the film (Bub, the 'zombie with a soul'). It's almost as if Romero has gone back to basics and made *Day of the Dead* as *White Zombie* with added gore.

There are a couple of fragments in the film, however, which are more interesting, appearing as they do to connect a post-Fordist political unconscious with the material conditions of film-making. The first is the scene where a couple of lower-echelon members of the base show off 'The Ritz', their kitsch facsimile of a mass leisure environment, complete with lounger, sun-shade and wooden trellis. The bunker scenes were all filmed in an abandoned limestone mine in Pennsylvania which since the end of the Second World War had been used as a storage facility for all sorts of consumer durables (boats, golf-carts, powdered milk, feature-film negatives). From industrial work-place to consumer garbage dump to film-set – the archaeological history of the site already anticipates the post-apocalyptic sub-text of the movie. To that extent, 'The Ritz' is a synecdoche of the collapse of the Fordist system.

The second loaded scene in the film is the sequence at the beginning where a chopper lands in a zombie resort town in Florida and a scientist steps out to hail survivors. The streets are littered with cardboard boxes, old newspapers and abandoned cars, the elegant buildings are distressed and dirty, the whole place has seen better days. And then the zombies start appearing. Parodic tourists dressed in loud Hawaiian shirts and idiotic sun-hats, they converge on the chopper and force it to leave. This sequence was filmed in Fort Myers in Florida, a core city suffering from urban blight as a result of capital flight to the outer suburbs in the Eighties. The film-makers did not have to do too much to dress their set. History had done it for them.

Romero has said of *Day of the Dead*: 'The community I had in the original script was always sort of representative of the new West or Florida, where cities now collapse in ten years instead of two hundred.' He was also much more specific about the exact social composition of this community in his original script. One element which never made it into the finished film was the idea of a surplus human population living in sleazy fenced-in stalags reminiscent of Florida retirement condos. Described by Romero as a 'cesspool of human dregs', its members are either used as slave labour or as fodder for the zombie soldiers. What is clear here is that the post-Fordist under-class has become completely detached as an unconscious political referent from the figure of the zombie. Now, it is simply referred to by the grotesque fantasy of 'human dregs'. It is no surprise to learn that this hysterical outburst was revised for the film.

But the semiotic instability of the zombie was there right from the beginning. One significant difference between Romero's *Night of the Living Dead* and the remake is that Savini permits a multitude of conflicting explanations for the zombie plague, from chemical weapons to the hole in the ozone layer. This is something Romero wanted to do in the original, but he didn't have sufficient confidence in his audience and ran with a B-movie cliché about radiation from Venus. Co-writer John Russo has said: 'At the time, every film we went to see in that genre had an explanation. It seemed that the masses couldn't live without some sort of explanation. So we gave them one.' But the Fordist 'masses' were not the individuals who would turn *Night of the Living Dead* into a cult hit on the midnight circuit. Did the film-makers really have such contempt for their audience? The suspicion remains that Romero failed to understand the fascination of his zombies. But then, maybe so did his audience. By the time he came to make his two sequels to *Night of the Living Dead*, Romero had no trouble casting his zombies. People would come from miles around for a chance to impersonate the living dead. Savini set up a make-up assembly line for applying masks and paint to the hundreds of zombie extras required for each film. A technician who worked on *Day of the Dead* has commented: 'People would come and stay all night. It was something to do. Instead of going to a midnight showing of *Rocky Horror*, they'd come to the mall and be zombies.' Who were these people? Members of a post-Fordist under-class eager to exhibit the signs of their abjection? An avant-garde generation of consumers burlesquing the conformist habits of the past? Were they zombies or were they survivalists?

Maybe they were indeed the Fordist 'masses' of Romero's fond imagining, come out for one last time to rehearse the spectacle of their own extinction by processing themselves through Savini's assembly-lines. It would certainly fit the profile of Romero's career. He started out making commercials for US Steel, Alcoa, Heinz and Duke beer, outfits similar to those whose mass-produced commodities he would later trash in *Dawn of the Dead*. His production company, Image Ten, was set up in 1963 within earshot of Pittsburgh's declining steel mills, and occupied an ambivalent position in the economic fabric of the town. Parasitic upon the local branches of big Fordist companies for employment, it operated flexible post-Fordist labour practices itself and was staffed by a small 'family' of highly skilled workers who treated the office as a home from home. It was within this makeshift environment that *Night of the Living Dead* was conceived, financed, filmed and edited. Schooled in selling corporations a flattering image of themselves, Romero took his revenge by defaming the reputation of the people they served.

COMMUNIST REVOLUTION
i-D, 176, june 1998

This year marks the 150th anniversary of the popular revolutions which spread across Europe from their epicentre in Paris before being suppressed by the dominant powers. Was it chance or necessity which saw to it that the *Manifesto of the Communist Party* by Karl Marx and Frederick Engels had been printed at offices in the City of London just a few months before? One thing is sure. No publisher can resist the lure of a quick cash-in and the original document has now been reissued in a smart new volume under its more familiar title of *The Communist Manifesto* (Verso) with an introduction by Eric Hobsbawm. Does it still speak to us today? Once it is understood that the history of the twentieth century from WWI to WWII to the Cold War is the history of the anti-Bolshevik war (and that the Soviet regimes of Eastern Europe practised a form of state capitalism which mirrored the warfare/welfare capitalism of the West), then everything falls into place. The late twentieth century returns us to the hard realities of multinational capitalism which prevailed at the end of the nineteenth century – all that's changed is the tech (something understood by steampunk SF which retools cyberpunk by swapping personal computers for anarchist printing presses). This makes Marx's vision of a transnational regime of mass production giving every region in the world a homogenous 'cosmopolitan character' remarkably prescient. It fits our experience of airport consumer culture in which all the old vertical holds (development/underdevelopment, First/Third World) have been replaced by horizontal bands of shifting intensity. But it did not really begin to occur until data comm tech had allowed assembly lines to be instantaneously shifted to cheap labour depots in the 1970s. It is this side of Marx – the side of him which admits to the revolutionary productive capacities of capitalism – which postmodern cyber-ideologues like Sadie Plant wish to rehabilitate. What is being attested to here is not the way that the contradictions of capitalism may crash the whole system but the way that they trigger semi-autonomous feedback loops which force it to evolve (Hobsbawm speculates that such a move towards a 'post-capitalist society' would necessitate 'a sharp shift away from private appropriation to social management on a global scale'). Anarcho-luddites like Hakim Bey will no doubt judge that if this is a revolution it is a revolution led by the bosses. The other side of Marx – the side of him which hypes the emancipatory powers of the proletariat as a universal class – is something which has been consigned by liberal fascists like Newt Gingrich to the ash-heap of history along with the welfare state. This ignores the fact that the threat of communism was only tamed when the organised labour movement cut a deal for its members with the boss class (not when Ronald Reagan won the Cold War). Now that deal is in ruins, now that poorer people begin to drop below the threshold of political visibility, now that molecular interest groups begin to infect the command-and-control systems of representative democracy, it might be said that an old spectre is again haunting not just Europe but the world.

VIRTUAL CAPITALISM
i-D, 135, december 1994

Where does techno-theory go from here? For the last few years, the name to watch on the pop philosophy circuit has been Arthur Kroker. A trendy Canadian academic who picks up where Marshall McLuhan left off (that's to say, on the edge of the place where the media, the body and cyberspace meet), he has pumped out a number of postmodern primers since the late Eighties, but it's only in the post-Cold War era of soft ideologies and virtual wars that his slogans ('crash television', 'excremental culture', 'panic bodies') have started to bite. Kroker is a slippery character. He main-tains that he does his best writing while tuned into CNN in McDonald's and while this gives a good indication of the hermetic concentration of his subject matter (basi-cally, American mass culture gone global), it also hints at the thin, textureless and rather insubstantial quality of his prose (as soon as you've swallowed one theory-byte, you've already forgotten what it tasted like and are ready for another). In his latest batch of apocalyptic routines, *Data Trash* (New World Perspectives), Kroker is on good form. Co-authored with Michael A. Weinstein, the book gets to grip with the media's big story of the year – the Internet – and comes to some gleefully pessimistic conclusions. Kroker doesn't buy the theory that the Internet – that parasitic elec-tronic messenger service which has developed on the back of the world's corporate computer networks – is a counter-public sphere in the making, a digital hideout for anarchists, subversives and hackers alike. It's already too late for that. According to Kroker, the romantic idea of the Internet as an electronic commune is just a come-on – a sales pitch – designed to make the punters sign up, log on and get virtual ('Like a mirror image, the digital superhighway always means its opposite: not an open telematic autoroute for fast circulation across the electronic galaxy, but an immensely seductive harvesting machine for delivering bodies, culture and labour to virtualisa-tion'). Who are the insidious people behind all this? The 'virtual class'. That's to say the usual conspiracy candidates – a techno-elite of corporate, banking and govern-ment types who want to run the world. Actually, this is to be slightly unfair to Kroker, who does go on to distinguish the interests of the virtual class (who want to trans-figure the base matter of the flesh into pure information) from those of the capitalist class (who, as ever, simply want to make money). Even so, his prose only really takes off when it is fuelled by the delirium of the 'will to virtuality'. It is here – whether cruising around the global data-banks of Taiwan, calibrating the recombinant virtu-osity of fashion viruses, or contemplating the jacked-in body refiled as 'data trash' – that Kroker really comes into his own. Where he falls down is in his failure to theorise how the bodies left behind by the flight to cyberspace – the surplus populations of Europe and America, the 'system-deleted countries' of Africa – might possibly come together to gum up the digital works. Kroker isn't interested in anything that's not plugged in. It means he misses a lot. But it means the stuff he does get is pure gold. Where else could you read a sentence like this: 'The information highway is paved with (our) flesh.' Read and enjoy.

CLASS WARFARE
i-D, 180, october 1998

The great value of Jacques Camatte's work is that it makes the link between occult Marxism, critical postmodernism and posthuman science fiction. Quite a neat trick. *This World We Must Leave* (Autonomedia) is the first volume of a projected three volume edition of Camatte's writings to be published. It consists of pamphlets disseminated in the wake of the insurrectionary events of May 1968 when Camatte was closely involved with Amadeo Bordiga and the Italian Communist Party. Together they offer a capsule analysis of the general fate of the Marxist critique. Here's how it goes. First, the antagonistic class couple of the bourgeoisie/proletariat benefits from the eclipse of the feudal mode of production by the capitalist mode of production. Then, there is the passage into one of two possible transitional phases. In the third volume of *Capital*, Marx speculates that the dialectical outcome of class war will deliver a dictatorship of the proletariat. In the *Grundrisse* he speculates that it will deliver instead an expanded capitalist mode of production. Camatte suggests that these two phases indicate nothing less than the differently articulated modulations of welfare state capitalism which prevailed across the East/West divide during the Cold War. He holds true to Marx's hope that this transitional state will (via the intercession of a superior mode of production) go on to liberate the progressive energies of the forces of production and establish a universal post-scarcity utopia. But he warns that there is the danger that this moment will benefit capital rather than humanity. It is from this point that Camatte's analysis begins to develop its dystopian edge. He goes back to the cybernetic legacy of Norbert Weiner to suggest that capital has become an out-of-control global entity which operates according to its own runaway logic. It is autonomous, 'fictitious', virtual – it has 'escaped' to establish its own despotic empire whose only parallel is with the metaphysical megamachines of Asia. What makes Camatte particularly valuable is that he refuses to celebrate this moment. Instead he offers up a whole series of critical lines of engagement. He ties the 'empire of capital' to an ecological crisis of overpopulation, pollution, resource-depletion and general unsustainability. He implicitly agrees with the French situationist Guy Debord that capital has passed beyond the fetish of the gold standard and is organising itself around 'ideal representation' or spectacle and the niche manufacture of recreational subjectivities but argues that the subversive potential of 'detournement' is always recuperated as fresh mystification. He runs with Baudrillard for a while when he suggests that it may be the subjectivity of the object world (as in the idea of a 'brand personality') which is becoming dominant. He comes out in favour of some post-modern social movements (hippies, regionalists, vegetarians) while remaining critical of others (drug users, anti-psychiatrists, mystics, queers) and ambivalent about femi-nism (which uncouples the reproductive capacities of the female sex from patriarchy only to deliver the productive capacities of the female gender to capital). More than anything else he suggests that 'the material community of capital' is responsible for subjecting humanity to sociobiological 'domestication' in the shape of mind control, media manipulation, neuro-linguistic programming and genetic resequencing. Now that the old bourgeois class has been replaced by the new middle classes of post-modernism and the proletariat has been structurally adjusted there is the sense in which the capitalist social designates a universal class of slaves marked by different 'hierarchies of inequality'. Camatte is post-Marxist to the extent that he excoriates the salvation myth of the proletariat as an elect class, but hyper-Marxist in the sense that he sees the new class war as an apocalyptic last battle between capital and humanity. It's an extreme hypothesis. But maybe an essential one in the struggle to establish 'not a new mode of production but a new mode of being'.

hermetic signatures

You are waiting in the Clerkenwell office of a trendy young graphic designer for your colleagues Jim and Matthew to turn up. Together you have been funded by metropolitan listings publisher Tony Elliott to produce a dummy issue of an electronic lifestyle magazine. The three of you can't decide on a name for it but know that it will have to compete with the UK version of Wired *being put together round the corner. Your nameless title folds before the first issue as the publisher takes fright at its failure to securely identify its target market and some years later after multiple relaunches its prospective competitor also implodes. The spread of ubiquitous computing is dissuading the cybercult scene from remaining at the edge of the media simulacrum. Instead it disappears into the culture. You refuse to accept this negation of your avant-garde theoretical position and make the move into non-nonfiction.*

GILLES DELEUZE & FELIX GUATTARI
i-D, 179, september 1998

Michel Foucault once famously said that the twentieth century would be known as
the Deleuzian century. We still live under the sign of that dispensation. The concepts
first theorised by Gilles Deleuze and his buddy Felix Guattari – desire as the principal component of a political machine, sexual identity as production rather than
representation, revolution as a micro-political or 'molecular' event – have come to
specify the operating system of postmodern subjectivity. *Chaosophy* (Semiotext(e))
– a recently translated collection of old interviews, essays and roundtable events –
is a useful little introduction to the duo's major works. It also includes a valuable
critique of their system by Pierre Clastres, the political anthropologist who theorised tribal subjectivity as a form of 'society-against-the-state'. Clastres knows that
Deleuze and Guattari's achievement is to have produced a political anthropology of
late capitalism. He also could not have avoided recognising the fact that the equation made in *A Thousand Plateaus* between capitalism and schizophrenia proceeds
through the route of primitive magic. Deleuze and Guattari explicitly access the
ethnographic data of anthropologist and Marcel Mauss disciple Marcel Griaule during
the course of their book. Griaule documented the West African Dogon people extensively during the 1930s and 1940s until he was finally initiated into the occult
meaning of their ritual practices by a tribal elder. The result of this encounter was
to produce a body of magical lore – the value of lines of force, 'nomos' rather than
logos, the multiple encoding of signs – which Deleuze and Guattari imported directly
into their analysis of late capitalism (so that, for example, 'surplus value' functions as
a form of prestige in the circuit diagram of sacrifice). This is the point at which Clastres begins his critique. He 'wonders whether the idea of Earth does not somewhat
crush that of territory'. Given that Deleuze and Guattari's ideas on 'deterritorialisa-
tion' and 'reterritorialisation' are explicitly identified with the nonplaces of the desert
it is no surprise to discover that – as the Critical Art Ensemble for one has recently
argued – cyberspace has been the most hospitable domain for the back-engineering
of these nomadic techniques of living into tools of capitalist appropriation. Clastres
also questions 'a theory that asserts the primacy of the genealogy of debt replacing
the structuralism of exchange'. He here implicitly attacks the whole system of pro-
scarcity politics which structure Deleuze and Guattari's understanding of the social.
The Dogon believed that the precious seeds for their crops had been delivered to
them as cargo from the sky gods – but then they did live in a relatively barren
cliff-top environment. Deleuze and Guattari have no such excuse. Their recourse to
the marginal utility school of economics (which disputes Marx's labour theory of
value in favour of a theory of molecular market demand) is an ideological manoeuvre
which designates capitalism as a cybernetic cargo cult and theorises Mauss' originally scandalous idea of 'gift exchange' as a feedback loop. It is perhaps only dissident surrealist Georges Bataille's notion of 'unproductive expenditure' (an imaginative
act of negation seeking not even the prestige of sacrifice) which points a way out of
the Deleuzian maze.

MANUEL DE LANDA
i-D, 174, april 1998

Manuel De Landa has written one of those rare brilliant books which single-hand-edly attempts to reconceive the history of philosophy from the ground up. *A Thousand Years Of Nonlinear History* (Zone) succeeds on its own terms. But it fails by every conventional academic yardstick (which makes it something to compare to Nietzsche's *Birth of Tragedy* or Walter Benjamin's *Origin of German Tragic Drama*). De Landa's central thesis is that all history is the history of a flow of 'matter-energy' which incarnates itself at various moments as animal, mineral or vegetable entities which themselves begin to 'complexify' and evolve. He supports his argument with a bold display of conceptual armour – Prigogine's nonlinear dynamics, Dawkins' neo-Darwinian theory of memetic evolution, Deleuze's ideas of molecular self-organisation – and models it across the three separate bands of geology, biology and linguistics. What really impresses about this is not just the inter-disciplinary breadth of learning – De Landa can move effortlessly from the part played by 'wind circuits' in the European conquest of the Americas to the way a 'microbial proletariat' has been harnessed to produce antibiotics – but the long view taken. De Landa writes in the tradition of the French historian Fernand Braudel, who would typically analyse the effects of capitalism over a four-hundred-year time-scale, and this clarity of vision allows him to produce a massively confident prose style ('The cities that began multi-plying in Europe at the beginning of the millennium were like so many islands in the middle of a large temperate forest in its climax state').

The problem arrives when De Landa claims that all the metaphors used in his book are meant to be taken literally, that they describe material processes which operate at the molecular level. This is his Lucretian swerve – the moment when he refers back to the Deleuzian 'engineering diagram' which makes it possible for him to say that a hurricane is powered by the same motor as a truck – and it is the move which takes his work into myth. De Landa suggests, for example, that Europe was able to colonise the Americas because (unlike with its earlier attempt to colonise the Middle East during the Crusades) it had the 'biological weapons' – in the shape of diseases like smallpox and the measles – which enabled it to 'ingest' the natives. He goes on to comment that about 27 million Mexicans died during this time (De Landa dedicates his book to his parents, who hail originally from Mexico). But if disease is industrialised in this way, then conversely, cultural events like the killing of six million Jews by the Nazis are implicitly naturalised and De Landa's rhetoric begins to do the job of retrieving a discourse like eugenics not as ideology but as science (flawed science, admittedly, but the paradigm shift has been made). There is an anti-humanism struggling to emerge here. When De Landa suggests that the European conquest of the Americas can be reduced to a story of peasant 'biomass' converting into industrial 'silver' which goes on to seduce the world he is plainly reproducing an alchemical narrative (he later refers to our planet as 'a mere provisional hardening in the vast flows of plasma which permeate the universe'). De Landa has produced an ambient cosmological myth for the twenty-first century. Enjoy with caution.

HAKIM BEY
i-D, 143, august 1995

I turn the dial and manage to catch Hakim Bey at the Virtual Futures conference at Warwick University in Coventry. His voice is quick, alert and New York dry. Interference ghosts the signal and I adjust the aerial.

'Hello, can you hear me?'

'I'm reading you fine.'

Hakim Bey is not a real person. He is an avatar invented by an American Sufi scholar, itinerant anarchist and self-styled poetic terrorist. You may have read some of his stuff. How about *T.A.Z The Temporary Autonomous Zone* (published in 1991 by Autonomedia). Or *Immediatism* (published in 1994 by AK Press). How about 'The Information War', 'Evil Eye' or 'The Permanent Autonomous Zone' (all posted on the Net). Even if you haven't read any of his books or essays, you're bound to have come across some of his slogans – 'ontological anarchism', 'art sabotage', 'psychic paleolithism', 'anarcho-mysticism', 'pirate utopias', 'democratic shamanism'. Hakim Bey is a conceptual alchemist who cross-breeds ideas taken from the intellectual underground (e.g. hermeticism, magick, Islam, gnosticism, anarchism, situationism) to form sturdy new hybrid memes which he then releases on the net. There is no copyright on any of his books. He wants the ideas he has broadcast to be taken up and used.

'I think it was Marcel Duchamp who said that if you have three ideas in your life, you're very lucky. I don't know whether I've really had any and I don't think the TAZ was one of them. I just put a nice handy label on something that was already going on and if that helped clarify people's thinking, then I'm happy.'

The idea of a Temporary Autonomous Zone – a nomadic, free-floating space which drifts through the wastelands of the dominant order assembling possibilities for pleasure, subversion and creative play – has certainly been an influence on the development of club culture. Was he aware of this? 'Yeah. I've found that the ravers are some of the people who really do understand what I'm talking about – the real ravers. I was told that there was a so-called rave in England that was sponsored by Pepsi Cola and that it called itself a TAZ. And I wanna say quite clearly that that is not a TAZ, that if Pepsi Cola is involved then that is by definition from the very start to the very finish not a Temporary Autonomous Zone. Maybe it's a zone and maybe its temporary. But it sure isn't fucking autonomous. 'What would be? What is a valid TAZ?' 'It's already going on. In response to the miseries of alienation and the immiseration of commodification – not to talk about neo-fascistic state power and the McDonaldisation or Disneyfication of society – in response to all of these things, people rediscover their friends and their bodies and suddenly it becomes intensely pleasurable not to be involved all the time in mediation. Right here and now I think that the TAZ is a very useful tactic. Because two minutes of freedom and pleasure is better than a lifetime of mediocre misery on your knees worshipping the idols of mediation.'

Hakim Bey – like Timothy Leary and Terence McKenna – is making links between the post-rave moment and an older Sixties-based tradition of hedonism, subversion and disalienation. (The difference is that he still has his marbles.) He is interested in the new psychotronic interfaces – drugs, music, dancing – but doesn't particularly groove to them himself ('The best thing about rave music for me is not the content – because I don't enjoy it – but the structure, the way it's made'). And he still carries a utopian baggage from the 1960s which identifies capitalism and all its works – commodities, media, technology – as the enemy. All of which contributes to the irony of Hakim Bey being a minor Net god who is not himself on-line. 'It's like that first sentence in *Society of the Spectacle* – everything that was once lived has moved away into representation. I don't care how much fun you can have on the Net (far be it from me to say that people aren't having fun just because I don't happen to enjoy it – let n flowers bloom to requote Mao), but if you're only living through representation in that way – well, the image that always occurs to me is from Gibson where the hacker is always plugged in and his avatar is off in cyberspace having a grand old time and the meat is dying. In fact the very concept of the body as meat is telling.'

So is the Net a bad drug? 'I would say that if commercial television is third grade heroin then the net is capable of being third-rate coke. It's exciting, but it's a third-rate kind of excitement. This is why it has a numb skin feel to it – for me. But that's just my personal taste. I'm not gonna make a generalisation about the people who think that it's good to be numb – either because they're the propeller-head type who can't face real life or because they're following some pseudo-gnostic approach where you celebrate the downloading of consciousness into the machine.'

Does he believe that's possible? 'It hasn't happened yet and I believe there may be reason to feel that it can't happen. I have an intuitive feeling that consciousness and body are linked. Although I'm by no means a defender of the pure body. The cult of the body in the sense of the pure body is just the flipside of the cult of immateriality – of pseudo-gnosis. In fact the whole idea of a pure body is a gnostic idea. I find myself defending impurity – and stupidity on a certain level – because to be too smart in a certain sense is to jack into cyberspace and leave Mother Nature behind.'

But surely the Net would seem like an obvious place for the TAZ to redefine itself? Look at the imaginary collectively-authored MOO environments, for example. 'The Net is only a metaphor. You can't go live there, you can't grow your turnips there. One place where a TAZ could emerge is from the place I call the no-go zone, the areas from which control withdraws itself. What you have in some parts of Newark or Detroit – or perhaps some of the cities in the north of England – is the spectacle of control. You don't have the reality of it anymore. Every once in a while the cops will come in and smash a few people and show it on television and hope that that will deter the rest but since all the services have been withdrawn, where is the reality of the state? So it's perhaps in zones like that where a more permanent autonomous zone could transpire.'

So the Net is a false god? 'What could be more *cogito ergo sum* than the Net? What's left of the old Cartesian paradigm but the pure *cogito*? Every ghost is always coming back to haunt us in some respect. I would just prefer to choose the ghosts who hold out some promise of a good party. So the concept of the living earth has great appeal to me. I'm not gonna twist my brain around and superstitiously believe in Mother Earth as some kind of hypostasised entity. But on the other hand it's alive.' What about McLuhan's old idea – recently revived by Kevin Kelly – that the global superstructure of the Net is itself alive? 'That goes back to the old Jesuit idea of the noosphere, something I've always felt a profound mistrust for. I associate it more with cyberspace than with some kind of evolutionary material development.

In fact, I think it's a parody of the noosphere. It's not the actual noosphere that all these fucking Jesuits were waiting for. It's a heaven of glass – something the Jesuits claimed the gnostics had always built. A false heaven.'

Let's forget about the Net. Let's talk about music and drugs. These are escape vectors which Hakim Bey sees as more positive because they connect with the reality of lived existence. 'Although, as you know, music and drugs can have all kinds of functions. I'm not a puritanical thinker about drugs like, say, Terence McKenna, who thinks "mushroom, good; coffee, evil". But there is a sense in which certain drugs relate to certain aspects of the social and not to others. And the same holds true for music. So music and drugs – yeah groovy. But heroin addiction – not so good, not really very positive in my view. I also have a problem with the tyranny of 4/4 rhythm and the blasted omnipresence of commercial rock. What was once a few minutes ago a celebratory form of partying in the Deleuzian sense, has simply become an omnipresent commodity tyranny. I was clocking it the last time I travelled from New York to London. I was almost never out of range of some goddamn 4/4 rhythm. I felt like I was being smashed with a hammer. It was on the airport, it was on the plane, it was on the bus from the airport, it was in the hotel when I arrived. I was never able for one moment to have a little silence and I call that a form of tyranny not a form of celebration.'

What about other forms of music like trance and techno? The 4/4 beat which so distresses Hakim Bey has been sloughed off in a lot of this material. What is explored instead is texture, polyrhythms, fractal dimensionality. 'It reminds me of the interest generated in Oriental music back in the Sixties. My parents could never listen to completely Oriental music the way that my generation could. It existed below the aural threshold for them. If anything made the difference, I think it was LSD. That enabled us to get off on the droning aspects of the music and hear those elements that my parents missed.'

Nomadism may be the key to Hakim Bey's cast of mind. He has coined a term – 'nomadosophy' – which sums up his interest in thinking on the move. 'Obviously, the Deleuzian nomadic thing is important. I think travel itself can become a zone-less TAZ, a multidimensional TAZ. You have the example of the travellers in England, people who are creating their own free space which is not in any one particular space. But which is in material space. And that's very important.'

How has it affected him? 'Let me put it this way. No matter what kind of revolutionary idea you have, 15 minutes later it's a McDonalds ad. Be it culture or ideology – no matter where you're drawing from – it's going to end up in that maw. That all-devouring maw. There may be forms of discourse that we can come up with which are indigestible by that monster, but it's very curious that we don't seem able to come up with them. Therefore you gotta drift, you gotta stay on the edge of the wave and always be – not trendy – but anti-trendy. Take a definite dialectical stance against whatever looks trendy. Which is stupid because then you're just a curmudgeon … What can I say? It's a dirty job but somebody has to do it.'

BILL VIOLA
i-D, 184, march 1999

North American video artist Bill Viola received the first comprehensive retrospective of his work at Amsterdam's Stedelijk Museum in 1998 and in recognition of this fact his collected writings from 1973 to 1994 have been reissued. *Reasons for Knocking at an Empty House* (Thames and Hudson) shows how far he differs from other video art luminaries like his contemporaries Nam June Paik and Bruce Nauman. What marks out Viola is his interest in filling the emergent medium of video with subversive ethnographic discourses – gnostic belief systems, Eastern spiritual disciplines, Renaissance memory protocols, shamanic trance practices – when it was still an open symbolic channel. In this he anticipates the same move which was made with regard to Nineties new media by psypherpunk writers like Erik Davis and Kodwo Eshun and it is worthwhile reading his texts in the shadow of the Internet, sampladelic systems and digital tech. What becomes clear after this is the key importance of his 1982 essay 'Will There be Condominiums in Data Space?'. Here Viola theorises the concept of cyberspace at the same time as William Gibson. Not only does he distinguish in semi-Deleuzian fashion between its coding as a linear 'branching' structure (like a narrative-dominant videogame) or an open-ended 'matrix' structure (like a VR walk-through), but he also goes on to make the connection with technoanimism which was such a constituent feature of *Mona Lisa Overdrive*. But whereas Gibson in his novel hooks cyberspace up to the spirit world of the Haitian voodoo cults, Viola comes up with the same idea of a digital dreamtime by plugging into Indian Tantric doctrines instead. This has great para-theoretical benefits. Gibson made the equation between the Haitian 'vever' or ritual graffiti tag and the circuit diagram; Viola goes one step further by discovering how the Tantric 'yantra' or divine energy diagram also links up with the 'mantra' or sonic invocation ritual. This emphasis on the audio interface with an embodied psyberspace is what animates many of the other texts in this collection. Viola suggests in 'The Sound of One Line Scanning' for example how a techno-genealogy of video situates its descent from the microphone (rather than from photography as is the case with film) and thus opens it out to a domain no longer dominated by objects but structured instead by a recording/broadcasting *field*. This then leads to a consideration of the acoustic space of architecture which ends via a reckoning of wraparound structures (Greek amphitheatres, whispering galleries, the Moog, the tambura, digital positioning satellites) with a theorisation of 'desert solitude as an early form of visionary technology'. How does Viola make this final leap? By referencing Mircea Eliade's conception of the shaman's ability to dissolve the upright posture of Enlightenment subjectivity – with its ego-fixated point-of-view, its four cardinal points and six-sided rooms – and reincorporate a forgotten wilderness sense of distributed lifeworld intelligence. Of course this carries its own dangers. Viola ultimately designates the limit structure of cyberspace as a paradox-riven 'schizo' model in which every pathway is simultaneously the same and not the same as any other. Users, he cautions, 'may become lost in this structure and never find their way out'. We have been warned.

ROGER CAILLOIS
i-D, 178, august 1998

The mythology of the serial killer is still over-determined by the image of Hannibal Lecter – damaged genius, mad outlaw, sacred monster – outsmarting his captors from the confines of his high-security cell. It's an image which reappeared every week in the first series of Chris Carter's post-*X Files* TV show *Millennium* in which psychic detective Frank Black hunts down an assortment of crazies, weirdos and mad prophets. The value of Mark Seltzer's *Serial Killers* (Routledge) is that it buries this myth once and for all. Eschewing the trading-card mentality which sees every Ted Bundy or Henry Lee Lucas as a marketing opportunity, Seltzer instead analyzes the serial killer as the limit event of postmodern subjectivity. In a world where there is no longer a charged interface between public and private, where inside and outside implode into a Baudrillardian feedback loop, the postmodern subject becomes a nodal point in an information network and the human individual feels like a ghost in the machine. This is the aporia of identity which the serial killer makes his natural habitat. Seltzer convincingly argues that the serial killer is not so much an outlaw as an oversocialised psychotic or hyperconformist idiot, a blank figure who is more normal than normal. He quotes a psychiatric consultant on Jeffrey Dahmer: 'Dress him in a suit and he looks like ten other men.' Or refers to Bundy's capacity to become the 'significant other' of any person he met. What all this suggests is that the serial killer organises their identity to a logic of neither production nor consumption but of simulation. In this sense 'identity' bleeds into a process of perma-identification in which the subject becomes completely mimetic. Seltzer quotes Jim Thompson from *The Killer Inside Me* on the social chameleon which is his alter ego: 'I leaned an elbow on the counter, crossed one foot behind the other and took a long slow drag on my cigar.' All this was theorised long ago by the ethnographic surrealist Roger Caillois. He speculated that there was a mimetic drive which went beyond the functional effects of camouflage and preceded even the instinct for self-preservation: 'mimicry would thus be accurately defined as an incantation fixed at its culminating point and having caught the sorcerer in his own trap.' It is at this moment of maximum danger that the subject-as-simulation is tempted to disappear into their own immediate environment and shelter a Pythagorean molecular hell. The serial killer escapes this destiny by committing what Seltzer calls 'suicide by proxy'. Their victim becomes a substitute for themselves in a sacrificial ceremony which because it is dedicated to individual rather than collective social renewal can never work. Instead it gets caught up in what Rene Girard has theorised as a monstrous scene of mimetic doublings (whose banal props and costumes are only significant as elements of a structural diagram but often misrecognised as literal fetishes). Infinite repetition is the curse of the serial killer. That's why they all court celebrity. The jail cell with the CU-SeeMe is the only way out.

MARCEL DUCHAMP
i-D, 183, february 1999

If late twentieth-century art practices – appropriation, simulation, decommodification – are just catching up with Marcel Duchamp that's because he was so far ahead of his time. The value of David Joselit's extended essay *Infinite Regress* (MIT) is that it deconsecrates the received mythology of the original French avant-garde artist by arguing that his later devotion to chess 'was not a renunciation of art but rather a means of rethinking its terms'. The arc of Duchamp's career is described by an astonishing series of paradigm leaps. His early Cubist paintings like *Sad Young Man on a Train* or *Nude Descending a Staircase* are already different from the perspectival involutions of Picasso and Braque in that they are explicitly conceived of as a graph of the moving human body considered as a writing machine. Duchamp based his method on the chronophotography of Etienne-Jules Marey and it prefigured an interest in the imaginative possibilities of the machine which would dominate his career (he did not fetishise machines like the Futurists – whom he called 'urban Impressionists' – but was interested in the processes they encoded). This move from representation to inscription allowed Duchamp to jettison the canvas altogether and make his connection with the commodity world as a new extended surface of engagement. His conception of the readymade was always based around the idea of a 'rendezvous' between the artist and a chance object rather than an act of aesthetic terrorism and his signed commodities – the urinal, the snowshovel, the bicycle wheel – record moments of subjective estrangement ('by planning for a moment to come – on such a day, such a date, such a minute – to inscribe a readymade, the readymade can later be looked for'). Joselit says that Duchamp was always interested in nested dimensions and points to *Handmade Stereopticon Slide* – where a polygonal volume is superimposed over a two-dimensional seascape – as an example of this. The suggestion is that the readymades in parallel fashion are events which implicate Einstein's fourth dimension of time ('Naturally inscribe that date, hour, minute on the readymade as *information*'). Whereas André Breton was prepared to be surprised by his found objects, Duchamp designated a gravitational field of attraction in advance. He began to map a psychogeography of space-time. This is why he made the final move into chess (check the photo of a chessboard hung on the wall of his Paris studio like a painting). The intersubjective dynamics of this fiendishly complicated game modelled a virtual topography which allowed Duchamp to fold the grid of space-time along specific axes (he was fascinated by 'end-game problems of possible games so rare as to be nearly utopian'). What happens next? It's possible to speculate that Duchamp's games with space-time conjured the possibility of transfer across the fifth dimension of hyperspace which had recently been theorised by the German mathematicians Theodor Kaluza and Oskar Klein in the 1920s. His great work *The Bride Stripped Bare by Her Bachelors, Even* then becomes the diagram of a (nearly) utopian vehicle capable of inscribing his own introjected subjectivity as a 'ready-found' to be objectified and discarded at some future date and a new subject position occupied. Which date? The inscription attached to *Fresh Widow* – Duchamp's model of a leather-paned French window which looks as if it had a black hole trapped inside

– reads: Fresh Widow COPYRIGHT ROSE SELAVY 1920. It was the first work to be executed by Duchamp's cross-dressing alter ego and marks the axis of his own career (Rose Selavy still awaits us).

STEPHEN HAWKING
i-D, 187, june 1999 (killed)

One of the great novels of the post-Sixties period of American traumatic realism is Joe Haldeman's *The Forever War* (originally published in the early 1970s it now finds itself reissued by Millennium). Haldeman was employed as a combat engineer in Vietnam from 1967 to 1969 and his novel about a thousand year war between the Earth nation and an alien race of Taurans is often interpreted as an allegorical account of American imperial involvement in South East Asia. What is often forgotten however is that Haldeman had studied physics and astronomy and that his speculations on the possibilities of faster-than-light hyperspace travel are exact. He accesses astro-physicist John Wheeler's idea of a 'wormhole' to theorise how passage from a black hole to an exit 'white hole' might be effected but introduces a new terminology when he designates both these zones as instances of a 'collapsar'. Beyond that he also suggests that a flightpath navigation system for a pre-programmed sequence of 'collapsar jumps' might be supplied by the pathworking techniques of the Jewish qabala. It is with this formulation that Haldeman makes his occult Deleuzian turn and specifies the collapsar jump as a technique for pursuing a line of flight from one subject position to another (Deleuze and Guattari: 'Every consciousness pursues its own death ... attracted by a black hole, and all the black holes resonate together'). The qabala is often called the 'tree of life' and in that sense resonates with the trunk-based root-and-branch diagrams often associated with shamanic cosmologies. Hyperspace may indeed have a schizoid or 'rhizomatic' structure but that doesn't mean that 'arborescent' navigation systems are not needed to successfully plot a course through its fiendish domains (just as an intelligent agent needs its source code to navigate the network of networks that is the Internet).

The mythical origins of the qabala are densely populated with orders of angels who tend to coalesce into the figure of Metatron – the archetype according to gnostic scholar Harold Bloom of all those wayfarers who engage in a 'heavenly ascent of the soul'. How might this occur? Theoretical physicist Paul Dirac speculated in 1928 that virtual particle-antiparticle pairs spontaneously appear from the fluctuations of space-time geometry in the quantum void and shortly afterwards disappear through an act of mutual annihilation. Astro-physicist Stephen Hawking updated this theory in 1971 when he suggested that a rotating micro-black hole might offer a type of gravitational singularity which would interrupt this process by preferentially capturing those anti-particles which have an opposite spin to its own so permitting the corresponding particles to survive. One way of solving this equation is to say the black hole evaporates. The other way of solving it is to say that the anti-particles disappear into hyperspace and reappear where a white hole condenses instead. In other words a wormhole is always blocked by a singularity which needs to be dodged in order for hyperspace travel to occur. This effectively means that a Metatron-like traveller must split their subjectivity and enact their own virtual death in order that the 'true name' of their 'archon' or angelic blocking agent might be discovered and safe passage through a collapsar achieved. Or as Haldeman puts it: 'I felt that I was at the same time being crushed and bloated'.

terminal futures

You have scored yourself a press pass to the Doors of Perception cybercult conference taking place at De Balie in Amsterdam. Over the next few days a parade of hackers, activists and professional technopagans takes to the stage and 'interpellates' (Louis Althusser) the new medium of the Internet with a collective imaginary of old utopian affects. You respond by digging deep into your review copy of Resisting the Virtual Life. Years later Dutch cyber theorist Geert Lovink turns up at the Post-Media expo in London to announce the closure of the electronic frontier. He says: The massification of the Internet has turned it into another adjunct of the society of the spectacle. You sense the leakage of aura. Soon afterwards you are offered work by an online retail store who are using the whole idea of the virtual community as a marketing tool to attract customers to their website.

ROCKET MAN
arena, 61, september 1996

An assorted collection of tech-heads, tattoo freaks and middle-class avant-gardists is filing into the dim pit of London's Institute of Contemporary Arts theatre to catch a rare appearance by the Australian body artist Stelarc. Each clutches a programme which explains that they are about to witness an 'Internet actuated and uploaded performance' called Ping Body which has only taken place once before in Sydney. People are nervous and excited. It's a bit like entering the sanctuary of an electronic church or the recess of a primitive control-and-command bunker. Nobody knows what to expect.

The object of this hushed anticipation stands spot-lit on stage wearing a head-mounted liquid crystal display unit with all the blind authority of an Easter Island statue. His nearly naked body is covered with a dense exoskeleton of trailing wires and electrodes which inevitably conjures Hollywood memories of Arnold Schwarzenegger in *The Terminator* or – further back – Boris Karloff in *Frankenstein*. Particularly striking is the Japanese-manufactured prosthetic hand attached to the artist's right arm. Its vicious stainless steel fingers look as if they could pull teeth.

Surrounding him in the semi-darkness is a host of equipment – three computers, three vidcams, two data-video projectors, a vision switcher and a sound mixer – which hum and wink like compact electronic familiars. They are to be his aids in this evening's performance. Ping Body intends to transduce the information traffic from thirty Internet Web-sites into a series of micro-signals which will take possession of the left side of Stelarc's body and cause it to twist and turn. The right side of his body, meanwhile, will be free to guide the sum total of the performance and activate the equipment around him.

It all sounds like so much cyber-voodoo. But what follows once everyone has settled into their seats is an elaborate choreography of machine-like gestures which is at once strange, haunting and, inevitably, a little boring. Stelarc lifts his feet, bends his arms and rotates his neck like a bionic mannequin wrestling with invisible demons. He activates his third hand and its glinting pincers grasp at thin air like a demented power drill. Other sensors attached to various parts of his musculature amplify the rush of blood in his arteries and translate the shifting geometries of his body into quasi-industrial sound effects. Add to all this the fact that a video remix of the performance is screened above the artist's head and uploaded to a special Web-site every 60 seconds and the stage is set for an audio-visual assault on the senses which is part cyberpunk circus act and part techno-shamanic ascension rite.

The next day in the bar, Stelarc appears without the weird gizmos to rap about 'alternative aesthetics', 'contestable futures' and his conviction that 'the human body is obsolete'. He is reassuringly kitted out in a long woollen waist-coat which looks as if it has been hand-knitted by his granny and has the distracted aura of a mad professor who has been released from an engineering basement somewhere on a 24-hour pass. That's to say, he is charming, affable and relaxed, but also prone to punctuating his wilder flights of fancy ('one thing which intrigues me is the idea of inserting a colony of micro-miniaturized nano-robots into my body') with demonic bursts of laughter.

One thing you soon learn about Stelarc is that he got to the whole techno-body art scene early. Back in the late Sixties when he was known as plain Stelios Arcadiou, he was already messing about with homebrew VR rigs at the Royal Melbourne Institute of Technology. He moved on from there to experiment with sensory deprivation stunts (he was sandwiched between two planks with his mouth and eyelids sewn shut at Tokyo's Tamura Gallery in 1979), suspension events (involving the 'exquisitely painful' piercing of his flesh with metal hooks) and internal body scans (he once inserted a sculpture into his stomach, discovered he had a polyps and had to undergo some unplanned emergency surgery).

But what has really grabbed people's attention in the last ten years has been his interest in developing software programmes which effectively virtualise the body as an interface and enable it to be modified, redesigned and transformed. The idea of connecting this interface to the Internet came more recently but it fits in with Stelarc's whole ambition to question the human body as 'a capable evolutionary structure' and think about how, as Marshall McLuhan put it, 'man is beginning to wear his brain outside his skull.' Stelarc nods at the mention of the Oracle of the Electronic Age. 'For me the Internet is not so much a sphere of information transmission but rather a means of externalising the central nervous system. The idea that in the future your body might be a host for clusters of agents spread over the net is a wildly romantic and beautiful notion.'

Stelarc once applied to NASA to become a mission specialist and 'give artistic expression to the experience of zero gravity'. He was (perhaps unsurprisingly) turned down, but outer space still holds as much of a fascination for him as cyberspace. Perhaps more. 'There are various things occurring now which generate unexpected possibilities and certainly one of them is the notion of designing a body that can survive in the varying atmospheric, gravitational and magnetic fields of other planets in the solar system. This has got nothing to do with sci-fi star-trekky go-where-no-other-body-has-gone-before kinds of fantasies. This is about planning intelligent survival strategies.' He looks at me, cracks off a laugh, and suddenly we're back on planet Earth.

SOFT SUBVERSIVE
i-D, 102, march 1992

The Meridien Hotel on Piccadilly looks like it belongs in an early Cronenberg movie. Plush, synthetic, molecular, one in an international chain, it is almost too designed, too purposeful.

Consec in *Scanners*: the corporation as a body of proliferating cells, a malignant growth. Starliner Towers in *Shivers*: a luxury apartment complex invaded by parasitic bugs, its lifeless inhabitants turned into a bunch of homicidal sex maniacs. The city of Montreal in *Rabid*: bland and bored, until seized by an epidemic of sexually transmitted rabies.

What strange creatures lurk in the even spaces of the Meridien? David Cronenberg sits in a room on the fourth floor, greying hair neatly parted, little round glasses flashing light. He is alert and polite. A tape unspools beside him.

'I am fascinated by the way we have never accepted anything as given to us,' he says. 'Take this hotel: we don't want to sit outside, we want to be somewhere where we can control the rain and the temperature. It's the same with our bodies. If we don't like the body's chemistry, we change it. We want to be involved in our own evolution. No other animal has done this and the cutting edge of it all is medicine.'

Cronenberg is in London to promote *Naked Lunch*, an adaptation of the mutant avant-garde novel by William Burroughs which has been gestating inside the director's mind ever since he made his first body horror movie. The original plan was to shoot the movie in Tangier, Morocco, the international zone where Burroughs had written most of the novel (after accidentally shooting his wife in 1951). The Gulf War changed all that and in the end the production never moved beyond Toronto.

Looking back, Cronenberg considers this to have been a happy accident. It forced him into a rewrite which heightened the movie's sense of internal drama and sharpened its hallucinatory edge. All very appropriate given that the thrust of the original novel has to do with the altered state of consciousness provoked by the systematic use of drugs. Burroughs wrote *Naked Lunch* in between shots of morphine and its jump-cut narrative style owes as much to the interrupted sense perceptions of the addict as any fancy theories about montage or random form.

At the same time, though, the novel is much more than a junky's testament. Burroughs is interested in how addiction serves as a metaphor for social conditioning, how human behaviour can be modified by indirect stimulation of the nervous system and what passes for reality manipulated by secret control agencies. In this sense, his text is recognisably Pavlovian in its cultural assumptions: reactions always come from the gut, opinions are nothing more than disguised bodily functions. Nobody is immune from some form of addiction, everybody is controlled by 'The Mark Inside'.

Peel back the beat lyricism, the vaudeville carnage and surreal slapstick, the cracked allegories and deadpan ironies of *Naked Lunch* and what is exposed are the Cold War innards of Eisenhower America. Burroughs' agents and pushers, his sinister control freaks like Doctor Benway ('a manipulator and co-ordinator of symbol systems, an expert on all phases of interrogation, brainwashing and control'), fit sideways into a wider world of wire taps and lie detector tests, truth serums and hidden persuaders. This is not the story that Cronenberg wants to tell. Burroughs' fictional alter ego, William Lee, is up there on the screen, a gaunt, croaking figure played with world-weary charm by Peter Weller. And so is Benway (a muted Roy Scheider). Even the aliens that crop up in the margins of the novel, the Mugwumps, are here, looking pooped, wrecked, strung-out, like ET on junk. The performances are great, the special effects are great, but this isn't an adaptation of *Naked Lunch* so much as a story of how the novel came to be written.

In some ways, Cronenberg had no choice. With its scenes of multiple murder, orgasmic violence, homosexual rape and mutilation, *Naked Lunch* is unfilmable. Any literal adaptation would, as the director admits, 'cost 400 million dollars and be banned in every country in the world'. So he has settled instead for 19 million dollars and a special effects version of a butt-fuck. The rest is an account of the internal dynamics of the act of writing, the psychology of the creative process. And that involves a lot of scenes with typewriters turning into crouching bugs which talk to Lee from sphincter-like holes in their bodies.

The structure is simple but strange. It's 1950s New York and William Lee is working as a cockroach exterminator. A nihilist in a three-piece suit, he hangs out with beatniks and is addicted to his own roach powder. His slatternly wife, Joan, is also addicted: one of the first scenes in the movie shows her injecting in her tit. Taken in by the cops, he is interrogated by a giant insect which claims to be his case officer. It tells him that he is a secret agent in an undercover operation and that his wife is working for the other side. Events fall into place and Lee accidentally shoots Joan in the middle of a drugged-out party.

Then he's on the run. He ends up in Interzone, a Tangier of the mind, where, through the mediation of his talking-asshole typewriter, he confronts the truth of his own aberrant impulses: his sexuality and creativity. He also gets caught up in the middle of a secret war for control of the international drugs trade. Before he knows it, he is compiling a series of reports on his covert activities: the first few pages of *Naked Lunch*.

Writing, in Cronenberg's hands, becomes a threatening, messy, visceral activity. As he says in the collection of interviews, *Cronenberg on Cronenberg*, recently published by Faber: 'When you see the list of movies about writers, it's quite extensive – everybody from F. Scott Fitzgerald to Dashiel Hammett to Kafka. But the problem is always the same: the act of writing is not very interesting cinematically. It's a guy, sitting. Maybe he's interesting, maybe he wears a hat, maybe he drinks and smokes. But basically he sits and types. It's an interior act. In order to really convey the experience of writing to someone who hasn't written, you have to be outrageous. You have to turn it out and make it physical and exterior.'

Nearly everyone in the movie is a writer. Besides the Lee-Burroughs composite, there are also disguised versions of Jack Kerouac and Allen Ginsberg, as well as characters based on the Tangier-based writer, Paul Bowles, and his wife, Jane. Despite the Mugwumps, the bugs and Benway, this is essentially a movie about character and psychology: devices repudiated by the novel in its effort to prosecute an entire society. It's no wonder that it fails to match up.

Cronenberg's thesis is clear enough. When he was using, Burroughs was collaborating in his own repression, he was attempting to literally exterminate himself. Only by owning up to his unconscious impulses was he able to free himself, only by writing could he survive. The death of his wife, ironically, was the trigger for this change.

As psychology this is unexceptional. It is also symptomatic of a narrowing of vision in Cronenberg's work from *The Fly* onwards. *Shivers* and *Rabid* are concerned with the violent transformation of whole societies; *The Brood* with the psychopathology of the nuclear family; *Scanners* and *Videodrome* with the spread of corporate control mechanisms; *The Dead Zone* with fantasies of assassination and nuclear incineration. *The Fly*, despite its high gross-out factor, is a movie about the deterioration of a relationship, while *Dead Ringers* is a study in the psychology of fratricide (at the same time, in purely aesthetic terms, it is Cronenberg's masterpiece).

Much more interesting than the narrative in *Naked Lunch* is the sideline conceptual labour performed by some of the special effects. In one stand-out scene, Benway presides over a dispensary where Mugwumps are suspended above the ground like so many carcasses, their phallic teats sucked on by a horde of slavering addicts eager to consume their jissom. All part of his master plan to corner the world market in drugs.

This is a wonderfully perverse moment which manages to catch some of the infernal energy of the novel. The blurring of the distinctions between nourishment and addiction as well as between male and female sex organs is presented as something sinister and malevolent. Quite the opposite, in fact, of the talking-asshole typewriters, which are ultimately in the service of a benign transformation.

And that is the difference between Burroughs and Cronenberg. The beat novelist may have provided the cult movie director with a reserve of imagery: bodily transformation, viruses, weird science, strange sex, insects, telepathic communication. But whereas in Burroughs, mutation is a grotesque allegory of conformism, in Cronenberg it is, more ambivalently, a possible symptom of post-human evolution. 'I really think that, quite some time ago, we seized control of our evolution without quite being aware of it,' he says. 'And perhaps the more conscious of it we are, the better off we're going to be.'

Take this whole business of the 'talking asshole'. In Burroughs it is a humorous fable. A guy teaches his sphincter to talk so he can make money as a vaudeville act; but pretty soon his mouth spontaneously seals up, his head atrophies and the asshole takes over. This is all presented, quite explicitly, as a metaphor of the vitiation of human potential by the cancerous spread of bureaucracy. In Cronenberg's version of events, however, it becomes the catalyst for a much more positive reaction.

As he explains: 'William Lee is an insect exterminator. He says, "Exterminate all rational thought." And that's what he's trying to do. He's trying to live straight – he's got a job, got a wife – but what he's really exterminating if he does that, apart from insects, is his unconscious, his homosexuality, his creative needs. So the typewriter as the insect, the insect unconscious – a sexual, sometimes sinister, sometimes funny, unpredictable thing – represents the strange and bizarre parts of himself he tried to repress.'

In the end, then – perhaps surprisingly – Cronenberg is more perversely optimistic than Burroughs. Not only are his movies attempting, as he has said many times before, to invent a new aesthetic which can accommodate things like the physical signs of disease (as in 'that's a fine, cancer-ridden young man') or the sight of the body's insides (as in the idea of a beauty contest for best spleen and best liver), they are actively engaged with the possibility that degeneration is a species of freedom.

Take the following remarks in *Cronenberg on Cronenberg*. 'The characters in *Shivers* experience horror because they are still standard, straightforward members of the middle-class high-rise generation. I identify with them after they're infected. I identify with the parasites, basically. Of course they're going to react with horror on a conscious level. They're bound to resist. They're going to be dragged kicking and screaming into this new experience. But, underneath, there is something else, and that's what we see at the end of the film. They look beautiful at the end. They don't look diseased or awful.'

All of this prompts the thought that if mutation in Burroughs is an image of the 'normalising' cancer infecting Eisenhower America, then maybe in Cronenberg it could be a metaphor of the 'polymorphous perversity' of the permissive society. This is something which hasn't escaped the attention of politically correct critics who, failing to understand how it's possible to 'identify with the parasites', convict Cronenberg of exhibiting tell-tale signs of 'phallic panic'. It is said that in his movies, the expression of female sexuality is typically stigmatised, the forces of law and order fetishised.

How does he respond to that? 'It's all coming back,' he replies. 'The whole political correctness thing. The right-wing feminist thing. The anti-AIDS thing. The ecology thing (I have a friend who calls them "eco-fascists"). Under the guise of saving the planet and so on, what's coming back is a lot of the puritanism that I recall from the Fifties. It's combined with talk shows where people talk about being a prostitute and a transvestite and God knows what else – which would never have been acceptable in the Fifties. But we're not so far away from that time.'

So does he feel vulnerable? 'Oh yes, absolutely. I'm sure that I'm going to be arrested at any minute by God knows who. I mean, definitely. It's a very strong feeling. A real feeling.'

NEW PURITAN TRANSSEXUALS
i-D, 175, may 1998

Kate Bornstein is the acceptable face of transsexual activism. His/her eclectic resume is less remarkable for the details of his/her gender switch (s/he was born Al Bornstein and has effected a M2F transition which means s/he is now recovering from oestrogen treatment) than for the fact that s/he has functioned in the past as a Scientologist and marketing director. Add it all together and what you get is *My Gender Workbook* (Routledge), an exercise in gender education which mixes autobiography, New Edge spiritualism and Dale Carnegie-style self-improvement. The whole thing is designed in the manner of Douglas Coupland's *Generation X* primer, with vox pop inserts, conceptual games and puzzles, cutecore slogans and Internet riffs layering the page. It's very postmodern (in many ways it's a pop remix of Judith Butler's seminal gender performativity text *Gender Trouble*). It's also very wholesome (thus distinguishing it from the hardcore musings of Bornstein's mentor Sandy Stone). What Bornstein is doing is taking queer theory to the mallbound middle-classes and s/he does it very well. His/her crucial theoretical recommendation is that we should distinguish the socially constructed norms of gender from the human activity of sex – which is 'fucking' plain and simple. Bornstein wishes to sidestep a whole series of unproductive debates by placing under erasure the 'sex-as-gender' designation (which focuses upon binaries like penis/vagina, androgen/oestrogen, XY/XX chromosomes). S/he is then able to move on to consider gender as a fluid process of signification which can take in basic signs – 'girl', 'tomboy', 'butch', 'femme' – and use them to concatenate more complex strings of code – 'transfag', 'hermaphrodyke', 'faggotdude', 'boychick'. This can result in the kinds of identity tags familiar from the Internet – like 'omnisexual omnigendered pervert fag transman in biofemale body'. It can also result in some bizarre assertions – like the claim that Jewish men and Christian men have different genders. At some undefined point in Bornstein's argument 'gender' simply becomes the master term in a familiar routine about postmodern identity politics. S/he fails to really open things up. But s/he does provide some interesting jumping-off points. It's possible (following Donna Haraway's insight that gender is a form of technology) to think about how the emergence of birth control tech has made gender obsolete and therefore paved the way for its comeback as a form of performance art. It's also possible (following the US Army's wetware/ hardware/software distinction and mapping it on to the familiar mind/body/ spirit distinction) to think about gender as a form of subjectivity programming exposed to the influence of media viruses and cultural memes. It's possible, in other words, to get to William Burroughs. Is all this going mainstream? Bornstein quotes a couple of pioneer identity hackers: 'what was once a potent means of communication among ourselves and others on the streets is now diluted into mainstream fashion trends – current accessorising fetishes used to be a semiotics of sexual proclivity – and people don't even know what they are doing (or SAYING) with their sartorial choices.' So there.

OLD FLAME WARS
arena, 64, december/january 1996/97

Richard Barbrook may be the 40-year-old head of the Hyper-Media Research Centre at the University of Westminster, but he likes to think of himself as a bit of an old punk rocker. It was with a dash of the belligerent spirit of '77 still in mind that he turned up at the Ars Electronica festival in Linz, Austria earlier this year, determined to take a pop at Richard Dawkins, Oxford University biologist, popular sage and esteemed author of *The Selfish Gene*. Dawkins took the stage prior to Barbrook and eloquently propounded his theory that human behaviour is to a large extent determined by 'memes', or self-replicating media viruses which are the neural equivalent of DNA. He went on to illustrate his point by referring to the vogue amongst some of his students for wearing their baseball caps backwards, arguing that this was an example of the bio-social conditioning or 'memetic engineering' he was talking about. Barbrook then got up and took Dawkins apart.

Sitting in his cramped academic quarters a month later snappily dressed in black suit, braces, Next polo-shirt and black brogues, he grins as he tells how upset Dawkins eventually became and it is obvious that he relishes the memory of their encounter. 'The thing I pointed out was that if you got up and said people's lives were controlled by angels and demons, people would think you were bonkers; but if you say they're controlled by memes and computer viruses it somehow seems to be scientific. What's interesting about Dawkins is that he's set himself up as a hyper-rationalist, but he's actually become the high priest of this pseudo-scientific cult. He's become a new L. Ron Hubbard.'

Barbrook laughs. 'I was being provocative. But because he's so fanatically anti-religious, it does force him to confront the weaknesses in his own position. I don't think he ever really gets challenged about this. I mean, he doesn't know anything about politics, sociology, economics, history, anthropology or psychology. He just has this simple idea. Now if he read some sociology, he'd know precisely why his students turn their baseball caps round – to annoy people like him, probably.'

With trademark black cap perched at a jaunty angle on his head, Barbrook is not exactly averse to annoying people himself. In fact, he has rather a talent for winding up the self-appointed gurus of the cyber-world. He recently accused the editorial mafia behind the avant tech magazine *Wired* (among them Kevin Kelly, Stewart Brand and John Perry Barlow) of promulgating a 'Californian ideology' whose blend of anarcho-capitalism and cyber-hippie libertarianism posited a 'digital nirvana inhabited solely by liberal psychopaths.' When his J'accuse was published in London's art-tech magazine *Mute*, it was head-lined with the slogan 'Never Trust a Hippy' and earned him a flame on the Net from *Wired* publisher Louis Rossetto. 'It made my week,' he says. 'I mean, you read *Wired* magazine and it pretends to be very hip and trendy and radical but it's basically arguing for all the unemployed to have their welfare benefits removed, to starve to death because it's good for them.'

Barbrook then punches up the HRC Web-site (http://www.hrc.wmin.ac.uk/) on his office Mac and shows me one of the 'Surrealist Games' he's designed along with partners in crime Andy Cameron and Jeremy Quinn. A series of baffling slogans scrolls past: 'Human Dissimulation Is Head-Mounted Anarchy', 'The Rotting

Physicalities Of The Privatised Bottom-Line Cancelises The Burnt-Out Interzone'. It turns out they've all been strung together by a random-text generator. The name of the game? 'Cyber-Bollocks.' Barbrook and Cameron put it together 'on a few bottles of beer and a few spliffs' after one cyber-conference too many had exhausted their patience with the arcane ramblings of McLuhanesque techno-theory. 'We thought, a machine could do this.' Then he shows me some of the 'Basic Banalities' he's written as a counter-weight to the Cyber-Bollocks. More slogans scroll past: 'Artist-Engineers Must Create Virtual Spaces Fit For Human Habitation', 'Cyberspace Is Where The Imaginary Can Become Real', 'The Beauty Of Digitised Human Labour Is That It Is Infinitely Reproducible', 'Desire For Union With The Machine Is Fear Of The Flesh', 'Your Taxes Built The Net: Thank The Agencies Of The State For Their Visionary Planning'. We both chuckle at that last one. ('It reminds me,' says Barbrook, 'of when I was down at Megatripolis and Timothy Leary was beamed into the club on a CU-SeeMe. Someone asked him why he thought computers were the LSD of the Nineties and he replied that it was because they were both invented by the American government. It's the one time I've agreed with him.')

The list of Basic Banalities pretty much sums up the HRC's working philosophy. Modernism, scepticism and pragmatism are the watch-words; William Morris and the Bauhaus the inspiration. The MA course which Barbrook and his partners are setting up this year is designed to equip students with the skills to become 'digital artisans' in the hyper-media economy of the future. They will be encouraged to work with businesses, community groups and public bodies during the course and once they are out in the real world there is the expectation they will feed their experiences and contacts back into the Centre. Barbrook has already fixed up a sponsorship deal which will enable one of his students to design an online version of London's Groucho club. Meanwhile, the HRC Web-site shows what has already been accomplished. 'J's Joint' was set up with Sony to publicise Jamiroquai's last album and includes material on the anti-road protest group Reclaim the Streets. ('Jay Kay wanted some green stuff on his site,' says Barbrook. 'It was only later we found out he drives a Ferrari.') There is also a collection of personal stories and art-terror postcards uploaded from the recent Bosnian conflict ('The postcard site won an Internet award which the Bosnians thought was pretty surreal at the time. They were basically getting electricity for an hour a day and they'd just won a prize in cyberspace'). Other treats include the Future Sound of London web-site and a version of Andy Cameron's wildly successful multi-media art project, *Anti-ROM*.

Barbrook has a whole pile of ideas about what a possible Ministry of Technology should be up to in the future. He describes himself as 'a card-carrying member of the Labour Party' and recently helped it to run through a draught of the Broadcasting Bill. He's also matey with Ken Livingstone (an old comrade from the heyday of the Greater London Council in the early Eighties) and is up to date with recent internecine party squabblings. So does that make the HRC an unofficial think tank for New Labour? 'Oh, I'm sure Tony Blair would be proud of us.' For the first time during the course of our interview, he actually appears rather bashful.

RETRO AVANT-GARDISM
i-D, 172, february 1998

If there's one thing that the recent Sensation show in London demonstrates it's the bankability of contemporary British art. Here is the private collection of a wealthy industrialist placed inside a public showcase of bourgeois art to the benefit of everyone involved. Charles Saatchi gets the official seal of approval, the Royal Academy makes money at the door, the artists see their stock rise. Marcel Duchamp commented on this kind of situation long ago: 'With commercialisation has come the integration of the artist into society, for the first time in a hundred years ... Today the artist is integrated, and so he has to be paid, and so he has to keep producing for the market.' All of this is another way of saying that the avant garde is dead. Its historic mission to close the gap between art and life has been effectively completed by the media, leaving no space for its critical impulses to survive. This at least is something understood by many North American artists. The recent 'Scene of the Crime' exhibition at the Armand Hammer Museum of Art and Cultural Center in Los Angeles probes the edges of the media simulacrum which the Sensation crew safely inhabit looking for signs of artistic life. Curated by Ralph Rugoff, it showcases the work of 39 Californian artists from the mid-Sixties to the present and reproduces the best of them in *Scene of the Crime* (MIT). The legitimising paradigm for this kind of move has to be Walter Benjamin's reinterpretation of Eugene Atget's empty photographs of Paris as forensic records of the untraceable ubiquity of the social crimes of history. Once this is understood then the key exhibit in *Scene of the Crime* is Mike Mandel and Larry Sultan's 'Evidence', a collection of black-and-white photos from the archives of police and fire departments, insurance underwriters' labs, aircraft manufacturers and scientific testing firms which makes its point – much like Duchamp originally did with his readymades – simply by shifting institutional boundaries. By comparison with the naked honesty of these images (characterised by Rugoff as 'craters made by explosions, burn marks, materials left over from various testing procedures, including "accidents" that appear to have been deliberately staged'), most everything else in *Scene of the Crime* – Lewis Baltz's wideframe shot of the road where the Rodney King beating occurred, Terry Allen's use of the detective's case progress board, Richard Misrach's manipulation of bullet-scarred porn mags, Barry Le Va's impacted glass sheets, George Stone's latex body-bags and even Anthony Hernandez's shots of abandoned homeless bashes under the freeways of Los Angeles – labours under the curse of belated self-consciousness (in which the crime to be investigated is the death – was it murder or suicide? – of the avant garde).

   If Benjamin is right to suggest that 'every spot of our cities' is the scene of a crime then it surely becomes the responsibility of the artist to lab-test – as Paul Virilio for one has suggested – a mobile 'ethics of perception'. Once this has been done then life begins to disclose its visionary moments like so many slashed eyeballs and the bunkers of art are revealed as mausoleums of dead capital.

very slow memes

You spend three years wandering through the open stacks of the Cambridge University Library on a psychogeographical 'derive' (Guy Debord). Scattered theoretical texts on Marx, Freud and Nietzsche morph in your imagination to code a heterogeneous operating system for your subjectivity. You find yourself hooked on the idea of turning your designated thesis into a total epistemological system but cannot bear the reduction into homogeneity this entails. You write enough to theorise the structural impossibility of media subversion. Then you spend the next ten years failing to prove yourself wrong. Your attempt to detourne the style press begins with editors requesting that you tone down the conceptual content of your work and ends with them begging you for more. The detour through your subjectivity doubles back on itself. You are passed by the media simulacrum.

AFRO-SHAKESPEAREAN PSYCHOGEOGRAPHY
i-D, 156,september 1996

Perhaps one of the last things you might think of reading for pleasure is a dictionary. Too boring, right? But dictionaries contain the archaeological deposits of the language and offer a disguised history of migration patterns, trade routes and the shifting borders of cultural identity. One of the best currently on offer is the *Dictionary of Caribbean English Usage* (Oxford University Press). Scrupulously edited by Richard Allsopp of the University of the West Indies, this is the first scholarly work to document the language spoken by 5.8 million people living in twelve independent nations. Read it and get wise. Find out if you're a 'spree boy' (fun-loving dude), a 'sport girl' (good-time girl), a 'nowherian' (wanderer), a 'pantyman' (queer) or a 'rang-a-tang' (tough guy). Understand when you're 'sprankious' (lively), 'sometimeish' (moody), 'humgrumshious' (bad-tempered), 'kicksy' (restless), 'pesterous' (irritating), 'half-and-half' (so-so) or 'trickified' (crafty).

The creative detourning of the language evident in each of these words shows how Caribbean English has thrived by not respecting the rules of the Queen's English. This doesn't make it a sub-language or a minority dialect. Far from it. It is positively Shakespearean in its wit, energy and inventiveness. This is no surprise. Allsopp points out in his introduction that the language of the region developed on the back of the 'triangular trade' in drugs and slaves which was routed between England, the Caribbean and West Africa from the 1560s. The English language was in many ways the first Elizabethan export. When Sir Francis Drake watered his ships at the island of St Christopher (now St Kitts) in 1585, it was uninhabited. It took an influx of West African slaves, English sailors and Irish bond servants into the island to effectively 'creolise' the language of the original colonialists. The same story can be repeated across many of the other islands. What this all adds up to is a story of the separate development of Elizabethan English in a kind of simulation chamber set apart from the imperium. It is a similar story to the one the Mexican-American theorist Manuel De Landa tells of the evolution of English from the time of the Germanic invasion of the British Isles onwards. Linguistic norms replicated across generations and transformed what was a soup of Germanic languages into Old English.

There was no command-and-control centre directing this development; it was an example of bottom-up self-organisation. Furthermore, it was the peasants who did all the work to make this happen; by the time of the Norman Invasion the boss class of aristocrats were all speaking French.

It's no different in the Caribbean. While the plantation owners sat on their porches doing the accounts and 'talking dicks' (speaking with proper diction), the language was changing all around them. In fact, Caribbean English can lay claim to being one of the more highly evolved forms of the English language. Check it out.

EJECTED METANARRATIVE

'Video Zombies, Carnival Clowns, Demobilizing the Masses' in Steve Beard, *Bloody Banquets: Trash Video, Jacobean Horror, Rewinding Foucault*, unpublished University of Cambridge PhD dissertation fragment, 1991

I   DOUBLE EXPOSURES

Loose talk about postmodernism and its discontents has become something of a commonplace over the last few years. Its mention has almost become something of an embarrassment, belonging back there with Reaganomics, power dressing and all the other media clichés of the last decade. But if the p-word is treated less as last year's favourite adland buzzword, a catch-all aesthetic used to tag the latest in everything from architecture to haute cuisine, and more as an attempt to get a handle on the possible emergence of a new historical epoch, then it still has some conceptual purchase. If postmodernity rather than postmodernism is the governing phrase, then an alert critical discourse – however constrained by the dictates of fashion, however 'commodified' – is once again made possible.

In the following chapter I intend to offer a new angle on an old debate by considering postmodern culture back to back with the culture of the early modern period in order to block out in parenthesis the Foucauldian archeology of modernity. The argument at its broadest is that just as the late sixteenth century was a period of cultural transition – the death throes of feudalism tied to the birth pangs of Foucault's disciplinary social under the sign of absolutism – so the late twentieth century is a similarly ambiguous watershed epoch – the decay of the Foucauldian regime structurally connected to the emergence of Baudrillard's cybernetic social under the sign of late capitalism. This in turn will be linked to a consideration of the rise and fall of the bourgeois public sphere in an attempt to give specific material definition to the contours of the argument. In this way, the Renaissance stage is figured as the crucible of modernity, of Foucault's disciplinary technologies, while the crisis of the cinematographic regime so evident in postmodern Hollywood, particularly in pause-button video culture, is figured as an equally historic event – the junking of the modern project, the testing of a new episteme.

II   FOUCAULT/BAUDRILLARD: SOFT COP/HARD COP

So what is the exact nature of the relationship between Foucault and Baudrillard? And how does it connect with the postmodern debate? The title of Baudrillard's celebrated 1977 polemic couldn't be more explicit: *Forget Foucault*. But this is an ambivalent injunction, an attempt to outbid rather than dismiss the Foucauldian conceptualisation of history. The reason why Baudrillard thinks Foucault should be forgotten is not that he is on the wrong discursive track but that he is lagging behind the times. His description of disciplinary power in *Discipline and Punish* is 'magistral but obsolete',[1] its grand microscopic sweep indeed the very sign of its superannuation. For 'if it is possible at last to talk with such definitive understanding about power, sexuality, the body, and discipline, even down to their most delicate metamorphoses, it is because at some point all this is here and now over with'.[2] The Foucauldian analysis 'comes to a halt right at the threshold of a current revolution of the system'.[3] It fails to acknowledge that discipline has been superseded by simulation as the governing mechanism of social control, the language of the social sciences by the rhetoric of marketing as the privileged discourse of power, the institutional regime of surveillance by the media modulation of feedback as the critical logic of subjection. Baudrillard seems willing to accept Foucault's key division of history – the shift during the early seventeenth century from a spectacular to a disciplinary economy of power – but only because he is able to trump it with one of his own – the parallel jump during the late twentieth century from that same disciplinary to a new cybernetic social formation.[4] All very convenient, but not a little disingenuous. Baudrillard is here making the same misguided assumption that Foucault did in such 'structuralist' texts from the Sixties as *Madness and Civilization*, *The Birth of the Clinic* and *The Order of Things* – history as the march past of epistemes, of regimented discursive blocs filing past with no sense of any causal connection.[5]

First the Renaissance with its ambivalent propitiations of the sacred leper, a liminal figure free to roam the margins of the city, socially excluded yet symbolically exhibited, a spectacle of abandonment, voyager on a 'ship of fools'; its casting of disease as allegory of sin, punishment and redemption, the signs of affliction poised challengingly between damnation and divine election; its scrupulous divination of the secret markings of a supernaturally ordained universe, the 'prose of the world'. Then in the early seventeenth century the Classical Age with its indiscriminate internment of the abject, the idle and the insane on the sites of the old lazar houses, the 'Great Confinement'; its figuring of infirmity as the propagation of sympathetic nervous disorder, 'unreason', a space of social contagion scanned by a clinical 'gaze'; its ordering of the natural world into exotic tables of correspondence, taxonomies of the monstrous and the mundane. Finally the Modern Age in the early nineteenth century with its separate institutional supervision of the delinquent, the disabled and the unemployed, the rehabilitation of madness as maladjustment; its individuation of illness as obscure organic pathology, solicited into being by the physician's penetrating 'glance'; its specification of human existence according to the language of the social sciences, the 'analytic of finitude', man as object of his own cognition – an age which Foucault acknowledged in 1966 may be 'perhaps nearing its end'.[6]

As if picking up his cue, Baudrillard goes on to supply a superbright episteme to round Foucault off. Now it's the late twentieth century and here comes the Postmodern Age with its modelling of genetic mutation as cybernetic control check, its coding of sickness as viral contamination, its fascination by the meaningless simulations of the media. That's to say, Foucault's Modern Age is obsolete on two counts. First because power is no longer securely grounded in institutions like the prison, the hospital, or even the university, but is dispersed across a series of communication networks, paraded as a flow of signs rather than administered as a relation of forces. And second because sexuality is no longer dragged from the depths of the unconscious by the nets of psychoanalysis – and therefore poised to burst free from social norms – but is conjured, channelled and in the end colonized by the trappings of the media, by fashion, design and advertising.

Simple. Except that in *Discipline and Punish* – Baudrillard's chief target in *Forget Foucault* (along with *The History of Sexuality*) – Foucault complicates the picture painted by his earlier texts and comes up with a much more subtle portrait of post-Renaissance history. Again there is the same tripartite schema – this time figured in terms of the history of punitive technique rather than of madness, medicine or systems of knowledge – but now the discursive blocs overlap at certain points rather than succeed one another discontinuously. To the extent that 'in the late eighteenth century, one is confronted by three ways of organizing the power to punish': sovereign terror, juridical humanism and normalizing detention.[7]

The first two technologies of power have already been described by me in 'Pop Theory, Bardolatry, Leaving the Twentieth-century Academy',[8] but the second requires elaboration. Juridical humanism recommended a method of punishment which was at once more lenient and more efficient than earlier forms. The spectacle of the scaffold, with its ritual markings of the body of the condemned, was criticised by eighteenth-century humanist reformers on the basis that its violent excesses were not only barbaric but also disruptive, tending to sanction the possibility of popular revolt. Their solution was to theorise crime not as an attack on the body of the sovereign demanding vengeance, but as a breach of the social contract requiring payment in kind. Punishment was then theorised in turn as a calibrated system of penalties – mainly centred around the idea of public works – exposed to the view of the general population, a 'punitive city'. In this way, the criminal became both the subject of social redress and the object of public instruction.[9]

Although the legacy of the 'gentle way in punishment' still survives today in all the pious talk about 'paying one's debt to society', the project itself never got off the ground. Instead it was almost immediately invaded, subverted from within, by the insidious micro-technologies of discipline – a process referred to by Foucault as the 'colonization of the penalty by the prison'.[10] Somehow it seemed so much easier to pay lip service to the 'juridical' rhetoric of the reformers in principle while resorting in practice to the simple political expediency of locking offenders behind bars irrespective of their crime.

In acknowledging that three 'technologies of power' were jockeying for position in the late eighteenth century, Foucault goes some way to accommodating his analysis of history to an understanding of how residual, dominant and emergent ideologies – or at least 'discursive practices' – can be embedded in the same culture.[11] Furthermore, there is scattered evidence in *Discipline and Punish* to support the view that it was the early seventeenth rather than the late eighteenth century that was the real historical sticking-point. Foucault points out that the oldest model of punitive imprisonment, the Rasphuis of Amsterdam, was employing disciplinary techniques like the time-table and the work schedule as soon as it opened in 1596.[12] But he needn't have stopped there. He could have gone on to mention Bridewell, the Elizabethan house of correction in London where rogues and prostitutes (as well as vagrants, invalids and children of the poor) were taken for supervision after public chastisement at the stocks.[13]

Unfortunately, Foucault rarely takes account of English – or even Protestant European – history in *Discipline and Punish*. A grave omission, given that countries like England, as well as the Netherlands, were at the cutting edge of Renaissance modernity precisely because they lacked the technologies of social persuasion built into traditional Catholic custom. As a result he fails to come up with any earlier evidence of humanist objection to the counter-productive excesses of public execution, evidence to match his discovery of the use of disciplinary techniques in early seventeenth century Amsterdam. But it's not hard to find. As early as the late sixteenth century the respected Elizabethan lawyer, Edward Coke, was complaining that exemplary punishment was increasingly ineffectual, because it not only advertised the frequency of popular transgression but also inured its audience to the spectacle of pain.[14] What was needed was a subtler disciplinary power to supplement the faltering spectacular power of the scaffold, a power which was to find its test-bed on the platform of the Elizabethan stage.

From this perspective, then, the submerged message of *Discipline and Punish* is that there are really two – as opposed to three – overlapping discursive blocs which go to make up the social map of post-Renaissance history. First the spectacular order of the sixteenth century which slowly peters out over the next three hundred years, and then the juridical-disciplinary regime which insinuates itself in the margins of the earlier social formation during the early seventeenth century. The history of democratic enfranchisement over the succeeding three centuries is thus also the history of the 'juridical coding of power'. That this is not a fanciful reading of Foucault is confirmed by a lecture he delivered in 1976, which clearly distinguishes the 'uniform edifice of sovereignty' from the 'multiple forms of subjugation' which emerge in the seventeenth century under the cover of juridical 'rules of right'.[15] In this way, the reforming jurists' notion of the 'punitive city' takes on the aura of a brightly shining myth, while the distinction between the Classical Age and the Modern Age so beloved of Foucault in his earlier texts recedes in significance. Discipline begins with the Great Confinement.[16]

At which point Baudrillard's troubled relationship with Foucault becomes clearer. It is the juridical-disciplinary regime which Baudrillard insists is obsolete - the rhetoric of liberal humanism on the one hand, the practices of discipline on the other. But obsolete in what way exactly? His 1978 essay, '...Or, The End of the Social'[16], provides some pointers. Here, Baudrillard speculates quite explicitly on the manner in which Foucault's disciplinary social – or simply 'the social' as he calls it – has been eclipsed, offering four possible scenarios. The first is (deliberately) idiotic, hypothesising that the social has never really existed but has instead been an illusion masking the stubborn persistence of an older symbolic order based on 'challenge, seduction and death'.[18] The fourth, which supposes that the social has imploded into the masses, is equally absurd and has been criticised by me at some length in 'Pop Theory, Bardolatry, Leaving the Twentieth-century Academy'.[19]

His second and third scenarios are more interesting. The second suggests that from as early as the late sixteenth century when the poor houses took charge of the impoverished, the lunatic and the sick, the social has always been a mechanism for cleaning up the human residue of society. Expanding its field of operations through history – with the charitable projects of the nineteenth century, the social security programmes of the twentieth century – it finally reaches saturation point and implodes. At this moment, 'the machine stops, the dynamic is reversed, and it is the whole social system which becomes residue'.[20] As a result 'we are in a civilization of the supersocial, and simultaneously in a civilisation of non-degradable, indestructible residue, piling up as the social spreads'.[21]

This spiral of entropic congestion has accelerated in the years since Baudrillard wrote his essay. To the extent that the supersocial today refers to a degraded public realm of hospital waiting lists, council housing queues, overcrowded schools, crumbling prisons and gridlocked streets. Take London. It has become a reservation for the dispossessed, a refugee centre for those left behind by the forced march of capital. Mental patients turfed out of shut-down hospitals wander the streets, homeless teenagers kicked off the dole crowd into the tube stations, tramps huddle for warmth in public libraries. These solitary, self-absorbed figures are avoided by the streams of commuters and eddying swirls of shoppers as if they were postmodern lepers.

Four hundred years after the Great Confinement comes the Great Expulsion. Having reached its point of maximum expansion in the late twentieth century, the social is now contracting, slowly expelling from its care those whom it first began to discipline four hundred years ago: the vagrant, the homeless, the unemployed, 'the sub-social'. These now form a new population, the residue of a residue, Cardboard City, a social surplus rather than a social remainder – everything that Baudrillard in his 1986 travelogue, *America*, consigns to the category of the 'Fourth World', the Third World which exists in the First World's own backyard.[22]

Everyone is pressurised by the squeeze of the supersocial, but those with the readies increasingly have the option of attempting to cut loose, of retreating into a new public realm of free-floating media and hyperreal grace, the sphere of what might be termed 'the para-social'. This is where Baudrillard's third hypothesis comes in, the one familiar from *Forget Foucault*, the idea that the social existed once as a regime of disciplinary power and productive sexuality, but exists no more. According to this scenario, the 'rational sociality of the contract … gives way to the sociality of contact … of a total dissemination, of a ventilation of individuals as terminals of information'.[23] Only Baudrillard protests too much. The social is obsolete in the sense that it is residual, not that it is extinct, while his cybernetic order of simulation and communication is very much an emergent and highly defensive social formation. He admits as much in *America*: '[t]he social order is contracting to include only economic exchange, technology, the sophisticated and innovative; as it intensifies these sectors, entire zones are "disintensified", becoming reservations, and sometimes not even that: dumping grounds'.[24] Come back, the silent majority. All is forgiven.

III POSTMODERNISM AND THE CULTURAL LOGIC OF CARDBOARD CITY

All this immediately ushers in the whole vexed problem of the economic rationale of postmodernism. At which point it is no longer possible to ignore Fredric Jameson, Grand Old Man of Western Marxism, First Prophet of Postmodernism, the only New Left theorist to remain unembarrassed by the breaching of the Berlin Wall. His celebrated long-playing essay from 1984, 'Postmodernism and the Cultural Logic of Late Capital',[25] is still the major text on this highly charged issue. For much of its length, Jameson is preoccupied with providing an empirical account of the constituent features of postmodern culture: depthlessness or 'waning of affect', a euphoric self-annihilation or 'fragmentation of the subject', pastiche in the sense of 'blank parody', the quote-happy simulations of 'libidinal historicism', nostalgia, the free-floating 'intensities' characteristic of a schizophrenic breakdown in the signifying process. All signs of the implosion of modernism into mass culture,[26] of the 'aesthetic populism' whose representative symbol is the mirrored-glass 'hyperspace' of an urban megastructure like the Bonaventure Hotel in downtown Los Angeles. There's no real arguing with Jameson on this score. He only begins to tread dangerous ground when he attempts to conceptualise postmodernism as the 'cultural dominant' of capitalism in triumphalist mode, as 'the internal and superstructural expression of a whole new wave of American military and economic domination throughout the world'.[27]

While there's no doubt that postmodernism is symptomatic of a radical shift in the global deployment of capital, a new 'mode of production', Jameson's model of expressive totality is far too monolithic to fully articulate the way changing patterns of international trade have altered the shape of the cultural landscape. Let there be no misunderstanding here. Jameson is not being criticised for homogenising cultural difference under the aspect of 'late capital', still less for implying that poststructural-ism's indeterminate play of signs has a quite determinate political referent.[28] It is, after all, precisely the point of his text, as he makes clear in his 1989 follow-up essay, 'Marxism and Postmodernism',[29] to establish 'a unified theory of differentia-tion'.[30] And in this he is perfectly correct. It's only necessary to remember the multi-purpose cross-branding of the Levi's ads, the multinational media events sponsored by Pepsi and the pop culture industries or the corporate multiculturalism of the United Colours of Benetton marketing campaigns to get his point. The only problem is that he doesn't go far enough. While taking account of the differences 'multina-tional capitalism' manufactures as a result of its own internal dynamic, his theory fails to articulate the much more significant differences which exist between emer-gent and residual social formations, between the para-social of the Bonaventure Hotel and the sub-social of Cardboard City.[31] For all its aesthetic populism, his strain of postmodernism is an exotic culture which blooms only inside the climate-controlled envelope of the new cybernetic society.

This is the point missed by sociological critics of Jameson such as Fred Pfeil. In his 1985 essay, '"Makin' Flippy-Floppy": Postmodernism and the Baby-Boom PMC', Pfeil conceives of postmodernism 'not as the inevitable extrusion of an entire mode of production but as a cultural-aesthetic set of pleasures and practices created by and for a particular social group at a determinate moment in its collective history'.[32] There is no theoretical incompatibility between these two views. All Pfeil is doing is boxing Jameson's cultural analytic into a social category, defined as the Baby Boomer generation or the Professional-Managerial Classes, the kind of guys who get off on *Saturday Night Live* as well as *Einstein on the Beach*. As far as postmodernism goes, Jameson is the product designer, Pfeil the market researcher, but they're both working out of the same building. The question never really addressed by either is whether the stragglers drifting past the mirrored glass walls of the Bonaventure Hotel are also plugged into some variant of postmodern culture. What about the kind of guys who get off on *Driller Killer* as well as *Saturday Night Live*? Don't they also patrol the space of aesthetic populism? Although postmodernism may indeed be defined as the cultural logic of late capital, this does not make it the exclusive property of a specific privileged class. Before it begins to manufacture cultural differ-ence, the postmodern mode of production is engaged first and foremost in the manu-facture of class division.

This is nowhere more apparent than in the material upheavals which reckless speculative development has inflicted on the developed world's major cities over the last ten years or so. Take Los Angeles. The urban theorist Mike Davis points out in his 1985 essay, 'Urban Renaissance and the Spirit of Postmodernism',[33] that the transformation of the city's sleazy downtown area into a financial control centre for the Pacific Rim economy, complete with skyscraper fortresses and pseudo-public corporate monuments, has proceeded side-by-side with a deterioration in the existing urban infrastructure, a massive influx of illegal Third World immigrants and a corresponding revival of primitive sweatshop capitalism. LA increasingly has the look of a city under siege. The heady expansion of its financial service sector during the Eighties is less an indication of capitalism's ascent to a higher plane of global homogenisation and more a symptom of generalised social collapse, a casting in concrete of class polarisation. As Davis emphasises, Jameson's theorisation of post-modernism 'as the surface content of a deeper structure of multinational integration in the capitalist world system ... misses the crucial point about contemporary capi-talist structures of accumulation: that they are symptoms of global crisis, not signs of the triumph of capitalism's irresistible drive to expand'.[34]

As if that weren't bad enough, Jameson also manages to get his chronology slightly confused. Citing Ernest Mandel's magisterial 1972 tome, *Late Capitalism*, as his economic authority, he traces the culture of postmodernism back to the Fifties, indexing its emergence to the post-war boom in the American consumer economy which was triggered off by the diffusion of new technologies of electronic reproduc-tion – particularly computers and television.[35] But, as Davis points out, Mandel in subsequent writings has made it clear that the point of rupture which most concerns him is the early Seventies, the moment of history when 'late capitalism' buckles under the weight of its internal contradictions.[36] As a result, the Sixties are not so much the start of a brave new world as the end of an era, the culmination of the 'long wave' of post-war economic growth.[37] Postmodernism is thus revealed as the cultural logic of a political economy which has superseded 'late capitalism', which may indeed have gone beyond capitalism as it is conventionally understood.[38]

This is a periodisation which fits quite neatly with the theory of the French Marxist 'regulation school' that the end of the Sixties marks the high point of assembly-line production as first conceived by Henry Ford in 1914 when he estab-lished his automated car plant in Dearborn, Michigan.[39] The originality of the Fordist 'regime of capital accumulation', according to economists like Michel Aglietta and Alain Lipietz, is not that it increased productivity by breaking down the manufac-turing process into component tasks – the benefits to industry of standardising labour routines in this way had already been documented three years earlier by F. W. Taylor's meticulously detailed time and motion studies[40] – but that it established a 'mode of regulation' which integrated the exigencies of mass production within a larger social framework geared to the stimulation of consumer demand. The emer-gence of Fordism which took place during the early Thirties in the States and the Forties in Europe and Japan was thus intimately connected with the fabrication of a new political order, a dovetailing of the interests of corporate capital, organised labour and the welfare state under the aspect of Keynsian economic management.

The implication of this thesis at its most radical is that consumerism is itself a mode of production, a system devoted to the serial manufacture of individual needs. It's at this point that Baudrillard can be slotted back into the argument. In his Marxist text from 1970, *La société de consommation*,[41] he criticises the common assump-tion that a 'human revolution' separates some heroic Age of Production from a new euphoric Age of Consumption, arguing instead that the 'same process of rationaliza-tion of productive forces which took place in the nineteenth century in the sector of production is accomplished, in the twentieth century, in the sector of consumption'.[42] The consumer is no idle pleasure-seeker liberated from the constraints of the work ethic but a busy shopper gripped by the imperatives of 'fun morality', a figure whose agonized prevarications before the supermarket shelves translate into an act of 'social labour'.

What this amounts to saying is that Fordism is the extension into the sphere of consumption of the technical calibrations of Taylorism. Which is where Foucault suddenly comes back into the picture. For the 'political anatomy of detail' which he claims distinguishes discipline is precisely the hallmark of Taylorism. As Frank Lentricchia has observed in his penetrating critique of *Discipline and Punish*, the 'phenomenon of Taylorism completes the portrait of discipline's long historical duration; its persistence grounded not in truth but in a power that produces truth as a detailed knowledge of individuals in their everyday activities'.[43] This, as Lentricchia admits, is to read Foucault against the grain of his text, for he explicitly repudiates the possibility of any accommodation with Marx. But it nevertheless makes sense.[44] Viewing this Marxist Foucault through the joint lens of Baudrillard and the regulation school, it thus becomes clear that the apogee of the disciplinary social is the Fordist regime, with its quotas of consumption and norms of expenditure, its hidden persuaders and conspicuous conformists.

This is the regime which according to the regulation school reached crisis point in the late Sixties. Saturation of domestic markets, union resistance to industrial redeployment and automation, increased competition from the newly industrialized nations of South America and South East Asia – all played their part in articulating the crisis. Meanwhile strains were imposed on the system by the protest movement, with excluded minorities demanding a union ticket into the affluent society on one side and counter-cultural activists voicing their dissatisfaction with its bland uniformity on the other. Things couldn't last. And they haven't. The last twenty years or so have seen the emergence of a new mode of social and political regulation – namely, deregulation – and a corresponding post-Fordist regime of accumulation marked by automation of productivity, 'flexible specialisation' and the transnationalisation of capital.

What this means is that while old assembly-line industries are exported to the low-wage climes of the Third World, contributing in the process to the recrudescence of what Alain Lipietz calls 'Bloody Taylorism', manufacturing in the developed nations increasingly makes use of small-scale flexible machines which can be easily modified to cater to the shifting demands of the service sector economy. As a result, the old blue-collar ranks of semi-skilled machine-minders have been segmented into a 'core' of multi-skilled personnel and a 'peripheral' pool of unskilled labour, often concentrated in sweatshops. As the cultural theorists Eric Alliez and Michel Feher point out, post-Fordism in its essence is characterised by 'the double process of the nomadisation of the marginalised population and the enslavement of the assimilated population'.[45]

All this offers a more plausible model than Jameson's of 'multinational capitalism'. It provides a rationale for the emergence of the Fourth World as the industrial reserve army of what Lipietz calls 'peripheral Fordism'. At the same time it makes clear that Baudrillard's hyperreal universe is actually a circumscribed and highly controlled environment inhabited by the international downtown salariat. The term post-Fordism also helps to focus the discursive limitations of the label postmodernism, which slips so confusingly between the registers of the theoretical and the journalistic. The mode of production which cuts across the class divide may more properly be called post-Fordist than postmodern. Postmodernism instead describes PMC culture of the mid- to late Eighties, a set of practices perhaps already past its sell-by date, absorbed by the spiral of fashion, transformed into new species of leisure. What needs to be looked at in order to fill out this analytic is the culture which exists on the downside of the post-Fordist divide, the culture of Cardboard City.[46]

From the perspective of post-Fordism, the relationship between Baudrillard and Foucault suddenly falls into place. In his 1976 book, *L'échange symbolique et la mort*, Baudrillard sketches in his own map of post-Renaissance history considered as three orders of simulation.[47] Corresponding to Foucault's spectacular order at the point of its maximum instability is Baudrillard's society of the 'counterfeit', a 'competitive democracy' of status symbols which succeeds the strictly codified hierarchies of feudalism. Here, the 'bound signs' of rank are transformed into the 'emancipated signs' of fashion proper to a new era of bourgeois social mobility, an era of 'the double, the mirror, of theatre and the play of masks and appearances'.[48] With the ascendancy of Foucault's disciplinary regime comes Baudrillard's order of production, the 'dominant scheme of the industrial era' geared to the serial manufacture of standardised commodities, a regime which still persists today in the residual social formations of Bloody Taylorism and peripheral Fordism.

Finally there is the order of simulation which takes off when 'serial production' is absorbed by the technologies of mechanical – and later electronic – reproduction to give rise to a process of 'generation by models'. This is the third order of simulation which Foucault was unwilling or unable to theorise, a regime defined by the flexible specialisations of post-Fordism where commodity-signs are designed with a view to the ease of their media reproducibility, their degree of diffraction from a generating conceptual nucleus or 'model'. Here, mass production has given way to batch production, the identical parade of brand names superseded by the distinctive competition between designer labels. Commodities are no longer defined as they were in the Fordist era by their degree of exchangeability with other commodities, but by their coefficient of conversion into media signs. If Fordism is conceptualised as the extension of the forces of production into the realm of consumption, then post-Fordism, as Baudrillard recognises, in turn conceptualises 'the realm of production, labour, and productive forces as basking in the realm of "consumption" – here taken as a generalised axiomatic, a coded exchange of signs, and as a general lifestyle'.[49]

IV   THE LIVING DEATH OF THE BOURGEOIS PUBLIC REALM

It's a long way from the theatres of early modern England to a postmodern megastructure like the Bonaventure Hotel. But it's possible to sketch in a direct line of descent between the two as part of a more wide-ranging genealogy of public space. The cultural historians Peter Stallybrass and Allon White have already laid the groundwork for such a task in their 1986 book *The Politics and Poetics of Transgression*. Tracing the emergence during the late seventeenth and early eighteenth centuries of new sites of bourgeois recreation and assembly like the coffee-houses, clubrooms and fashionable resorts of Georgian England, they emphasise how much this reinvention of public space was implicated in a cultural project of controlled exchange of speech and regulation of codes of conduct, a complete reformation of manners and mores. The bourgeois public realm was not simply a thing of bricks and mortar, it involved 'a re-territorialization of places and bodies, a realignment of domains, discourses, manners and states of mind'.[50]

Stallybrass and White initially tie this 'Great Reform' to the development of a bourgeois ideology of taste, the invention of an aesthetic of 'purity' which, according to the French sociologist Pierre Bourdieu, refuses the visceral or the sensational and so distances itself equally from the vulgarity of both the court and the masses.[51] More significantly, they go on to link it to what the German sociologist Norbert Elias calls the 'Civilizing Process' – the elaboration of social standards of restraint governing eating, washing, coughing, sneezing, spitting, urinating and defecating, a process measuring the gradual advancement of the 'threshold of shame' over the centuries which begins with the expropriation of private vengeance by the state.[52] So that Stallybrass' and White's Great Reform goes beyond the ideology of aesthetics, connecting the physical, the subjective and the social into 'a zone of transcoding at once astonishingly trivial and microscopically important'.[53]

This is a process concerned in its most acute detail with the ingestion and elimination of foreign substances from the body. Which is the cue for Stallybrass and White to graft the theories of Elias and Bourdieu on to those of the Russian folk historian Mikhail Bakhtin. Bakhtin distinguishes the 'grotesque body' of the carnival – mobile, heterogeneous, impure, open to invasion, polymorphous, disproportionate, protruberant, collective – from the 'classical body' of the bourgeois public realm – monumental, homogenous, pure, self-enclosed, unitary, symmetrical, individual – almost as a point of formal principle. The grotesque body exhibits everything the classical body furiously wishes to erase, from panting tongues and popping eyes to pot bellies and uncontrollable physical spasms. Revelling in the exposure of orifices, gaps and all their associated symbolic filth – shit, sweat, piss, vomit, other bodily fluids and, in the opposite direction, food and drink – it piles into one gloriously fecund dung heap everything nominated by Bakhtin as belonging to the 'lower bodily stratum'.[54]

What Stallybrass and White do is draw out the historical tensions in Bakhtin's formal opposition. Their Great Reform becomes the story of the transformation of the grotesque body of the old absolutist regime into the classical body of the ascendant bourgeois order, the invention of a 'sublimated public body' distinct from the dominions of Church and State on the one side and the taverns, streets, fairgrounds and market-squares of the mob on the other. It's a long hard effort. According to Stallybrass and White, bourgeois culture is always driven by the struggle to expel, purify or tame the grotesque, which it symbolically castigates as 'low-Other'. Their point of critical interest, the moment which subverts the course of this struggle, is then defined by what they call the 'poetics of transgression'.

This is not simply a ritual strategy of hierarchy inversion on the part of subordinate social groups, the substitution of their domains and discourses for those of the dominant in a wild explosion of saturnalian energy. That would be to mistake licensed misrule for popular revolt, holiday for revolution. Instead it is something more complex, a strategy which 'generates the possibility of shifting the very terms of the system itself, by erasing and interrogating the relationships which constitute it'.[55] A mode of hybridisation rather than of inversion, the poetics of transgression aggravates the inherent instability of symbolic hierarchies of taste as they exist within dominant constructions of discourse, the body and social place, exposing the way in which 'what is socially peripheral is so frequently symbolically central'.[56]

So far, so good. Unfortunately, Stallybrass and White lapse into incoherence when they attempt to expand upon these ideas. They make the obvious point that the Great Reform is the flipside to the 'institutionalizing inventiveness' of Foucault's Great Confinement, but theorise the link inaccurately in terms of some Freudian return of the repressed. According to this scenario, Foucault's confined population belong to a 'bourgeois imaginary' of the grotesque, they are the 'contained outsiders-who-make-the-insiders-insiders' and as a result function as a primary erotic constit-uent of bourgeois fantasy. 'High discourse' in attempting to expel 'low discourse' as Other ensures that it returns as a grotesque object of 'phobic enchantment' and so disables itself from the very beginning.[57] The problem with this is that the grotesque is theorised twice over – first as the symbolic filth repressed by the Great Reform, second as the imaginary threat which returns to beguile it[58] – when it only needs to be theorised once. The link between the Great Reform and the Great Confine-ment is capable of being made without resort to Freud.[59] Stallybrass and White miss Foucault's essential point about the Great Confinement, which is that its benefit to the bourgeoisie was expressed not in the exclusion of an unproductive population but in the invention of techniques of discipline. As he puts it in his 1976 lecture, 'the bourgeoisie has never had any use for the insane; but the procedures it has employed to exclude them have revealed and realised ... a political advantage, on occasion even a certain economic utility'.[60] The techniques which oppress the insane are the very same techniques which, once employed by the bourgeoisie on their own minds and bodies, become empowering precisely in the way analysed by Elias. The grotesque creatures herded into houses of confinement during the seventeenth century are mere laboratory specimens. The real threat to the bourgeois reformation of manners arises from the unreconstructed mass of bodies crowded into the brothels and palaces of the early modern city. But these cannot be 'reformed' or disciplined until the bourgeoisie have first learned to discipline themselves.

All of this suggests that the possibility for a 'poetics of transgression' is greatest at that moment when the bourgeoisie first begin to try out the techniques of disci-pline, on the boards of the Elizabethan stage. The logic of 'phobic enchantment' is something which belongs exclusively to the nineteenth century. Stallybrass' and White's failure to recognise this stems from their assumption that the Civilizing Process is a process of increasing sexual repression when, as Foucault makes clear in his critique of the 'repressive hypothesis' in the introduction to *The History of Sexuality*, it is instead a process of increased 'cultivation of the body'. The bourgeois appropriation of disciplinary technique contests the aristocratic 'symbolics of blood' by inventing an 'analytics of sexuality', a personal regime of health and hygiene and a politics of medicine and sanitation. The masses were not granted a discursively sexualised body until they were recruited by capital and put to work in the factories of the nineteenth century.[61] Only at this point does the bourgeois imaginary begin to be haunted by the displaced erotic charge of the sweaty, labouring body. Think of Freud's case histories or the reforming social documents of Henry Mayhew and Edwin Chadwick.[62]

The reason why 'socially peripheral' discourses became 'symbolically central' in the early modern period has nothing to do with fantasy and everything to do with power. As Steven Mullaney argues in *The Place of the Stage*, the public playhouses of London emerged 'at a time when traditional hierarchies were breaking down, and neither they nor the plays they fostered were thus contained by the customary antitheses of rule and misrule, order and disorder, everyday and holiday'.[63] Built on the threshold of London, in the Liberties beyond the city walls or south of the Thames in the suburbs,[64] they existed outside of the jurisdiction of the city authorities yet their players were licensed to perform at court. Exercising a determinate effect on the economy and the pageantry of the city, theatres like the Rose, the Swan and the Globe nevertheless occupied an indeterminate zone of authority. They drew London's citizens away from work on weekdays and away from the pulpit on Sundays, confusing communion with carnival, leisure with illicit time off, offering the experience of holiday without liturgical or municipal sanction. Elizabethan drama was 'hybridised' in the sense that it was the material embodiment of cultural contradiction.

The playhouses encouraged absenteeism, riot and public drunkenness, they were a form of what Mullaney calls 'incontinent theatre'.[65] This is what so outraged Puritan pamphleteers like Stephen Gosson, John Northbrooke and Phillip Stubbes, all of whom laboured furiously in the service of that Great Reform of manners and mores analysed by Stallybrass and White. They castigated the theatres as 'resorts of idleness', spaces of promiscuous minglings and immoral couplings, category confusions and symbolic filth.[66] And they were right.[67] The Elizabethan theatres were indeed the site of scandalous licence and grotesque exhibition, places where kings consorted with clowns on stage and artisans rubbed shoulders with aristocrats in the pressing throng beyond.[68] If Shakespeare's history plays and romantic comedies were, in the words of the humanist playwright John Lyly, such a 'mingle-mangle', then that was because its public was such a 'hodge-podge'.[69]

The structural ambivalence of the playhouses was duplicated by the public scandal of the performers themselves. The stage offered the sight of players personating kings, boys playing girls, boys playing girls playing boys, a carnival parade of signs which put the traditional marks of rank and gender into a spin. Even off-stage, actors occupied an ambivalent social position. Both entrepreneurs involved in the business of entertainment and retainers notionally engaged to aristocratic patrons, they were 'masterless men' exempt from the Vagabond Acts by royal decree, celebrities of no fixed cultural abode. Successful actors grew rich and dressed above their station, shamelessly violating the Sumptuary Laws which attempted to legislate an archaic feudal dress code, standing tall at court one day and diving into the taverns of the city the next.

Here was Baudrillard's 'counterfeit order of simulation' in all its ambivalent splendour. Yet, as Mullaney demonstrates, this was something historically anticipated. When the public playhouses first opened for business in the 1570s and 1580s, they were capitalising on a tradition of cultural licence which already existed in the Liberties, in its gaming-houses, brothels, bear-baiting arenas and archery greens, its hospitals, scaffolds of execution and lazar-houses. These were 'the preserve of the anomalous, the unclean, the polluted and the sacred'.[70] The popular stage appropriated and made manifest a latent subversive potential which had always intermittently troubled the margins of the city. Which is as much to say that they put it to use, made it available, colonised it according to a 'self-consuming logic of "exhibition"'.

This logic belongs to a larger dynamic, the 'rehearsal of cultures' which Mullaney claims characterised the pastimes of the early seventeenth century.[71] Just as the lazar-house was an ambivalent rehearsal of the signs of affliction prior to their disappearance, just as Bedlam Hospital was a public rehearsal of the spectacle of folly prior to the Great Confinement, so the Elizabethan theatre was a rehearsal of a hybrid popular culture prior to its subjugation. Like Foucault's houses of confinement, the playhouses were proto-disciplinary institutions, developing a series of experimental techniques and practices in the residual social field. Unlike the houses of confinement, however, they were also cultural institutions which traded in the vocabulary and the imagery of society at large; they were in a position to articulate their predicament and examine the paradox of their own spectacular ambivalence. The same disciplinary techniques which would be later employed for their own profit by the bourgeoisie were also the dramatic techniques which so outraged and disgusted the Puritan divines and city fathers of early modern London.

The Elizabethan and early Jacobean theatre thus provide scope for exactly the 'poetics of transgression' defined by Stallybrass and White. The grotesque body politic which so offended the Puritans was paraded on the stage as an object of ambivalent scrutiny, simultaneously hostage to a developing disciplinary consciousness and tribute to displaced carnival affectivity. This is something particularly evident in the revenge tragedies of the period, plays like Thomas Kyd's *The Spanish Tragedy*, Shakespeare's *Titus Andronicus* or Cyril Tourneur's *The Revenger's Tragedy*. Here, the theatre of the state banquet, the execution and the court masque fuse into an obscene celebration of Bakhtin's 'lower bodily stratum', a corrupt ball of flesh which both repels and attracts the divided figure of the revenger. A shadowy 'analytic of sexuality' emerges under the sign of his furiously complex language, a proleptic figuration of the bourgeois classical body which contests the grotesque inflations and degraded festivities of an older aristocratic 'symbolics of blood'.[72]

Take *The Revenger's Tragedy*. The cross-currents of lust, appetite and disgust in this play are multiple. Vindice is a court intriguer determined to avenge the memory of his fiancée after she was poisoned by a gluttonous Italian duke for failing to respond to his advances. To this end, he disguises himself as a procurer, falls in with the duke and waits for his moment to strike. His purity of intention supposedly guaranteed by his position on the margins of the court, he insinuates himself into a grotesque economy of exchange – of food, words and bodies – only to be consumed by his own actions and voided from the reconstituted social ('Away with 'em').

Throughout the play, the category confusions of carnival are figured as symbolic filth by Vindice. Revelry and feasting are associated with the sign crimes of the court, are even bound up with the spectre of incest ('Any kin now, next to the rim o'th'sister/Is man's meat in these days'). The problem for this 'strange-digested fellow', however, is that he aspires to a state of personal grace which can never free itself from the degraded culture of the court. In the cramped social arena in which he is forced to perform, it is the sublimated public body of classical imagining rather than its grotesque underside which is 'socially peripheral'. The difficulty is not, as it is for the immaculate bourgeoisie of the Restoration, that a language of physical delicacy is contaminated by social disgust, but that a dominant vocabulary of grotesque inversion bears witness to an impossible desire for purity.

What becomes 'symbolically central' for Vindice is not some demonised 'low-Other' but a fantasised realm of chaste manners and clean living. As a result, his language is shot through with paradox and unforced contradiction. The duke, for example, is characterised as a 'juiceless luxur', image of 'grey-haired adultery', while his fiancée's untouchability is fetishised as a consuming void ('O she was able to ha'made a usurer's son/Melt all his patrimony in a kiss'). It is the play's cruellest joke that her 'purer part' should be reduced to the bare dimensions of a skull, that the desired sublimation of offensive body parts should be imagined as a complete divestiture of flesh. Even in this absolute state, however, purity remains an impossible dream, for the skull retains symbolic value only as a *memento mori*, as the warped mirror of carnivalesque excess ('Advance thee, O thou terror to fat folks').

It is when the skull is employed as a prop in Vindice's act of revenge against the duke that its symbolic contradictions fully emerge. Lured by Vindice into a tryst with what he fondly imagines is a painted lady, but which is really the skull lined with poison, the duke is consumed by desire in the most literal fashion. Just as he disfigured Vindice's fiancée, so he himself is destroyed after he kisses her 'purer part' – his teeth eaten away, his mouth peeled and rotted. The wages of sin could not be more graphically illustrated ('those that did eat are eaten'). At the same time, though, revenge is staged as a repetition of the original offence and purity measured by the symbolic excrement of carnival. When Vindice nails the duke's panting tongue to the floor with a dagger and forces him to watch his bastard son consorting with his wife – appropriately enough at a banquet seasoned with the 'taste of sin' – he has created a spectacle of degradation which mimics the very grotesque scenography he wished to repudiate ('now I'll begin/To stick thy soul with ulcers').

The subversive 'incontinence' of the public playhouses did not survive the reign of James I. As the second decade of the seventeenth century elapsed, popular drama came to occupy a less ambivalent place in the cultural landscape.[73] The transfer in 1610 of the King's Men from the Globe to the Blackfriars for its winter season marks the symbolic turning point, the moment when theatre began to migrate from the periphery to the centre of the city. By then the Rose had already been pulled down, the Swan vacated and the granting of theatrical licenses established as a royal monopoly. At the same time, smart new theatres like the Hope and the Phoenix began to spring up in the fashionable end of the city, exclusive social establishments charging a higher admission price and catering for a more discerning clientele.[74]

These private theatres, as they were known, differed from the old public theatres in size and structure.[75] Whereas the Elizabethan playhouses were essentially open-air amphitheatres capable of holding an audience of up to three thousand, the new theatres were enclosed halls built to contain less than a thousand spectators, each of whom was assigned a specific place rather than allowed to roam through the crowd. In the public theatres, the groundlings mingled freely before the raised stage while the wealthier patrons were accommodated behind them in the galleries; in the private theatres, there was a graded seating system which ensured that the higher the price of entry, the closer the view of the stage, with additional seats available on the stage itself. As the theatre historian Andrew Gurr mentions in his 1987 book, *Playgoing in Shakespeare's London*, the Blackfriars 'established for the first time in England the disposition of seat prices which still rules in every modern indoor theatre'.[76] The Blackfriars audience was no longer an unruly mob, but an assembly of attentive citizens, a mass of disciplined bodies.

Partly as a result of this participation on the part of the theatre in the Civilizing Process, Puritan attacks on the stage declined. As the critic Martin Butler points out in his 1984 book, *Theatre and Crisis 1632–1642*, during the late 1620s and 1630s the theatres became sites of political dialogue and public association for a new gentry class eager to seize on its privileges, stops on an emerging social round, fashionable resorts rather than riotous dens. They functioned as 'neutral zones, independent of the court ... both public settings and areas of unrivalled personal exchange, environments where manners and mores could be determined and established on a communal level'.[77] The comedies of manners of Richard Brome, Philip Massinger and James Shirley were instrumental in this respect. Offering the Caroline audience flattering images of themselves at play in parks, squares and gaming-houses, they acted as arbiters of correct conduct, miniature models of social behaviour to be scrutinised and emulated.

Butler goes out of his way to demonstrate that such plays carried subversive ideological messages when the real force of his argument lies in its implication that they encouraged a bourgeois 'cultivation of the body'.[78] This is nowhere more apparent than in the transformed cultural status of revenge tragedy in the late Jacobean and Caroline theatre. Plays like James Shirley's *The Traitor*, Philip Massinger's *The Fatal Dowry* and John Ford's *The Broken Heart* differ from *The Revenger's Tragedy* in their attempt to purge the act of revenge of any lingering filth or sweat, to restage its effervescent violence as an aesthetic exercise in blood-letting, a forensic interrogation of the flesh, rather than a carnivalesque whirl of mangled limbs and severed heads. The trope of the wounded physis no longer occupies Bakhtin's 'lower bodily stratum' but has ascended to a more 'classical' theatrical plane of sculpted carnage and meticulously detailed distress.[79]

Take *The Broken Heart*. Set in post-civil war Sparta, this is a play about broken promises, broken families and the binding ties of self-inflicted violence. The set-up is simple enough. The noblewoman Penthea had been promised to the high-ranking Orgilus as a sign of accord between their warring clans, but this 'firm growth of union' was crushed by her brother, Ithocles, when he married her off to a third party in order to slight Orgilus and satisfy his own pride ('whose ripened fruit hath ravished all health'). The drama thus begins with the sense of symbolic blockage and interrupted growth, of infected matter clogging the veins of the body politic.

Unlike *The Revenger's Tragedy*, however, this swollen body politic is purged not through deception – although Orgilus is enough of the conventional revenger to disguise himself – but through heroic display. The play's violence is concerned with the bleeding of infected parts rather than the aggravation of open wounds. Carnage becomes a refined spectacle, an aristocratic blood sport, and the category confusions of the grotesque disappear. There is none of Vindice's seething language in *The Broken Heart*. Instead it is full of promises, petitions, commands and curses - codified speech acts which provide the violent tableaux of the play with the appropriate gloss. A broken contract is the source of all the trouble, for example, while the expounding of a Delphic oracle is the sign of its conclusion.

All the deaths in the play are similar, collapsing the imagery of physical evacuation and public display into the master trope of suicide. Penthea protests against the enforced slavery of her desires by starving herself to death. She seals her body off from a hostile world, stopping the flow of blood which she considers polluted ('Her blood – 'tis just – be henceforth never heightened/ With taste of sustenance'). Once dead, she is worshipped as a 'hallowed shrine'. It's the same with the rest of the deaths in the play. Orgilus stages his revenge in a succession of portentous gestures.

He unveils Penthea's corpse to a shamefaced Ithocles, traps him in a chair alongside her, and proceeds to slowly pierce his flesh with a dagger. With a clear understanding of the emblematic value of this scene ('Sweet twins, shine stars forever'), he surrenders to an aesthetic appetite which Ithocles is by now more than willing to share ('if the wound close up,/ Tent it with double force'). Next it is Orgilus' turn. When he confesses to his crime he is sentenced to death but granted the privilege of choosing his means of execution. He elects to be bled to death – penetrated like Ithocles, evacuated like Penthea. He willingly opens the first vein himself and again there is the implication of self-sacrifice in this suicide, as real suffering is restaged as symbolic pain ('look upon my steadiness').

The final suicide scene also seeks to transform death into an edifying spectacle as Calantha, the daughter of the king of Sparta, dies of a broken heart after hearing of the death of her beloved Ithocles. Her death – again self-willed, a kind of martyrdom – is figured in redemptive terms because it explicates the significance of the cryptic Delphic oracle delivered at the very beginning of the play ('the pith of oracles/ Is to be then digested, when the events/ Expound their truth'). But its real meaning lies in its conceptualisation of violence as a matter of good digestion, of death as a matter of good manners. By the end of the play, a series of staged suicides has purged the body politic of its infected blood not by any transcendent means but by refashioning the imagery of the 'lower bodily stratum' into an abstract notion of 'good heart'.

All this does not mean that the older tradition of rowdy public performance was no longer visible in Caroline London. Playhouses such as the Red Bull and the Fortune in the north of the city continued to do a roaring trade among the nut-cracking masses but they belonged to a recognisably residual social formation. Demonised by the more fashionable playwrights as sinks of unregenerate behaviour and crowd-pleasing rough stuff, strewn with filth and populated by 'stinkards',[80] they functioned as that symbolic 'low-Other' necessary to the emergence of bourgeois cultural identity. If the Puritan stigmatisation of the public playhouse as a grotesque popular body had by this time evaporated, this was partly because the playwrights were doing their job for them.

This is where Bourdieu slots back into the picture. The bourgeois rejection of popular revelry was as much a matter of taste as of manners, with the split between the theatres in the north and south of the city gauged in terms of differences in repertory as well as in audience. The Fortune and the Red Bull became renowned for a blood and thunder idiom which was thought to be too clamorous and excessive, too redolent of the tavern and the bear-baiting pit to be appropriate for theatres now equipped with candle-light and musical interludes. Staging revivals of old Elizabethan favourites, carnival jigs and patriotic romances, as well as new plays by the likes of John Webster and Thomas Heywood, the Red Bull offered a very different cultural fare from the private theatres, with their tragicomic romances, disguised ruler plays and comedies of manners.[81]

The dramatist John Fletcher captured the aesthetic distinction precisely in his preface to *The Faithful Shepherdess*, where he redefined tragicomedy in terms not of some grotesque interpenetration of 'mirth and killing' but in the lightness of touch with which death is introduced as a dramatic spectre only to be banished at the last moment.[82] His immediate target was the kind of intermingling of bloodshed and buffoonery characteristic of an Elizabethan dramatist like Christopher Marlowe. But what was being castigated ultimately was the popular tradition of antic violence which the public playhouses inherited from the medieval period, the combination of game and insult, laughter and terror familiar to folk custom and rural pastime, everything the distinguished critic Muriel C. Bradbrook has labelled 'eldritch diabolism'.[83] Which is as much to say, everything likely to unsettle the frazzled nerves of the bourgeoisie.

It was this popular tradition which was effectively suppressed by the closure of the theatres by act of Parliament in 1642.[84] By the time the theatres opened again in the Restoration, the tradition of 'mirth and killing' was a cultural embarrassment. Even the poetic carnage of a dramatist like Ford would be considered too much. The threshold of shame had advanced. The objections on the part of critics and dramatists to the violence of the Renaissance stage was now phrased explicitly in terms of sensibility rather than of culture, the sign of an unhappiness with what the eighteenth century critic Joseph Addison called 'cruel temper'.[85] Renaissance drama was previously only ever censored if, in the words of the Master of the Revels in 1633, it contained 'offensive things against Church and State'.[86] By the time of the Age of Reason, however, it was censored for being an offence against public decency.

The story of the Great Reform of manners and mores from the eighteenth century onwards is the story of the trickle down of its canons of aesthetic decency and rules of proper behaviour to the masses. This in turn coincided with an expansion of the bourgeois public realm. Just as the grand narrative of social enfranchisement and increased human rights is also Foucault's secret history of increased discipline, so the public face of the nineteenth century was as visible in the civic architecture of its libraries, museums and town halls, public parks and paved streets as in the stonework of its prisons and factories. The reactionary logic of the bourgeois project is dialectically interwoven with its progressive logic. This is the message of Stallybrass and White re-routed via Foucault. The granting of a discursively sexualized body to the lower orders in the nineteenth century coincided with the mobilization of a whole administrative and technical machinery of discipline to keep them safely under surveillance: schooling, housing, public hygiene and transport, institutions of relief and insurance, what Foucault calls 'the generalized medicalization of the population'.[87] That's to say, everything completed by the public welfare programmes of the mid-twentieth century corporate state, everything consigned by Baudrillard to the historical category of the 'social'.

Any consideration of the slow spread of the social cannot avoid taking into account the special importance of cinema. The ascendancy of Hollywood marks the moment when Fordism, discipline and the expanded public realm all intersect. The dream factory itself was modelled on explicit Taylorist principles by movie mogul Thomas H. Ince in the 1910s. This was evident not only in the day-to-day functioning of the studio system, with its backlot assembly-lines staffed by interchangeable rosters of scriptwriters, directors, cameramen and editors, but also in its year-round output of standardised genre movies, its mass produced Westerns, gangster pictures, musicals and screwball comedies. Here was one instance of Baudrillard's 'industrial simulation' in action.

The fact that Taylorist management techniques stretched from pre-production and post-production through to distribution and exhibition is what made Hollywood cinema properly Fordist. The system of vertical integration which dominated the States from the Twenties to the Forties meant that the studios owned the backlots where films were made and the picture palaces where they were screened. Picture-making was therefore concerned quite as much with the regulation of consumer demand, the manufacture of the desire to go to the movies, as it was with the steady ticking-off of production quotas. Hence the emergence of things like block booking and blind buying. They ensured that independent exhibitors took whatever Hollywood threw at them without complaining.[88]

Like the department stores which often faced them in the centre of a city, the picture palaces showcased the same wares simultaneously across the country. Sites of bourgeois recreation on a mass scale, they were institutions geared to the regula-tion of urban manners and mores, pleasure machines devoted to the sexual policing of a newly industrialized labour force. This was nowhere more apparent than in the normalizing function of the star system, especially as it developed after Hollywood's adoption of the Hays Code in the Thirties. Movie stars not only entertained audi-ences, they also instructed them in the fashionable way to make love, dress, walk, talk, work and consume. As a result, their private lives were often as manufactured as the movies they appeared in, exemplary instances of social responsibility and clean living. Patrons were expected to step out from the cinema feeling good about themselves.[89]

Mass attendances at picture palaces were in many ways the cultural equivalent to Foucault's 'generalized medicalization of the population'. Cinema was a glamorous disciplinary machine devoted to the production of attentive consumers, an engine of the Civilizing Process. Everything surrounding the weekly ritual of movie-going attests to this: the queue to get in, the allocated seat number, the taboo against noise or movement, the darkened auditorium focussing attention exclusively on the brightly lit screen. These informal inhibitions added up to a collective exercise in self-restraint on the part of the audience, a 'discipline of silence' which the sociologist Richard Sennett traces back to the bourgeois theatre of the nineteenth century.[90]

There thus seems to be a clear line of descent from the private theatres of early seventeenth century England to the picture palaces of the mid-twentieth century, a field of power-knowledge relations which amounts to a genealogy of the bourgeois public realm. This defines the material face of the modern episteme, the cultural axis described by Foucault and Elias. Now, as Baudrillard has noted, things are shifting into reverse, the social contracting as the economy implodes. Coinciding with the passage from a Fordist to a post-Fordist regime of capital accumulation is what Mike Davis in his 1990 book on postmodern Los Angeles, *City of Quartz*, has called the 'privatization of public space'.[91] Selective redevelopment of not just Los Angeles but of other world capitals, including London, has seen a new public realm of shop-ping malls, leisure centres, corporate plazas, museums and galleries – Baudrillard's mediatised environment[92] – constructed on the back of the old. The spaces which remain untouched by the growth of this new service sector economy, the urban left-overs, are simply allowed to rot.

Cinema has not been immune from this restructuring process. The Fordist crisis may have been most conspicuously expressed in the factory closures and assembly-line shutdowns of the last ten years, but it also took its toll on the picture palaces, which were largely abandoned or sold off during the same period. At one point in the mid-Eighties, it seemed as if cinema might be a thing of the past. That, however, was before the arrival of the multiplex. Located in the greenfield sites of the new public realm, alongside shopping malls, leisure centres and out-of-town retail parks, these functional multi-screen cinemas have reintegrated movie-going into a wider lifestyle economy. Once slotted into a hyperactive round of consumption which makes it possible to pick up a pizza and a pair of 501s before catching the latest Schwarzenegger movie, cinema divests itself of the discipline associated with the old picture palaces and begins to participate in Baudrillard's logic of preprogrammed solicitation. Not only do the multiplexes offer a choice of up to eight different movies, but multi-point ticket booths and credit card booking systems have eliminated the need for queuing, while the 'discipline of silence' in the theatres has been eroded by the kind of slam-bam special effects movies which encourage cheers, whistles and applause at the appropriate fetishistic moments.

This transformation in the cultural fortunes of cinema has affected the way movies are produced as well as consumed. The decline of the dream factory can be traced all the way back to the 1948 Supreme Court decision which effectively broke the studio choke-hold on vertically integrated production, distribution and exhibition. The gradual abandonment of the Hays Code and the slow death of the contract system were also significant pointers. But it was not until the Seventies that new post-Fordist production techniques began to invade the Hollywood machine. As the backlot assembly-lines have ground to a halt, talent has gone freelance. At the same time, the studios continue to exercise a near-monopoly on distribution. Agents spend months working the phones in an effort to put together script, director and star into an attractive sales package, but it's always the studios who put up the money for these independently produced movies. In a textbook instance of post-Fordist deregulation, Hollywood has become more highly controlled precisely by becoming less centralised.

One result of this is that fewer movies get made than before. Film production has increasingly been superseded by speculation of the type governing the stock market. Paper deals are traded between studios without a movie necessarily seeing the light of day. The films which are produced are either star vehicles, movies built around one performer, or 'high concept' efforts, movies built around a one-sentence proposition. As a result, movie stars are no longer the normalising icons of the past, but enhanced simulations advertising their difference from one another in a crowded marketplace. They no longer instruct the cowed spectator in the arts of refinement but compete for the attention of the distracted consumer. The dark secrets of their personal lives, once hidden from the public gaze, are now splashed over the pages of the newspapers, are often manufactured – all in a desperate effort to raise their commercial profile. It's the same story as far as the old genre system is concerned. Movies are no longer mass produced year after year according to a preconceived formula. Instead, they are batch produced in rush runs according to prevailing fashions. The steady supply of Westerns and musicals familiar from the past has been replaced by a manic turnover of over-designed gimmick movies: body swap movies, underwater movies, cop-and-dog buddy movies, ghost movies. As soon as a trend is targeted, then five or six movies based on the same idea are manufactured all at the same time.

A post-Fordist regime of capital accumulation has quite naturally emerged in Hollywood to match this new deregulatory mode. The watchword here is conglomeration. Over the last twenty years, the major studios have diversified into related industries like TV, music and publishing, their distribution chains incorporated into global merchandising networks. As a result, any movie nowadays gains a significant percentage of its revenue from spin-offs and tie-ins, becoming part of a larger multi-media event which takes in the soundtrack album, the comic-book, the novelisation, the toy range, the poster, the T-shirt. Product placement also plays its part in this process, transforming a movie into a *mise-en-scène* of commercials before a script has even been prepared.[93]

Hollywood has become less of an industry and more of a business, the paradigmatic instance of Baudrillard's third order of simulation. Movies increasingly slot into a logic of 'generation by models', pre-programmed according to a design nucleus rather than manufactured according to an industrial blueprint. No longer celluloid fodder block booked for a mass audience passively shuffling along in a cinema queue, they are instead mobile media events targeting the alert, postmodern consumer. The discipline of the dream factory and the picture palace has given way to the spiralling simulations of the hype machine and the multiplex – something more than evident in the way that the final cut of a movie is often made only after its test screening in a preview theatre. Here, audience response is captured in advance and fed back into a film in an attempt to forge an integrated media circuit. Movies becomes a sub-department of market research.

According to this scenario, the sexuality of the consumer is no longer a bundle of impulses which demand policing but a flux of signs which require massaging. In Baudrillard's hyperreal universe of 'total dissemination', Foucault's 'analytics of sexuality' has been detached from the raw nerves of the flesh and plugged into the free-floating circuitry of the media. Bodies are transformed from engines of labour into reservoirs of symbolic capital, cybernetic organisms, human commodities. This is the Civilizing Process gone hyperreal. Having triumphed over the need to regulate an ethics of socially acceptable public behaviour, the great labour of bourgeois culture is now to fashion an aesthetics of cosmetically sustainable self-invention. The threshold of shame has advanced to the point where Bakhtin's bourgeois 'classical' body must be hermetically sealed against the creeping signs of erosion and neglect, strategically nipped and tucked, surgically enhanced according to the latest fashion. It's not sloppy table manners which are the great source of personal embarrassment in the sleek confines of the new public realm, but flabby muscle tone and sagging jowls.

This new hyper-advanced 'cultivation of the body' marks the emergence of a concept hardly dreamed of by Foucault, something which might be termed a 'symbolics of sexuality'. Many Hollywood spectaculars of recent years attest to this, especially hyperviolent sci-fi movies like Paul Verhoeven's *RoboCop* and *Total Recall* or James Cameron's *Aliens*. The hero of *RoboCop*, for example, is a cyborg put together from the remains of a dead cop. Clad in a titanium shell with power joints and a host of computerised accessories, he is the first member of a new cadre of officers in the privatised police force of a crime-plagued Detroit.

The interesting thing about *RoboCop* is his ambiguity. He cleans up the streets in a furious display of violence, complete with exploding windows, fireballs, broken bodies, fountains of blood and spills of toxic waste. A vigilante cop in a company town, he represents a reversal of Elias' Civilizing Process – the violence first expropriated by the state now returns to private hands. At the same time, however, he is a hermetic organism completely sealed off from the dirty work of policing. In that sense, he marks an advance of Elias' threshold of shame. He contrasts pointedly, for example, with the vile, sweaty bodies seen in the precinct locker-room at the start of the movie.

This ambiguity is focused around his only two orifices – his wet, vaginal mouth and the phallic muzzle of the gun which is holstered inside his right leg. Starting out as a symbolic denial of Bakhtin's lower bodily stratum, RoboCop becomes a compound auto-erotic object ('What did you think? That you were an ordinary police officer? You're our product'). A curious point is that he is fed on a specially prepared faecal paste which has the texture of baby food. He eats purest shit and pumps out bullets. The usual bodily functions obviously presume far too much contact with the outside world for this immaculate being. Genital activity is displaced, anal elimination becomes orally inverted.

A creature with a bullet-proof body and a shattered mind, RoboCop is an unexpected variation on Stallybrass' and White's bourgeois imaginary. The most suggestive scene, in this respect, occurs when he discovers who he really is by plugging himself into the police computer and dredging the files. As the images shuttle past on the monitor, there is the sense of an alienated search for identity mutating into an ecstatic semiotic voyage, a prosthetic video game. It almost acts as a metaphor for the postmodern condition – Jameson's schizophrenic buzz of signs wrapped up in a protective titanium shell. As such, it's certainly more insightful than the movie's 'situationist' chorus of TV ads and news blips.

But how does this fairly constricted image of cinema link up with Stallybrass' and White's 'poetics of transgression'? Where is the postmodern equivalent to the 'hybridised' culture of the Elizabethan playhouses? To suggest a possible answer to this question, it's necessary to look a little closer at the exhibition side of Hollywood – beyond the multiplex to the VCR. For video is that dispersed realm where the cultural contradictions of late capital begin to emerge. Not only is it an alternative outlet for postmodern Hollywood product – whether rented or purchased – it also offers space for independent production companies to bypass the studio distribution chain and knock out their own low-budget, low-return trash for a cult audience. Often these are splatter movies, horror films built around cheap special effects, absurdist humour and grotesque violence. The connection with the Marlovian tradition of 'killing and mirth' is striking and is perhaps best made by the film critic Kim Newman who, in his splatter inventory *Nightmare Movies*,[94] comes up with such resonant mutant movie genres as the 'Weirdo Horror Film', the 'Cannibal Zombie Gut-Cruncher' and the 'Down-Home, Up-Country, Multi-Implement Massacre Movie' in order to classify splatter movies like David Cronenberg's *Videodrome*, George Romero's *Dawn of the Dead* and Tobe Hooper's *The Texas Chain Saw Massacre*. Mixing horror and comedy, side-splitting gore and gut laughs, these films responded to the affectless blast of postmodern Hollywood with a carnivalesque lunge. Here is the culture of Cardboard City, grungy, acidic, elastic, the flipside to Fred Pfeil's PMC culture.

This whole aesthetic belongs to a video rental subculture which sprang up in the UK during the early Eighties. Again the cultural contradictions are rampant. The rental stores which stocked these movies were often located in areas of high unemployment, in the back-streets of the degraded public realm, yet functioned as ramshackle sites of entrepreneurial activity, flexible small-scale businesses serving local needs. As for the customers, they belonged to the sub-social but had managed to plug into a piece of electronic hardware which belonged to the 'long wave' of technological innovation and economic growth which kicked off in the early Eighties. The marketing of video as a consumer good coincided with the emergence of an industrial reserve army after the 1979–1982 recession. Here was a technology

literally in the hands of the Fourth World, a device which enabled them simultaneously to escape the disciplinary snares of the broadcasting net by slotting a tape
in over the top of television's white noise and bust out of the integrated circuit of
postmodern Hollywood by choosing to watch movies that failed to enter their calcu-
lations.[95]

Hence the 'video nasty' scare of 1983. A moral panic whipped up by the
tabloid press and exploited by frothing Parliamentary backbenchers, this offers a
perfect example of how a culture which is 'socially peripheral' becomes 'symbolically central'. Employing a vocabulary of disgust familiar from the Puritan offensives
against the Elizabethan playhouses, the authors of the scare publicly repudiated the
most popular form of video entertainment – the splatter movie – in an attempt to
promote a bourgeois ideology of good taste and engineered the passing of the censo-
rious Video Recordings Act in 1984. But as Stallybrass and White have demon-
strated in their reading of Bourdieu, an explicit concern with an aesthetic of 'purity'
always masks a deeper political interest. The intention of the Act may have been to
legislate against 'obscenity and offences against public decency'.[96] Its effect was to
monitor and control the scandalous cultural exchanges occurring daily in the back
streets and corner shops of the sub-social.

Just as the Puritans recognised that the 'incontinence' of the playhouses threatened the cultural momentum of the Civilising Process, so the new middle classes,
Pfeil's professional-managerial types, suspected that the 'nastiness' of video was the
sign of a wider cultural disaffection. They weren't wrong. The Great Expulsion which
ejects the poor and disabled from the confines of the disciplinary social has been
matched in recent years by a Decivilising Process. The old public realm exists today
as a 'lower bodily stratum' in Bakhtin's sense, a sunken landscape of crumbling
estates, gaping potholes and swelling garbage bags. Its inhabitants are the homeless
and the dispossessed, Baudrillard's 'residue', obliged by cuts in public services to
eat, sleep and even piss in the street with a diminishing sense of embarrassment. For
them, Elias' threshold of shame has retreated to the point of careless self-abandon.

The splatter movie provided a convenient handle for the symbolic castigation of
this whole grotesque scenography as 'low-Other', for the construction of a hierarchy
of discourse, the body and social place which freed the climate-controlled public
realm from the desperate clutches of the sub-social. It's the same story with drugs –
a real social crisis sponsors a fake moral panic as an alibi for political inaction. The
difference is that the splatter movie is a discourse as much as a commodity. It is in
a position to comment on its own ambivalent cultural situation, to articulate a sense
of what it means to be maintained as low-Other. Bakhtin's grotesque body erupts in
these movies not as the repository of some bourgeois imaginary but as a means of
contesting symbolic hierarchies of taste, of aggravating the cultural frictions of post-
Fordism.

Take *Videodrome*. A counterblast to the 'symbolics of sexuality' on display in
a film like *RoboCop*, this conceptual splatter movie deals instead with what might
be called an 'analytics of blood'. The set-up is complicated and difficult to summarise. Max Renn is the owner of a sleazy cable TV station on the lookout for new
product. When a technofreak pal unscrambles the signal of a sex-and-violence pirate
station called Videodrome, Renn attempts to track down the source of its transmission, only to discover that it is responsible for causing a brain tumour which triggers pornographic hallucinations. After that, he becomes involved in a mutating and

ultimately indecipherable corporate conspiracy as he attempts to understand why he has been exposed to the signal. Cronenberg's chief theoretical reference for *Videodrome* is fellow Canadian Marshall McLuhan, but the movie can also be interpreted as a critique of Baudrillard. One of its most resonant tableaux occurs when Renn is persuaded to wear a bulbous recording helmet which tapes his hallucinations for later transmission on Videodrome. Sporting black visor, eye tubes and a strobe-lit cranial dome, he sits in a vacant room slowly moving his trapped head from side to side. Effectively functioning as an input/output station in an integrated media circuit, he is the perfect image of Baudrillard's mass viewer. Except that he looks grotesque.

Throughout the movie, Cronenberg employs an imagery of amputation and wounding, of grotesque sexual coupling, in a way which implicitly criticises Baudrillard's classically inscribed notion of seamless media feedback. Television sets become veined and tumescent – in one scene, for example, Renn is attracted to a swelling screen showing a disembodied pair of lips ('Come to me') and ecstatically slips his head into its electronic embrace. Meanwhile, in another scene, his body mutates into a walking video machine, complete with messy stomach slot and biomorphic cassettes ('They can play you like a video tape-recorder'). He becomes a programmed assassin despatched on a round of public slaughter. His gun is fused to his hand; his body becomes a lethal weapon, it even bites – as one of his handlers discovers when he inserts a cassette into his abdominal cavity and gets his hand chewed off.

Renn becomes both the viewer and the viewed, hardware and software, input and output. But the 'code' governing this feedback loop is not, as Baudrillard would have it, some metaphysical absent cause. Instead it is graphically visceral and highly dysfunctional. There are leaks in the circuit. This is made clear by the fact that as the movie goes on, Renn's interactions with the screen become increasingly violent and incoherent. The formal breaks between fantasy and reality begin to fray and dissolve until it is impossible to figure out what is going on. Who is programming whom? What is the status of any given image? The final scene just about sums things up. A TV set shows Renn blowing his brains out before itself exploding in a fountain of blood and internal organs; only for Renn to repeat the suicidal gesture he has just been watching; only for Cronenberg to frame it in exactly the same way. This is Cronenberg's comment on Baudrillard's 'ventilation of individuals': a terminal image loop endlessly repeating the scene of its own erasure, a *mise-en-abyme* of video suicide.

The comparison between the 'classical' techno-body of *RoboCop* and the 'grotesque' bodily ventilation of *Videodrome* is instructive. But where Stallybrass and White become particularly useful is in their theorisation of how cultural events shift across 'distinct discursive domains'. This is an important consideration for any theory which attempts to articulate some sense of the divided post-Fordist cultural landscape, with its hermetic blocks of defensible space divorced from the crowded streets of the city, its fortress hotels and public wastelands, suburban enclaves and open-air squats. They make the important point that displacement does not occur – as poststructuralism would have it – across some historically inert 'signifying chain'. This free play of signifiers is something confined to the Bonaventure Hotel, it's Fred Pfeil's sociological definition of postmodern culture. Instead they argue that 'the most significant kinds of displacement are across diverse territories of semantic material and always appear to involve steep gradients, even precipitous leaps, between socially unequal discursive domains'.[97]

Joe Dante's fantasy movie, *Explorers*, provides a good example of this kind of cultural displacement in action. A response to the 'libidinal historicism' which Jameson sees as the constituent sign of postmodernism, it rephrases PMC culture as a grotesque nursery obsession. Dante marks out his bases clearly enough. The movie begins with a trio of disaffected pre-teens building a spaceship from bits and pieces of garbage they have scavenged from the local junk yard: an old carnival tilt-wheel, a trashcan, car tyres, washing machine doors, a TV screen, car lamps and street signs. This is a utopian vision of the sub-social – recycled garbage made productive by a collective dream. The fact that the ship is christened 'The Thunder Road' in honour of an old Bruce Springsteen blue-collar anthem only serves to emphasise the point.

Then comes Dante's twist. The ship is drawn into the maw of an alien space-craft, which, far from being classically streamlined, is bulbous and mottled, a grotesque artefact. Wandering through its interior, the boys are frisked by a security droid before finally making contact with the resident alien – a green slimeball who greets them with a line from an old Warner Bros. cartoon ('Nyah! What's up, Doc?'). Things get worse. Soon, the alien is standing before a jumbo TV screen shuffling images picked up from the earth's communication satellites – the only form of human culture he is familiar with. He has ingested the full freight of American pop trivia and spews it out at random in an attempt to communicate with the boys.

Here is Jameson's culture of quotation and pastiche reproduced as an arbitrary slew of jingles, advertising straplines, jokes, Hollywood sound-bites, cartoon effects and game show routines. Dante's message is not the banal one – that the Aliens R Us – but more subversive. The boys are symbolic emissaries from the Fourth World, the security-coded alien craft a kind of floating Bonaventure or postmodern media playpen, while the alien is a caricature of Baudrillard's hyperconformist consumer, a Jeff Koons in orbit. Literally occupying a 'black hole' in space, he takes the world's media flak unprotected and reduplicates it in a destructive act of 'hypersimulation'.

The figure of the alien illiterate has cropped up in other sci-fi movies, notably Ron Howard's *Splash* and John Carpenter's *Starman* – but always as a holy innocent in a fallen world. What makes *Explorers* transgressive is its hybridised poetics, its scrambling of the familiar cultural markers. While the pre-teens are clean-cut and media literate ('But this is just the movies'), the alien is a pinhead with an obscene paunch, phallic hind-quarters, tentacular fingers, eyes on stalks and plug-hole ears. They are the Fourth World as hip innocents, he is the postmodern channel-hopper as autistic slob. And whereas the boys' hometown is a cartoon wonderland, the alien environment – standing in for the cybernetic social – is figured in the familiar grotesque idiom as all steam, clanking pipes and industrial smells and belches.

Explorers thus links up intriguingly with Mullaney's notion of the 'rehearsal of cultures'. Just as the Elizabethan theatre was a 'self-consuming' exhibition of a folk culture prior to its disciplinary subjugation, so *Explorers* suggests, in reverse fashion, that the nostalgic exhibition of pop iconography which, according to Jameson, distinguishes postmodernism is the sign of its simulated extinction. Perhaps PMC culture in its entirety is a mere curiosity in some Bonaventure Wunderkammer, an exhibition of the remains of a collapsing society. Although postmodernism unquestionably defines the contemporary cultural dominant of post-Fordism, the question which unexpectedly demands to be answered is whether it belongs to a social formation still in the emergent or whether it is the last gasp of a bourgeois social now wrapped in a cybernetic shroud. Are the new middle classes unknowingly condemned, like the aliens in *Explorers*, to vanish from the face of the earth? Does the future, after all, belong to the Fourth World?

V   METABOLIC HANDICAPPING: CLOWNS AND ZOMBIES

It is impossible to supply a definite answer to such questions. A possible response can only begin to be formulated by supplementing Foucault's genealogy of modernity with the speculations of the maverick French cultural historian Paul Virilio. A difficult task. Whereas Foucault's texts are impeccably disposed, from the orderly succession of epistemes which is their subject to the mathematical precision of their syntax, Virilio is much more scattershot, a hit-and-run commentator rather than a commander of the theoretical field.

Unlike Foucault, his conception of modernity is not determined by a logic of space but by the logistics of time and perhaps as a result his texts are stop-start affairs, full of breath-taking conceptual leaps and jolting lapses. Arguments are dropped almost as soon as they are raised, metaphors extended to the point of paranoid fantasy, facts juggled and figures rolled.[98] Just as Foucault's texts reflect his belief that the unearthing of buried discourses from the sediment of history is itself a political act, so Virilio's texts – primarily 1977's *Speed and Politics*, but also the collection of interviews which make up 1983's *Pure War* – are symptomatic of his conviction that any revolutionary gesture is always an art of interruption, 'picnolepsy', the erection of barricades in time rather than space.

This provides a good starting point for attempting to graft Virilio on to Foucault. Whereas Foucault is concerned with the management of bodies in space, Virilio is much more fascinated by the regulation of bodies in time. For the Great Confinement, read the 'Dromocratic Revolution'; for discipline, read 'the bourgeois dictatorship of movement'; for power-knowledge relations, read 'power-moving' vectors. For surveillance, read speed. Speed is Virilio's Big Obsession. He virtually rewrites the whole of Marxist political economy according to this imperative. Exploitation is not so much the extraction of surplus value from labour by capital as the usurpation of mass mobility by state mobilisation. Power is connected with speed before it has anything to do with the accumulation of capital, wealth is always first and foremost a ballistic force. According to this logic, revolutionary demand translates into popular agitation while the development of the bourgeois social is a matter of the ordered flow of bodies, goods, services and, ultimately, signs. In the final analysis, the true enemy of the people is not the fat capitalist but the implacable traffic cop.[99]

Virilio seems to think his analytic supersedes Foucault's when it can quite easily be viewed as the missing half of the equation which goes to make up the history of the disciplinary social. According to *Speed and Politics*, the Dromocratic Revolution was instituted by the transformation of the 'freedom of movement' of the early days of the French Revolution, with its random assaults and mob rioting, its 'dromomania', into the 'dictatorship of movement' of the first co-ordinated mass uprising of 1793. What started out as a revolt against 'the constraint to immobility symbolised by the ancient feudal serfdom' quickly became a more insidious form of subjection – the 'obligation to mobility'.[100]

Whereas for Foucault the model of bourgeois power is the penitentiary, a machinery of discipline which distributes individuals in space under the gaze of an imaginary despot, for Virilio it is the public highway system, a machinery of 'poliorcetics' which regulates the serial movement of individuals in transit through the city according to a system of tolls, traffic lights and speed limits. Poliorcetics operates by 'confusing social order with the control of traffic (of people, of goods), and revolution, revolt, with traffic jams, illegal parking, multiple crashes, collisions'.[101] Virilio is not arguing that 'dromomania' is a revolutionary act in itself but that it is perceived to be so by the dominant classes, that its subversive potential lies in its ability to interrupt the smooth running of the dictatorship of movement.

How does this all connect with the early modern period? How should the link between the Great Confinement and the Dromocratic Revolution be theorised? Foucault's notion that confinement was significant less for its exclusion of an unproductive population than for its invention of a series of disciplinary techniques can be supplemented by Virilio's own thoughts on the subject. The bodies of the confined are scandalous for Virilio not because of their confusion of epistemological categories, their simultaneous display of the signs of abjection, idleness and insanity, but because of their 'kinetic disorder'. It was the great labour of bourgeois culture to normalise their aberrant behaviour by co-ordinating their spastic gestures, to discipline them by literally straightening them out. The body of the confined became a 'metabolic vehicle', while the attempt to tame it was the equivalent to an act of 'piracy', a 'boarding of the metabolic vehicle'.[102] When he refers to 'the arsenal of treatments inflicted daily on these soulless bodies by their owners, executioners, judges or doctors',[103] Virilio is thus offering an alternative analysis to Foucault's of the function of the disciplinary social.

The task now is to forge a theoretical link between this 'disciplinary-dromocratic social' and the Great Reform of domains, discourses, bodies and states of mind described by Stallybrass and White. It's a tough job, given that Virilio is so elliptical, but it can be done if the text of *Speed and Politics* is opened out a little. The starting point for such an interpretative shakedown must be Virilio's assertion that power for the early modern state 'appears beyond the accumulation of violence as an accumulation of movement'.[104] The broader implication of this remark is that the state monopoly of violence which Elias suggests inaugurates the Civilising Process is as much dromocratic as disciplinary. Just as Foucault claims that the bourgeoisie appropriated discipline for their own ends under the sign of a 'cultivation of the body', so the gestural technologies described by Virilio were hijacked in order to promote what might be called a 'mobilisation of the body'. By sexually cultivating their bodies, the bourgeoisie were effectively treating them as metabolic vehicles to be boarded, piloted and controlled. The elaboration of social standards of restraint governing public behaviour can thus be considered as a 'poliorcetics' of the body, a policing of the traffic in food and fluids which occurs at its points of ingestion and evacuation, its folds, slits and orifices. Bakhtin's explanation of how the 'grotesque' is converted into the 'classical' body during the course of the construction of the bourgeois public realm becomes an exercise in self-empowerment only because it's first an exercise in self-control.

Having theorised this much, the relevance of *Speed and Politics* to the 'incontinence' of the Elizabethan playhouses becomes easier to understand. By the late sixteenth century, the Liberties of London had become a place of refuge not only for struggling bands of players but also for a heterogeneous assortment of outlaws, misfits, peddlers, entrepreneurs, vagrant scholars, beggars, jugglers and victims of the enclosures – everyone represented by the grotesque figure of the 'many-headed multitude'.[105] The anxiety of the city authorities over the mob riots and traffic jams frequently associated with the playhouses was thus the sign of a wider 'poliorcetic' crisis, an identification of theatrical simulation with the spectacle of urban 'dromo-mania'. That this was an act of cultural misrecognition is made clear by Virilio when he describes how the dominant classes typically trip over themselves by 'confusing the mass's ability to move with its ability to attack'.[106] For while playhouses like the Rose and the Swan were indeed domains marked by social atomisation and urban drift, sites of displaced mobility, they were also proving grounds for the dictatorship of movement, strategic traffic islands, sluice-gates regulating the flow of vagrant bodies.

The cultural ambivalence of the theatres is reflected in the plays themselves, which comment obliquely on their compromised status as triggers of social mobility. Especially significant in this respect is the clown, a subversive figure who defines a circumscribed 'poetics of transgression' with his every dumb gesture. Advertising his stupidity in extravagant displays of physical impropriety and linguistic perversity, he resists dromocratic incorporation by his deliberate 'refusal to understand', as Michael D. Bristol puts it in his 1985 book, *Carnival and Theater*. The clown's determined insistence upon anarchic idiocy effectively makes real the imaginary threat of dromo-mania and puts a brake on the bourgeois 'mobilization of the body'.[107]

This kind of spasmodic foot-dragging is most effective when it interrupts the forced ideological march of tragedy. Take Christopher Marlowe's *Doctor Faustus*. The real struggle in this play is not between God and Lucifer for possession of Faustus' soul, but between a tragic and a comic phrasing of his seduction. Its trajectory is not metaphysical but metabolic. The good doctor sells his soul to Mephostopholis less for knowledge or pleasure and more for the promise of unrestricted mobility ('I'll be great emperor of the world/And make a bridge through the moving air'). Faustus is the world's first dromocrat, an ambivalent figure poised between subjection to Virilio's 'dictatorship of movement' and anarchic mobility.

The tragic side to his story is easily told and is the one preferred by the Chorus. Faustus circles the cosmos in eight days on a chariot drawn by dragons. It's a whirl-wind trip which takes him to 'the height of Primum Mobile', the still point of the turning world. The terms of his contract specify that when his 24 years are up he is obliged to surrender his body to Lucifer. However, when the time comes, Faustus wants only for all motion to stop ('Stand still, you ever-moving spheres of heaven'). He wants to wrest control of his body back, only to find it has been boarded by an infernal intelligence ('O I'll leap up to my God! Who pulls me down?'). Faustus discovers that selling his soul has transformed his body into an automotive vehicle. Mobility was what he craved and it catches up with him in the end.

But there is another side to the story – the one described by the comic subplot. When two drunken clowns conjure Mephostophilis 'in jest', transporting him from one side of the world to the other, his irritation is subordinated to their wilful perver-sity ('How am I vexed by these villains' charms!'). The movement he dictates in the main plot has been deflected by their anarchic mischief. This is something enjoyed by Faustus himself in those scenes of the play where tragedy descends into farce. After he has been made invisible by Mephostophilis, for example, he is able to run rings round the guests assembled at a state banquet in Rome ('Do what thou wilt, thou shalt not be discerned').

As he snatches the food from the Pope's mouth and boxes his ears, he offers an explicit rebuke not only to Catholic sensibilities but to the 'dictatorship of movement' defined in its most elementary form. Instead of the regimented parade of good table manners there is an explosion of panicky gestures. Disorder replaces discipline, panic subverts 'poliorcetics'.

The radically divided nature of Faustus' body – as automotive vehicle, as trigger of instability – means that by the end of the play it is literally torn to pieces. As three scholars mournfully contemplate the spectacle of his limbs distributed across the face of the earth ('All torn asunder by the hand of death'), the tragic note predominates. There is the sense that Faustus has indeed been repossessed 'body and soul' by Lucifer. But at the same time – bearing in mind previous slapstick episodes where he has conjured an extra limb from thin air or run around headless – it is possible to wonder whether he hasn't had the last laugh.

The supercession in cultural importance of the public playhouses by the private theatres, the shift from an 'incontinent' to an 'interstitial' staging of urban mobility, signals the moment when the theatre began to function less as a clogged social sieve and more as a kind of porous crowd control mechanism. By the 1620s, the fashionable theatres of the West End had put an end to the promiscuous minglings of the untamed multitude by inserting the newly empowered bourgeoisie into a strategic economy of motion, ferrying their pampered bodies across the city on a highly organised round of social stop-offs and public engagements. Here was the bourgeois dictatorship of movement in prototype, an anticipation of the Dromocratic Revolution to come during the eighteenth century.

This development is trailed in a play as early as Shakespeare's *Coriolanus*. If Faustus is the dromocrat as antihero, Coriolanus is the dromocrat as nihilist. A warrior unable to rest on his laurels, he spends most of the play in perpetual motion between his native Rome and the enemy camp of the Volsces. But the difference between the two – like the difference between God and Lucifer in *Doctor Faustus* – is a distraction. Just as God and Lucifer struggle for possession of Faustus' 'body and soul', so the Romans and the Volsces struggle to capture Coriolanus – his body, his mind, his very name. He begins the play as Caius Martius and ends it 'a kind of nothing, titleless' even as he insists throughout upon his singularity.

The significant conflict in the play takes place between Coriolanus and the mob. His tragedy is that he is constitutionally unable to mobilise the 'many-headed multitude' of Rome. In the victory over the Volsces which opens the play, he is unable to persuade his soldiers to storm the enemy city of Corioles and so takes it alone – thus gaining himself a new name. When he returns victoriously to Rome and runs for the position of consul, he is expected to display his wounds before the people in the forum but is wary of transforming his body into a public monument. He has sway over neither the military nor the proto-industrial proletariat. The 'dictatorship of movement' he exercises is confined exclusively to his own body ('When he walks, he moves like an engine'). A fighting machine possessed by the urge to perpetually extend his conquests, he refuses to keep still ('Pray now, sit down').

The mob attempt to deflect Coriolanus from his dromocratic orbit when they maul him in the forum, but, unlike Faustus, he refuses to submit himself to the spontaneous anarchy of 'dromomania'. He understands that popular acclaim for his achievements is based upon a wilful 'refusal to understand' their seriousness. Condemned as a potential tyrant by the tribunes of Rome, who are willing to manipulate the mob in a way he is not, Coriolanus is banished from Rome. But even when banished, he will not be swayed ('I banish you'). He joins up with his former enemies and advances on Rome, at which point the mob changes its mind and gives him a hero's welcome into the city. The self-interest which motivates this flip-flop of popular opinion is comically transparent but fails to interrupt the irresistible momentum of Coriolanus' tragedy. There is no margin reserved in *Coriolanus* for anarchic idiocy as there is in *Doctor Faustus*.

Coriolanus is destroyed because he switches sides once too often. He is consumed not by his stubborn inflexibility, his pride, but by his restlessness, his carelessness, his monstrous self-indulgence. After being petitioned by his mother, he refrains from sacking the city which lies at his feet and betrays the Volsces as he had earlier betrayed Rome. Passions rise on all sides and he is quickly overwhelmed ('Tear him to pieces'). It is a particularly appropriate irony that he should only be able to mobilise the mob around the prospect of his own extinction. Like Faustus, Coriolanus is dismembered, but there is no possibility of interpreting this as some carnivalesque thrashing. His tragic status remains inviolate. Coriolanus in the end becomes a cautionary lesson in the proper organisation of the 'dictatorship of movement', a reminder that the bourgeois 'mobilisation of the body' must shuck off the mob and reform the body politic if it is to survive.

The development of the 'disciplinary-dromocratic social' in the nineteenth century can be theorised in relatively simple fashion by direct reference to *Speed and Politics*. Whereas Foucault takes a detour to explain this expansion of the bourgeois public realm in terms of the discursive sexualisation of the masses and the corresponding extension of disciplinary institutions, Virilio is more direct. He suggests that this is mass mobilisation pure and simple, a matter not so much of disciplining bodies suddenly intensified by sex as of strategically disabling bodies suddenly empowered by speed. The link with Marx on industrial capitalism follows easily enough. Taylorism, for example, is more than an anatomy of detail in the Foucauldian sense; it is a calibration of time and motion according to a political logic of speed, with the coordinated movements of the assembly-line a strategic exercise in what Virilio calls 'metabolic handicapping'.

The idea that Fordism shifts the dromocratic intensities of Taylorist productivity into the realm of consumption during the twentieth century is also easily accommodated by Virilio. His figure of the 'consumer-producer' is quite explicit testimony to the continuities which persist between Taylorism and Fordism. With the emergence of the consumer society, the 'metabolic vehicle' of the labouring subject is boarded by the hidden persuaders of the advertising industry, piloted into the expanded public realm and programmed to compete for distinctive signs in Baudrillard's second order of simulation. This theorisation of Fordism is significant not only for the way it slots into a Keynsian economy of demand management but also for its phrasing of the consumer society as a festival of handicapped movement, a regime of package tours, commuter flows and mass assaults on the supermarket shelves. The significant thing all the way down the line is the 'poliorcetic' co-ordination of gesture, the precise policing of the vagaries of mass mobility.

The next obvious theoretical step is to understand Hollywood cinema not only as a Fordist engine of the Civilising Process but as the ultimate dromocratic device, pummelling subjects into position and streamlining bodies through ticket booths in mass formation. But Virilio complicates things by adding an unexpected conceptual twist. In his 1984 book, *War and Cinema*, he conceives of the stereotypical picture palace of the Thirties as a kind of urban troop ship designed to keep the masses in military harness after demobilisation. According to this slightly baffling scenario, cinema functions as a dromocratic call to arms, a form of 'perceptual logistics'. While the Hollywood star system becomes the perceptual arsenal of this military machine, with the sex symbol figured as a kind of irresistible image bomb, its big guns are defined by the musical comedies of the period, especially the all-singing, all-dancing spectaculars of Fred Astaire. It was the task of movies like *Top Hat* and *Follow the Fleet*, Virilio argues, 'to imbue audiences with fresh energy, to wrench them out of apathy in the face of danger or distress, to overcome that wide-scale demoralisation which was so feared by generals and statesmen alike'.[108]

This odd and rather implausible couching of cinema in battle dress is not to be taken too seriously and is really nothing more than a brilliant extended metaphor. At the same time, though, it links up with elements of *Speed and Politics* in ways which deserve serious attention. One thing of vital importance Virilio adds to Foucault's analytic of the bourgeois social is an understanding of what might be called the 'militaristic social'. Foucault strays into this area when he mentions in *Discipline and Punish* that the typical barracks of the early seventeenth century was one of the first disciplinary institutions and that discipline as the art of training bodies took its most visible shape in the eighteenth-century fashion for army manoeuvres and exercises. But in the end, all he is willing to argue is that the military dream of the 'perfect army' provided one model for the implementation of disciplinary techniques throughout civil society.[109]

Virilio goes much further. For him, civil and military society emerge simultaneously as two sides of the same historical impulse and continue to develop in parallel. The mobilisation of the 'military proletariat' is the counterpart to that of the 'industrial proletariat', the former serving an officer class, the latter a middle class, one concerned with logistics, the other with manoeuvres. There is a distinct division of labour – 'the new commercial bourgeoisie tends to enrich itself by amassing the productive movements (actions) of the industrial proletariat ... while the military class amasses the destructive act of the mobile masses'.[110] The important point Virilio makes in *War and Cinema* is therefore more broadly concerned with the Fordist industrial regime than with cinema. He seems to be arguing that Fordism during the Thirties explicitly orchestrated a convergence of the military and industrial proletariats as an exercise in mass mobilisation, going on during the Cold War era to hitch the planned economy of the consumer society to the demands of the defence industry under the auspices of 'military Keynesianism'.[111]

Virilio's interest in speed and politics means he is much better placed than Foucault to theorise the emergence of post-Fordism and the Fourth World. The Great Expulsion which accompanies the retrenchment of the bourgeois social is essentially a 'poliorcetic' crisis, a mass exercise in demobilisation triggered by the abandonment of the 'metabolic vehicle' of the 'consumer-producer' by late capital.[112] The Fourth World is thus revealed as the repository of an obsolescent industrial proletariat, a 'social bestiary' of unemployed workers, homeless teenagers, tramps, gypsies, vagrant hippies and illegal aliens. At best it becomes a kind of military proletariat once removed, charged under the auspices of such state-sponsored schemes as workfare with literally going through the motions of industrial labour while actually producing nothing.[113] More often than not, though, the nomadic caravans of the Fourth World are simply policed out of urban existence. Postmodern society terminates the Dromocratic Revolution by the simple expediency of ensuring that '[s]urplus populations disappear in the obligatory movement of the voyage'.[114]

It is the subliminal fear of the Fourth World which explains the fashion for fortress architecture in the privatised public realm. The monumentality of the Bonaventure Hotel is again the key symbol, although London's groundscraping Broadgate complex provides an equally resonant example. In such new 'public' spaces as these, patrolled by security guards and bordered by surveillance cameras, anyone whose face doesn't fit is typically classed as a vagabond and summarily expelled. Drifters are understood to be social undesirables who belong on the reservation, in the old public realm, and a whole micro-technology of deterrence has evolved to keep them perpetually in check.[115]

According to Virilio, the ultimate consequence of the termination of the bourgeois dictatorship of movement is 'endo-colonisation', the colonisation by the state of its unproductive population.[116] The world of tower blocks, inner city streets and public parks is in the process of being consigned to Third World status, becoming an internal colony to be administered by the social services and secured by the police – perhaps the only public services the new 'minimum state' will provide in the future.[117] This is much more than a poliorcetic or even a disciplinary crisis, it's a crisis of liberal democracy – as evidenced by the increasing indifference on the part of the dominant classes to the continued 'juridical coding of power' which Foucault sees as the mainstay of the bourgeois social.[118] Human rights don't come free like they used to.

All this provides another angle on the 'video nasties' scare – the importance of 'moving-power' in addition to power-knowledge relations. The most important effect of the Video Recordings Act of 1984 according to this scenario was the power it granted the state to monitor and control new media of communication rather than intercept individually 'offensive' messages. What provoked the anxiety of the dominant classes was not the existence of videos like *Driller Killer* or *The Evil Dead* but the possibility of tape exchanges functioning as a form of unregulated communication amongst the unemployed. Neighbours swapping tapes in pubs, the daily trip round the corner to the local video shop – this, it was thought, could lead to the establishment of unlicensed routes of communication, informal circuits of exchange. The 'video nasties' scare thus provides another classic instance of the dominant classes 'confusing the mass's ability to move with its ability to attack' – as the language of the Act suggests with all its talk about the 'dangerous spread' of cassettes.[119]

This pathological language of contamination and abuse is critically interrogated by the splatter movies which sponsored the 'video nasties' scare. Take George Romero's zombie movies. In *Dawn of the Dead* and *Day of the Dead*, packs of zombies hunt for human flesh in the evacuated urban badlands of America. Dispossessed, shambolic, grotesquely dysfunctional, they define an inadvertent 'poetics of transgression' in their very gait. Their intended victims are the last chance survivors of social catastrophe – armed, mobile, coolly amused, and more than ready to wipe out any interfering zombie by sending a bullet through their brain. The combination of professional cynicism and casual terrorism on the part of the survivalists defines a sensibility beyond 'enlightened false consciousness' – one best characterised by the

Canadian postmodern theorist, Arthur Kroker, as 'viciousness for fun'.[120] On the one side, then, the solitary technicians of movement, on the other, the herds of milling zombies – separated by chain-link fencing and a string of barbed one-liners. The black comedy which permeates the conflict between them is an unconscious recognition of the threat posed by the Fourth World to the new middle classes, who, in Virilio's words, always make the comical error of 'confusing social order with the control of traffic'.

A degraded social assortment of specific sociological types from suburban teenagers to Krishna disciples, Romero's zombies are no longer representative of the faceless masses. Spastic, raw, blown apart and exposed, dribbling and bleeding, they are completely different from the Fordist zombies which crop up in the alien invasion movies of the Fifties. In films like *Invasion of the Body Snatchers* and *I Married a Monster from Outer Space*, aliens take over the bodies of innocent small-town consumers in a glassy-eyed replication of the contours of Middle American conformity. The resulting match between bodily dysfunction and ideological slip is flawless. Any deviation from the social norm is a transparent index of unconscious thought-crime.

In *Body Snatchers* the giveaway signs include the meter-man calling at breakfast time, someone's father working late in the basement, a gas station attendant checking the trunk of a car. Meanwhile the incriminating evidence in *I Married a Monster* is even more ludicrous – the alien hubby doesn't drink, can't make small talk, forgets to turn on his headlights late at night. The sub-text to all this is a pop-up blank. The synapses of innocent Cold War conformists have been hot-wired by malicious Hidden Pesuaders from Madison Avenue, from Russia, from the floor of the House Committee on Un-American Activities. From Outer Space. Any way you fill in the blank, the result is the same. As Virilio says, in a slightly different context, 'bodies are guilty of being out of synch'.[121]

The twist with Romero's zombies is that the connecting nerve between ideology and the body has been severed. The zombies of *Dawn of the Dead* are not bodies guilty of being out of synch but abandoned vehicles guilty of obstruction – their imperfections are material and grotesque rather than metaphysical and classically signifying. Most of the action takes place in a Pennsylvania shopping mall and there are plenty of scenes of zombies bumping into each other, falling over, stumbling up the escalators, knocking over display cabinets and crushing goods under-foot. The confusion is all very comical, but this is not a satire on mindless consumerism. It is an oblique commentary on precisely the loss of those smooth reflexes which sustain the Fordist economy. The zombies are victims of a Decivilising Process, lost bodies which no longer know how to consume ('Some kind of instinct, memory, what they used to do – this was an important place in their lives').

The contrast with the hyperactive survivalists could not be more explicit. Whereas the zombies can barely take two steps without falling over, the survivalists race round the mall, skidding round bends and sliding down escalators. Their consumer instincts are pathological. When they're not shooting zombies, they're looting the mall, grabbing dresses, confectionery, watches, hats, and jackets, seizing cheese, salami, spices and coffee beans. They also make excessive use of the mall's indoor leisure facilities, playing basketball and golf, going ice-skating and, most significantly of all, playing video games. Here, they manipulate buttons, levers and steering-wheels in a simulation of that now obsolescent act of piracy described by

Virilio – the boarding of the metabolic vehicle of the proletariat. The movie suggests that the class struggle is no longer politically or economically mediated. The relation between the survivalists and the zombies is instead directly material, a matter of turf battles and body invasions. Appetite is the only claim the zombies have on the survivalists ('These creatures are nothing but pure motorised instinct'). Meanwhile, the survivalists attempt to turn the mall into a fortress by exterminating its internal population of zombies in a fairly graphic image of the privatisation of the public realm described by Davis. Trucks are used to seal its borders and there is a lot of comical splatter while this happens as zombies which get in the way are casually sideswiped and pulped. In an act which makes clear how mass consumption has reached a terminus in mass extermination, the zombies are shot and stacked in shopping trolleys – their useless bodies regaining a final value, as entertainment rather than labour, in the moment of their spectacular extinction. 'Viciousness for fun' just about says it. The zombies are the equivalent of postmodern lepers.

The link between Virilio and the Fourth World has been forged. But how does he connect with postmodernism on the other side of the post-Fordist divide? How does the crumbling of the bourgeois dictatorship of movement impinge on the debate between the Pop Theorists and Baudrillard sketched out by me in 'Pop Theory, Bardolatry, Leaving the Twentieth-century Academy'?[122] What kind of power-moving relations operate inside the Bonaventure Hotel? It's a question which needs to be answered but which Virilio's key concepts are unable to address. Whereas the zombies of the Fourth World have been expelled from the dromocratic social to become shambolic, vacant hulks, driverless metabolic vehicles, the players in the para-social have escaped the dictatorship of movement in a very different way. No longer Fordist 'consumer-producers' they are instead post-Fordist operators, their bodies less pirated vehicles than self-propelled vectors, touch-sensitive steering mechanisms. Baudrillard's hyperconformist careerist, the Pop Theorists' radical consumer – these are opposite sides of the same social type, the media switch-hitter, the enlightened cynic skilled at converting output and input, an acrobatic figure shimmying through the integrated circuits of late capital.

The French cultural critic Michel de Certeau provides the theoretical vocabulary necessary to round off this figure of the hyperactive consumer, although it involves reading his texts radically against the grain. Championed by some as the necessary response to Baudrillard's supposed nihilism,[123] a theorist concerned with the 'pragmatics' rather than the 'semiotics' of postmodern existence, de Certeau nevertheless reveals himself to be Baudrillard's secret accomplice. Once read via Virilio, his interest in vectors of speed and mobility emerges as the parallel to Baudrillard's interest in hyper-involved sign systems.

In his key 1984 text, *The Practice of Everyday Life*, de Certeau proposes to demonstrate the way in which the ordinary working stiff is able to outwit the system by a process of insinuation, trickery, diversion, tenacity and opportunism.[124] All these are interpreted as radically subversive gestures available to the ordinary city dweller, a figure empowered by his dexterity in the kinds of 'everyday virtuosities' and 'polymorph mobilities' which define his existence. De Certeau's master trope is '*la perruque*', which he defines as 'the worker's own work disguised as work for his employer'.[125]

This is where the problems begin. As George Yudice points out in his 1988 essay, 'Marginality and the Ethics of Survival', 'such "tactics" are wielded not only by workers but by the very same managers … who enforce the established order'.[126] '*La perruque*' is a practice which is much more profitable for a money broker with access to inside information on the stock market than to a company secretary who uses the office notepaper for his personal correspondence. The high rollers are much more expert at bucking the system than the scurrying low-level workers in a company. De Certeau's 'polymorph mobilities' finally emerge on the side of late capital as the counterpart to Baudrillard's 'generation by models', his third order of simulation. The link with the Pop Theorists' rhetoric of subversive consumption is obvious and the same charge can be made – that in attempting to outwit the system, '*la perruque*' merely invigorates it by providing new input.

But this much is in fact evident in the text of *The Practice of Everyday Life*, which spectacularly deconstructs itself as it attempts to widen its angle of theoretical approach. De Certeau distinguishes 'tactics' from 'strategy' in order to thrash out the issues involved. Strategy is the dominant exercise of power, the marking off of territory, the construction of an inclusive field of vision, whereas tactics is the popular subversion of power, the manipulation of boundaries, the diversion of established lines of sight.[127] Or in other words, strategy is to the dominant culture as tactics are to sub-culture. All the arguments levelled against the Pop Theorists thus also apply to de Certeau. Just as the dominant culture now only exists as a busy affray of mediated subcultures, so the strategic field of power has been completely usurped by the proliferation of tactical pathways.

De Certeau even admits as much. He speculates that the strategic model of the social has been 'defeated by its own success', becoming 'the scene of the Brownian movements of invisible and innumerable tactics' equivalent to the emergence of a 'cybernetic society' defined as 'the proliferation of aleatory and indeterminable manipulations within an immense framework of socioeconomic restraints and securities'.[128] This is a perfect definition of Baudrillard's third order of simulation locked inside Jameson's Bonaventure Hotel. The irony is that in supposing that '[t]here is no longer an elsewhere', de Certeau is ignoring the existence of the public realm outside of the Bonaventure, home to the shambling zombies of the Fourth World. The intriguing question then emerges. Does an anamorphic variation on the strategic model begin to re-emerge here on the other side of the post-Fordist divide? If the new middle classes now dominate precisely as a result of their tactical ingenuity, does the zombie occupy a new strategic field – one which circumscribes the tactical pathways of the experts? Isn't the only revolutionary power-movement vector defined nowadays not by the 'everyday virtuosities' of the individual but by the mass stampedes of the Fourth World?

Again this is a difficult question to answer. One point which can made is that de Certeau's opposition between tactics and strategy is the counterpart to Virilio's distinction between the dromomaniac and the dromocratic. All that is required is for this equation to be historically inflected. The 'tactical' virtuosities of dromomania are subversive for the masses only at the moment when the bourgeoisie is first shakily extending its grip on the 'strategic' field of the social. Hence the genuine troublesomeness of the Elizabethan clown's 'refusal to understand'.[129] Once the social has been more fully colonised by disciplinary-dromocratic mechanisms this opportunity for subversion vanishes. Tactical ingenuity is strategically handicapped, dromomania loses its edge and the negative capability of the Elizabethan clown is replaced by the positive disability of the Jacobean tragic hero.

As the bourgeois social begins to contract in the late twentieth century, however, the old signs suddenly reverse polarity. Just as de Certeau's strategic field is usurped by the proliferation of tactical pathways, so Virilio's dromocratic order is broken up by the emergence of a reinvigorated dromomania. Except that it no longer defines the subversive effervescence of the mob but the semiotic acumen of the new middle classes. The post-Fordist era consigns the old consumer-producer to an evacuated strategic field and releases the new postmodern operator into an air-conditioned realm of tactical upward mobility. This is the final irony of reading Virilio via a deconstructed de Certeau – his investment in the revolutionary potential of speed is turned against itself. This is nowhere more apparent than in the dromomaniac excitements of post-Fordist Hollywood. The strategic aims of the studio production line have been superseded by the tactical demands of the multi-media deal. Projects are talked up, turned around, fine-tuned and expertly targeted. Niche marketing replaces block booking. The mass mobilisation of a docile population gives way to the serial distraction of an atomized crowd. Bored consumers scan the multiplexes in the same way they browse the mall – with a poised, discriminating, tactical eye. But whether they take in the film-of-the-book or pick up the tie-in T-shirt is no big deal for the movie industry. The number of bodies filed by the box office counts for less in the final reckoning than the number of connections made by the merchandising chain.

The way in which the casual gestures of 'everyday life' are converted into the productive signs of late capital finds its ideological inflection in the careerist office movies of the Eighties. With their attachment to the 'power-moving' vectors operational in postmodern commercial space, films like Herbert Ross's *The Secret of My Success* and Mike Nichols' *Working Girl* condense de Certeau's acrobatic fantasy of bucking the system into a career game-plan. They accurately register *'la perruque'* as a third order simulation, but fail to place it in context. What is omitted from their linear narratives of upward mobility is any understanding of the complicity which exists between the 'tactics' of the careerist and the larger 'strategy' of the corporation he serves. The 'secret' of the success they advertise has nothing to do with the hidden machinations of capital and everything to do with the aesthetics of the smart career move.

The careerist office movie defines the conformist flipside to the 'poetics of transgression' traced by Romero's zombie movies. No longer represented as the last desperate sanction of the survivalist, 'polymorph mobility' is instead the first resort of the career player. His dexterity in the elevated art of *'la perruque'*, with all its dodges, sidesteps, runarounds and backflips, is the tautological sign of his advancement up the career ladder rather than – as Yudice points out – the index of his compromised position within a status hierarchy. It is also what makes him stand out from the crowd, no longer figured as a staggering herd of crazed Fourth World zombies but as an assembly of meek Fordist drones. The office effectively becomes his personal gymnasium, a corporate platform where he is free to go through the motions of the yuppie work aesthetic. Any sense of a public realm existing beyond the air-conditioned expanse of the cybernetic social has evaporated. Or as de Certeau blithely comments: 'there is no longer an elsewhere'.

The plot of *The Secret of My Success* is simple enough. Kansas farm-boy, Brantley Foster, seeks fame and fortune in New York, secures a job in the mailroom of his uncle's corporate conglomerate and quickly rises to the top by virtue of his fancy footwork. Occupying an empty office, he hops from casuals to a sharp suit, invents a smart new identity and passes himself off as a corporate high-flier. The secret of his success has less to do with nepotism, insider dealing or favour pulling than with the adroit manipulation of image. He is more concerned with ordering personalised notepaper and an office nameplate, for example, than he is with getting down to any actual paperwork ('I need some poster-boards, some coloured pens, some coloured pushpins and pencils, lots of pencils').

Foster succeeds because of his grace, his dexterity, his economy of mobility. All the charging round the building in order to escape detection – the sartorial quick-changes in the elevators, the sliding down staircases and ducking in and out of doorways – contrasts sharply with the unproductive mass movements of the other company executives. Whereas he is moving on up, they are running on the spot. Check the herds of identikit commuters streaming obediently from the subway to the office, the flunkies jogging round and round the perimeter of the office roof garden as they are drilled by their boss or the ranks of executives on the conveyor-belt running machines in the company multi-gym.

The mobility reserved for Foster is more productive because more artful and alert. Devoted to the cultivation of the appropriate gesture, it is best expressed by the montage of images showing him on the move to the strains of (appropri-ately) 'Walking on Sunshine' by Katrina and the Waves. Here, Foster engages in a literal choreography of power – glad-handing secretaries as he spins past their desks, zipping through office corridors greeting colleagues with hand-shakes and body-checks, bouncing file cabinets closed with his elbow as he grooves along. It is entirely appropriate that the final scene – a boardroom coup organised by Foster against his uncle – should be conducted as an exercise in engineered motion. Bursting into the board meeting with his cronies, Foster circles the table explaining the details of the changeover to the seated and highly startled executives ('You mind if I stand up? I think better when I'm moving around'). After his uncle has been carted off by security, he is finally invited to occupy the vacant chair at the head of the table. This is the movie's abiding fantasy – that power can be as fun and simple as a game of musical chairs.

But all this defines a debate which has partially been overtaken by events. Consumption for the new middle classes is becoming passé even in its hyper-evolved postmodern phase. Virilio suggests as much in *Speed and Politics* when he states that the consumption of signs and commodities has been surpassed in economic significance by the 'consumption of security', that the responsible citizen is 'no longer the one who enriches the nation by consuming, but the one who invests first and foremost in security, manages his own protection as best he can, and finally pays more to consume less'.[130]

On one level, Virilio is asserting that the crisis of the old Fordist regime pres-aged a mutation in patterns of consumption, that it's no longer consumer durables like television sets and cars but security devices like radio pagers and alarm systems which become 'the target of the whole merchandising system'.[131] But in some ways he is claiming much more – that the pathological prosperity of the Eighties repre-sented the last desperate fling of the consumer society.

The stark possibility must be entertained that consumption as a means of socialisation is drawing to an end. According to Virilio in *Pure War* technological development now pays more dividends in the war economy than in the consumer economy. More than that, it 'entails the non-development of society in the sense of civilian consumption'.[132] This is something which is becoming increasingly evident now that the Cold War has ended and the troops and munitions which underwrote the ideology of deterrence exit the realm of simulation to regain an explosive use value. In the Fourth World the aim of such militarisation is to control the circulation of surplus bodies, in the Third World it is to maintain the supply of scarce resources. But whether it's cops in battle-dress roaming the inner cities or grunts flying the flag in foreign deserts and jungles, the message is the same. Civil society is now under military jurisdiction.

The Green Dream of a 'steady state economy' is the ideology which organises this double deployment. It polices both the excesses of careless Fourth World consumption and the vagaries of irresponsible Third World production in the name of protecting the global environment. Which means that some poor slob can be condemned for spluttering away in his dirty old Ford in the same breath as newly industrialising countries like India and China are criticised for their reluctance to cut down on belching smokestack emissions. As Virilio points out, there is a match between the concerns of ecology and 'eco-logistics'. Post-Fordist society is 'heading toward a generalised development which, in terms of war economy, is similar to zero growth in ecological terms'.[133] The ecological obsession with clean air, the eco-logistical fixation with global immunity – both target new objects of grotesque revulsion. Both signal the hypertrophied development of Stallybrass' and White's 'bourgeois imaginary'. Some things don't change. Welcome to the wonderful world of Pure War.

VI   DYSTOPIA/UTOPIA

It's time to take stock. So far post-Fordism has been defined by a series of hierarchical oppositions. The Bonaventure Hotel and Cardboard City, the para-social and the sub-social, the new middle classes and the lumpen unemployed, the core and the periphery of the service sector economy, smart operators and dumb zombies, postmodernism and pap culture, military and civil society, the global city and the Fourth World, individual virtuosities and mass panics, multinational capitalism and the Third World. In each case the first term is the dominant one, the second is the point of theoretical resistance. Fine. It all adds up to a legible cognitive map of the world we live in.

But this still leaves unanswered the question thrown up by the earlier reading of *Explorers*. Which is the emergent and which the residual social formation? Capital may have holed up in the Bonaventure Hotel, but is it prepared for a long siege or a last stand? The zombies of the underclass may have been disenfranchised, but are they massing for the last big push or the final dissolution? If the Marxist class narrative is nearing its close, can there still be a happy ending? For us all? The remnants of Capital and Labour face each other across the wreckage of the modern project. Maybe the only theoretical task left is to mythologise their struggle as a manichean contest, a symmetrical history. A dystopian epic. What it loses in accuracy, it gains in force.

EJECTED METANARRATIVE FOOTNOTES

1 Jean Baudrillard, *Forget Foucault* (New York: Semiotext(e), 1987), p. 16. Baudrillard's 1977 essay was initially translated as 'Forgetting Foucault' in *Humanities in Society,* vol. 3, no. 1 (Winter 1980), pp. 87–111.

2 Ibid p. 11.

3 Ibid p. 16.

4 'With the simulation device we are no doubt as far from the strategy of transparence as the latter is from the immediate, symbolic operation of punishment which Foucault himself describes', Ibid p. 16.

5 Michel Foucault, *Madness and Civilization* (London: Tavistock, 1971; orig. 1961); idem., *The Birth of the Clinic* (London: Tavistock, 1976; orig. 1963); idem., *The Order of Things* (London: Tavistock, 1974; orig. 1966).

6 Foucault is quite explicit about this periodization in an interview he gave to Raymond Bellour in 1967: 'I can ... define the classical age in its own configuration through the double difference that opposes it to the 16th century on the one hand and to the 19th on the other. On the other hand, I can define the modern age in its singularity only by opposing it to the 17th century on the one hand and to us on the other ... From this modern age which begins around 1790–1810 and goes to around 1950, it's a matter of detaching oneself, whereas for the classical age it's only a matter of describing it'. See Michel Foucault, *Foucault Live (Interviews, 1966–84)* (New York: Semiotext(e), 1989), p. 30. Baudrillard would no doubt suggest that by the time of *Discipline and Punish* Foucault had moved on to 'describe' a social formation – modernity – from which his earlier texts had already 'detached' him. The problem with Baudrillard's own writings – as he acknowledges – is that they attempt to detach him from a culture which he can only describe.

7 Michel Foucault, *Discipline and Punish* (Harmondsworth: Penguin, 1979; orig. 1975), p. 130. Foucault goes on to summarize these three 'technologies of power': 'We have, then, the sovereign and his force, the social body and the administrative apparatus; mark, sign, trace; ceremony, representation, exercise; the vanquished enemy, the juridical subject in the process of requalification, the individual subject to immediate coercion; the tortured body, the soul with its manipulated representations, the body subjected to training. We have here the three series of elements that characterize the three mechanisms that face one another in the second half of the eighteenth century ... three technologies of power', ibid. p. 131.

8 Steve Beard, *Logic Bomb: Transmissions from the Edge of Style Culture* (London: Serpent's Tail, 1998), pp. 163–204.

9 'The reforming jurists ... saw punishment as a procedure for requalifying individuals as subjects, as juridical subjects; it uses not marks but signs, coded sets of representations, which would be given the most rapid circulation and the most general acceptance possible by citizens witnessing the scene of punishment', Foucault, *Discipline and Punish*, p. 130.

10 Ibid., p. 117.

11 This is something emphasized by Peter Spierenburg, who notes that while

public execution continued in Europe up until the 1860s, imprisonment as a disciplinary technique was introduced certainly as early as the seventeenth century. See Peter Spierenburg, *The Spectacle of Suffering: Executions and the Evolution of Repression: From a Preindustrial Metropolis to the European Experience* (Cambridge: Cambridge University Press, 1984), p. viii.

12 Foucault, *Discipline and Punish*, p. 121.

13 See Gamini Salgado, *The Elizabethan Underworld* (London: J. M. Dent, 1977), p. 186.

14 'We have found by wofull experience that it is not frequent and often punishment that doth prevent like offenses ... Those offenses are often committed that are often punished, for the frequency of the punishment makes it so familiar as it is not feared', cited in Steven Mullaney, *The Place of the Stage: License, Play and Power in Renaissance England* (London: University of Chicago Press, 1988), p. 94.

15 Colin Gordon (ed.), *Power/Knowledge: Selected Interviews and Other Writings by Michel Foucault, 1972–1977* (Brighton: Harvester, 1980), pp. 92–108. Foucault here extends his point about the colonization of the penalty by the prison to the larger process whereby 'the procedures of normalisation come to be ever more constantly engaged in the colonisation of those of the law', ibid., p. 107.

16 It should be admitted that this conclusion goes against the grain of much of *Discipline and Punish*. Foucault sometimes prefers to see the nineteenth century as the real historical threshold: 'If it is true that the leper gave rise to rituals of exclusion, which to a certain extent provided the model for and general form of the great Confinement, then the plague gave rise to disciplinary projects ... The exile of the leper and the arrest of the plague do not bring with them the same political dream. The first is that of a pure community, the second that of a disciplined society ... They are different projects, then, but not incompatible ones. We see them coming slowly together, and it is the peculiarity of the nineteenth century that it applied to the space of exclusion of which the leper was the symbolic inhabitant (beggars, vagabonds, madmen and the disorderly formed the real population) the technique of power proper to disciplinary partitioning,' Foucault, *Discipline and Punish*, pp. 198–9.

17 Jean Baudrillard, '... Or, the End of the Social' in his *In the Shadow of the Silent Majorities... Or The End of the Social* (New York: Semiotext(e), 1983; orig. 1978), pp. 65–91.

18 Ibid., p. 70.

19 Beard, *Logic Bomb*, op. cit., pp.163–204.

20 Baudrillard, '... Or, the End of the Social', p. 75.

21 Ibid., p. 73.

22 'Enfranchisement was an historical event: it was the emancipation of the serfs and the slaves, the decolonization of the Third World and, in our societies, the various social and political rights: workers' rights, the vote, sexual liberation and the rights of women, prisoners and homosexuals – things which today have been won everywhere. Human rights have been won everywhere. The world is almost entirely liberated; there is nothing left to fight for. And yet at the same time entire social groups are being laid waste from the inside (individuals too). Society has forgotten them and now they are forgetting themselves. They fall out of all reckoning, zombies condemned to obliteration, consigned to statistical graphs of

endangered species. This is the Fourth World', Jean Baudrillard, *America* (London: Verso, 1988; orig. 1986), p. 112.

23 Baudrillard, '... Or, the End of the Social', p. 83.

24 Baudrillard, *America*, p. 113.

25 Fredric Jameson, 'Postmodernism, or The Cultural Logic of Late Capitalism', *New Left Review* 146 (July/August 1984), pp. 53–92. An earlier, much abbreviated version of this essay was published as 'Postmodernism and Consumer Society' in Hal Foster (ed.), *Postmodern Culture* (London: Pluto, 1985; orig. 1983), pp. 111–125. Meanwhile, just to add to the confusion, these two essays were themselves combined and published as 'Postmodernism and Consumer Society' in E. Ann Kaplan (ed.), *Postmodernism and its Discontents: Theories, Practices* (London: Verso, 1988), pp. 13–29. The most up-to-date remix is 'The Cultural Logic of Late Capitalism' in Jameson's magistral collection of essays, *Postmodernism, or, The Cultural Logic of Late Capitalism* (London: Verso, 1991), pp. 1–54.

26 Jameson is more than willing to get specific about what this means: 'The postmodernisms have in fact been fascinated precisely by this whole "degraded" landscape of schlock and kitsch, of TV series and *Readers' Digest* culture, of advertising and motels, of the late show and the grade-B Hollywood film, of so-called para-literature with its airport paperback categories of the gothic and the romance, the popular biography, the murder mystery and science-fiction or fantasy novel: materials they no longer simply "quote", as a Joyce or a Mahler might have done, but incorporate into their very substance', ibid., p. 55.

27 Ibid., p. 57.

28 Something he spells out quite clearly in his 1984 essay, 'Periodizing the 60s' in Fredric Jameson, *The Ideologies of Theory: Essays 1971–1986; Volume 2: The Syntax of History* (London: Routledge, 1988), pp. 178–208. See pp. 194–201. The essay is reprinted from *The 60s Without Apology / Social Text* (New York: University of Minnesota Press, 1984), pp. 178–209.

29 Fredric Jameson, 'Marxism and Postmodernism', *New Left Review* 176 (July/August 1989), pp. 31–45. Five years on, Jameson has little to revise in his original thesis and mainly uses the essay as a chance to respond to his critics – both those avant-garde art critics who dismiss him for the vulgar reductionisms supposedly typical of Marxism and those uncomprehending comrades who accuse him of reneging on Marxism altogether. He does take the chance, however, to acknowledge his indebtedness to Baudrillard. Something he expands on in the revised and much longer version of the essay published as 'Secondary Elaborations' in *Postmodernism*, op. cit., pp. 297–418.

30 Ibid., p. 34.

31 To be fair, Jameson does concede the point in his 1989 essay, but it feels like too little too late: 'a mode of production is not a "total system" ... and includes a variety of counterforces and new tendencies within itself, of "residual" as well as "emergent" forces, which it must attempt to manage or control ... Thus differences are presupposed by the model, something which should be sharply distinguished from another feature which complicates this one, namely that capitalism also produces differences or differentiation as a function of its own internal logic', ibid., p. 39. The major part of the 1984 essay was concerned with the latter form of differentiation and hardly mentioned the former.

32 Fred Pfeil, '"Makin' Flippy-Floppy": Postmodernism and the Baby-Boom PMC' in his *Another Tale to Tell: Politics and Narrative in Postmodern Culture* (London: Verso, 1990), pp. 97–125. See p. 98.

33 Mike Davis, 'Urban Renaissance and the Spirit of Postmodernism' in E. Ann Kaplan (ed.), *Postmodernism and its Discontents*, op. cit., pp. 79–87.

34 Ibid., pp. 82–83. This is something conceded by Jameson in the closing pages of 'Periodizing the 60s', when, in good dialectical fashion, he suggests that the expansion of 'global capitalism' is simultaneously accompanied by global 'proletarianization'. However, in focusing on 'the dreary realities of exploitation' in the Third World, he tends to miss the equally iniquitous forms of oppression which are taking place much closer to home. See Jameson, 'Periodizing the 60s', op. cit., p. 208.

35 Jameson, 'Postmodernism', pp. 53, 77–79.

36 Davis, op. cit., p. 81.

37 The theory that the history of capitalism is the history of successive 'long waves' of economic growth was conceived by N. D. Kondratieff and popularized by Joseph Schumpeter. Mandel suggests that three such waves have broken since the industrial revolution of the late eighteenth century, each of them heralded by their own 'technological revolution'. The third begins with the introduction of electronic and nuclear powered machinery in the Forties and ends in the Seventies. See Ernest Mandel, *Late Capitalism* (London: Verso, 1978; orig. 1972), pp. 108–146.

38 Mandel almost suggests as much: 'Late capitalism, far from representing a "post-industrial society", thus appears as the period in which all branches of the economy are fully industrialized for the first time ... we have here arrived at the absolute inner limit of the capitalist mode of production', ibid., pp. 191–207.

39 See Michel Aglietta, *La fin des devises cles: essaies sur la monnaie internationale* (Paris: La Decouverte, 1986); idem., *A Theory of Regulation: the US Experience* (London: NLB, 1979; orig. 1976); Alain Lipietz, *Mirages and Miracles: The Crises of Global Fordism* (London: Verso, 1987); idem., *The Enchanted World: Inflation, Credit and the World Crisis* (London: Verso, 1985), *Crise et inflation, Pourquoi?* (Paris: Francois Maspero, 1979); idem., 'New Tendencies in the International Division of Labour: Regimes of Accumulation and Modes of Regulation' in Allen J. Scott and Michael Storper (eds.), *Production, Work, Territory; The Geographical Anatomy of Industrial Capitalism* (London: Allen and Unwin, 1986), pp. 16–40; A. J. Scott, *New Industrial Spaces: Flexible Production Organization and Regional Development in North America and Western Europe* (London: Pion, 1988); Robert Boyer (ed.), *The Search for Labour Market Flexibility: The European Economies in Transition* (Oxford: Clarendon, 1986); Michael J. Piore and Charles F. Sabel, *The Second Industrial Divide: Possibilities for Prosperity* (New York: Basic Books, 1984). For a useful summary of these arguments see Eric Alliez and Michel Feher, 'The Luster of Capital' in Michel Feher and Sanford Kwinter (eds.), *Zone 1/2: The Contemporary City* (New York: Urzone, 1986), pp. 314–359.

40 F. W. Taylor's *The Principles of Scientific Management* was first published in 1911. A highly influential tract, it described how labour productivity could be significantly increased by accumulating a detailed knowledge of the minute particulars of the manufacturing process. Taylor's thinking has a long heritage, stretching all the way back to the works of mid-nineteenth century writers like Ure

and Babbage.

41 Jean Baudrillard, *La societe de consommation* (Paris: Gallimard, 1970). For a partial translation see 'Consumer Society' in Jean Baudrillard, *Selected Writings*, Mark Poster (ed.) (Oxford: Polity, 1988) pp. 29–56.

42 Baudrillard, ibid., p. 50.

43 Frank Lentricchia, 'Michel Foucault's Fantasy for Humanists', in his *Ariel and the Police* (Wisconsin: University of Wisconsin Press, 1988), p. 61.

44 'If Marx gives us the theory of pure capitalism, then Foucault, on discipline, gives us the theory of practical capitalism whose essential category is detail', ibid., p. 60.

45 Eric Alliez and Michael Feher, 'The Luster of Capital', op. cit., p. 355. The literature on post-Fordism continues to accumulate. Opinions are mixed as to whether it marks a radical break with Fordism or is merely a symptom of its mutation. The urban theorist David Harvey takes the narrow view, seeing 'the flexibility achieved in production, labour markets, and consumption more as an outcome of the search for financial solutions to the crisis-ridden tendencies of capitalism, rather than the other way round', p. 194. See David Harvey, *The Condition of Postmodernity* (Oxford: Blackwell, 1989), pp. 119–197. The sociologists Scott Lash and John Urry seem to be more on the ball when they argue that the late twentieth century has witnessed a transition from 'organized capitalism' to 'disorganized capitalism'. Contrary to Harvey, they suggest that post-Fordism is a solid transformation rather than a temporary fix, although they fail to face up to the Baudrillardian paradox that capitalism is becoming more organized precisely through its increasing dispersal. See Scott Lash and John Urry, *The End of Organized Capitalism* (Cambridge: Polity, 1987). Meanwhile, the messianic contributors to the British periodical, *Marxism Today,* continue to celebrate post-Fordism as the harbinger of wonderful 'New Times' for all. See Stuart Hall and Martin Jacques (eds), *New Times: The Changing Face of Politics in the 1990s* (London: Lawrence & Wishart, 1989).

46 A provisional shopping list might include hip hop and house music, with their electronically deconstructed sounds and sampled blips; the cyberpunk science fiction novels of William Gibson and Bruce Sterling; David Cronenberg's body horror movies; future shlock movies like *Blade Runner* and *Repo Man*; the stripped down superhero comics of Alan Moore and Frank Miller; trash fashion as featured in magazines like *i-D*; salvage art; computer-generated graffiti; the industrial baroque architecture of Nigel Coates; TV shows like *The Simpsons*. This is a culture which can quite easily be indexed under the sign of Jameson's aesthetic populism but which fails to figure much in the PMC playpen. It is a variant of postmodernism needing to be distinguished from the one which includes the avant funk of Talking Heads; the dirty realist fiction of Raymond Carver and Bobbie Ann Mason; the pop modern movies of Spike Lee or Jim Jarmusch; the poetry of John Ashbery; Jean-Paul Gaultier's glossy comic strip fashion; the conceptual art of Jeff Koons or Cindy Sherman; the scattershot video imagery of Nam June Paik; the deconstructivist architecture of Frank Gehry; opera like *Einstein on the Beach*. To avoid confusion, a new tag is needed. Pap Modernism?

47 See 'Symbolic Exchange and Death', pp. 135–147 in Baudrillard's *Selected Writings*. The three orders of simulation correspond to three laws of value – the natural law of value, the commodity law of value, the structural law of value

– and to three expressions of value – use value, exchange value, sign exchange value. It might be possible to label these three orders more conventionally as the regimes of mercantile capitalism, commodity capitalism, and simulated capitalism or 'hypercapitalism'.

48 Ibid., p. 138.

49 Ibid., p. 134.

50 Peter Stallybrass and Allon White, *The Politics and Poetics of Transgression* (Ithaca, New York: Cornell University Press, 1986), p. 90.

51 Pierre Bourdieu, *Distinction: A Social Critique of the Judgement of Taste* (London: Routledge, 1984; orig. 1979). 'This pure aesthetic is indeed the rationalization of an ethos: pure pleasure, pleasure totally purified of all sensuous or sensible interest, as remote from concupiscence as it is from conspicuous consumption, is as opposed as much to the refined, altruistic enjoyment of the courtier as it is to the crude, animal enjoyment of the people', p. 493.

52 Norbert Elias, *The Civilizing Process: Sociogenetic and Psychogenetic Investigations Volume 1: The History of Manners* (Oxford: Blackwell, 1978; orig. 1939) and *Volume 2: State Formation and Civilization* (Oxford: Blackwell, 1982; orig. 1939). Stallybrass and White do not dwell on this matter of the state monopoly of violence, but it provides an interesting slant on the periodization of modernity. According to the historian Lawrence Stone, the royal monopoly of violence was not enforced simply as a result of the legislative fiat of Henry VII but took until the early seventeenth century to accomplish. It was a gradual process involving the reduction of the size of the nobility's armed retainers, the breaking up of the great territorial empires, the moratorium on the building of castles, the persuasion of the nobility that violence was not only impolitic but dishonourable and of their dependents that their first loyalty lay with the crown. The Civilizing Process was as much concerned with habits of mind as force of arms from its very inception. See Lawrence Stone, *The Crisis of the Aristocracy 1558-1641* (Oxford: Clarendon, 1965), pp. 199–270; idem., 'Interpersonal Violence in English Society 1300-1980', *Past and Present*, no. 101 (November 1983), pp. 22–33.

53 Stallybrass and White, op. cit., p. 90.

54 The terms are taken from Bakhtin's *Rabelais and His World* (Bloomington: Indiana University Press, 1984; orig. 1936).

55 Stallybrass and White, op. cit., p. 58.

56 Ibid., p. 5.

57 'A recurrent pattern emerges: the 'top' attempts to reject and eliminate the 'bottom' for reasons of prestige and status, only to discover, not only that it is in some way frequently dependent upon that low-Other ... but also that the top includes that low symbolically, as a primary eroticized constituent of its own fantasy life', ibid., p. 5.

58 Stallybrass and White recognize this, but fail to see it as a problem. They admit that it is necessary to distinguish 'the grotesque as the "Other" of the defining group or self, and the grotesque as a boundary phenomenon of hybridization or inmixing, in which self and other become enmeshed in an inclusive, heterogeneous, dangerously unstable zone ... a fundamental mechanism of identity formation produces the second, hybrid grotesque at the level of the political unconscious by the very struggle to exclude the first grotesque', ibid.,

p. 193.
59 Stallybrass and White make the essential point with admirable succinctness. 'The creation of a sublimated public body without smells, without coarse laughter, without organs, separate from the Court and the Church on the one hand and the market square, alehouses, street and fairground on the other – this was the great labour of bourgeois culture, complementary to that institutionalizing inventiveness of the same period which Foucault has mapped in *Madness and Civilization* and *Discipline and Punish*', ibid., pp. 93–94.
60 Colin Gordon (ed.), *Power/Knowledge*, op. cit., pp. 101–102.
61 Michel Foucault, *The History of Sexuality, Volume One: An Introduction* (Harmondsworth: Penguin, 1981; orig. 1976), pp. 17–49;115–131;145–150.
62 These are precisely the examples used by Stallybrass and White, which just goes to show how their instincts are better than some of their theoretical judgements. See Stallybrass and White, op. cit., pp. 125–187.
63 Mullaney, op. cit., p. 49. Mullaney points out that it was the theatre which had been culturally dominant before the construction of the public playhouses – 'interstitial' rather than 'incontinent' – which was bound by this saturnalian logic. This was the theatre of the innyards, the academic theatre of the university colleges, schools and Inns of Court. It takes in the run of the children of the royal chapels at Blackfriars from 1576 to 1584 as well as the stationing of the 'little eyeasses', a troupe of boy players, at the same theatre from 1600 until 1608.
64 James Burbage's Theatre was built in Shoreditch in 1576, soon after the Red Lion had been opened in 1567 by his brother-in-law and partner, John Brayne. Between 1576 and 1598, when the Theatre was demolished and reincarnated as the Globe in Bankside, three theatres opened in London: the Curtain, the Rose and the Swan. None of them, with the exception of the Curtain, lasted long. The Swan staged plays for just two years (although it continued to be used for feats of activity until 1637) while the troupe acting at the Rose moved to the Fortune, in the north of the city, in 1600. The only new public playhouse to be opened in the seventeenth century was the Red Bull at Clerkenwell around 1605. See Andrew Gurr, *Playgoing in Shakespeare's London* (Cambridge: Cambridge University Press, 1987); Michael Hattaway, *Elizabethan Popular Theatre: Plays in Performance* (London: Routledge, 1982).
65 Michael D. Bristol makes a similar point about the 'structural ambiguity' of the public playhouses. See Michael D. Bristol, *Carnival and Theater: Plebeian Culture and the Structure of Authority in Renaissance England* (London: Methuen, 1985), pp. 111–13. 'A pragmatically illicit or unauthorized use of time (idleness) coincides with an altered representation of time (anachronism) leaving open the possibility of revisionary and therefore seditious misinterpretations of both past and present', ibid., p. 112.
66 For material on the Puritan pamphleteers see Mullaney, op. cit., p. 51. See also Margot Heinemann, *Puritanism and Theatre: Thomas Middleton and Opposition Drama under the Early Stuarts* (Cambridge: Cambridge University Press, 1980), pp. 18–47. With regard to the cultural opposition to the theatres, Heinemann observes that it 'has been customary to regard Puritan doctrinal objections as the primary reason for opposition, and the authorities' practical worries about plague, riots and traffic jams as mere excuses. In fact, it appears often to have worked the other way round,' ibid., p. 35.

67 They were right to be scandalized, but wrong to trick this up in the language of moral disgust. The theatres were not morally offensive so much as socially polluting. For the difference between 'moral rules' and 'pollution rules', see Mary Douglas, *Purity and Danger* (London: Routledge, 1966), pp. 129–139. If the theatres were unclean, that was because they contravened social order. As Douglas famously observes, dirt does not exist in itself, it must be defined structurally as 'matter out of place,' ibid., p. 35.

68 See Alfred Harbage, *Shakespeare and the Rival Traditions* (New York: Macmillan, 1952). Harbage's idea that the audiences at the public playhouses represented a cross-section of Elizabethan society has in the last forty years been subject to revision but remains more or less intact. The most strenuous objection has been made by Ann Jennalie Cook, who argues that the audiences at the public playhouses were drawn from the upper levels of society. See Ann Jennalie Cook, *The Privileged Playgoers of Shakespeare's London 1576–1642* (Princeton: Princeton University Press, 1981). However, her thesis has been convincingly rebutted by Martin Butler. See Martin Butler, *Theatre and Crisis 1632–1642* (Cambridge: Cambridge University Press, 1984), pp. 293–306.

69 'If wee present a mingle-mangle, our fault is to be excused, because the whole worlde is become an Hodge-Podge'. Quoted in Robert Weimann, *Shakespeare and the Popular Tradition in the Theater: Studies in the Social Dimension of Dramatic Form and Function* (London: Johns Hopkins University Press, 1978), p. 173.

70 Mullaney, op. cit., p. 23.

71 Ibid., pp. 60–87. Mullaney argues that the popular stage was the site of a 'rehearsal' of folk and rural pastimes prior to their erasure by Puritan tracts and sermons, city ordinances and Statutes of the Realm protecting the Sabbath.

72 Leonard Tennenhouse works the equation differently. He links the classical body with an aristocratic body of blood contested by the grotesque body of the masses. As a result of this, he concentrates his critical energies on Shakespeare's history plays and romantic comedies, arguing that they enact a purification of the mass body so as to make it fit to participate in rituals celebrating hierarchical power. See Leonard Tennenhouse, *Power on Display: The Politics of Shakespeare's Genres* (London: Methuen, 1986), pp. 17–101. This is fine as far as it goes, but it is rather literal and veers dangerously close to reduplicating Foucault's power couple as it exists on the scaffold. That's to say, Tennenhouse takes little account of the historical beneficiaries of this struggle: namely the bourgeoisie.

73 'Popular drama owed its birth ... to an interim period in a larger historical transition, a period marked by the failure of the dominant culture to rearticulate itself in a fashion that would close off the gaps and seams opening on the margins of its domain. Such a historical interlude could not last long, however, and it was beginning to draw to a close in the first decade of the Jacobean period.', Mullaney, op. cit., p. 137. At the beginning of the seventeenth century, there occurred what Mullaney calls a 'narrowing-down of the theatrical'.

74 After the first decade of the Jacobean period, a second wave of theatre construction took place. Between 1608 and 1629, no less than seven new theatres were built. Not only was there the reconstruction of the Globe and the Fortune after they burnt down, there was also the remodelling of the Globe's companion theatre at Blackfriars and the opening of the Hope in 1614. To these can be added the conversions of the Whitehall Cockpit into the Royal Cockpit,

of the Cockpit in Drury Lane into the Phoenix Theatre, as well as the Whitehall Cockpit-in-the Court conversion of 1629. By 1630, the only surviving public playhouses were the Fortune and the Red Bull in the north of the city (the Curtain had closed its doors to actors in 1627). See Gurr, op. cit.; Keith Sturgess, *Jacobean Private Theatre* (London: Routledge, 1987).

75 The distinction between the public and private theatres was first made by Harbage and has since been subject to critical revision. Gurr, for example, suggests that the proper distinction should be between 'amphitheatres' and 'hall theatres', op. cit., pp. 13–31. Meanwhile, Butler prefers to distinguish between 'popular' and 'elite' theatres', op. cit., p. 132. This seems like so much academic sandpapering. I intend to stick with Harbage's nomenclature.

76 Gurr, op. cit., p. 27. For details on the material conditions of the private theatres, see pp. 13-48.

77 Butler, op. cit., p. 110. It should be noted that whereas Harbage was broadly right to suggest that a socially mixed audience attended the public playhouses, he was wrong to insist that the private theatres were the preserve of a 'coterie' audience. Butler offers a convincing critique of this myth of the 'Cavalier audience', pointing out that the private theatre audiences, although retaining strong links with the court, were drawn from the same social classes as Parliament, op. cit., p. 100. Perhaps all the arguments about the exact social composition of theatre audiences should be subordinated to the observation that patrons in each type of theatre would have been expected to behave in very different ways.

78 Butler is here taking his lead from Heinemann, who argues that an 'opposition drama' – represented in its highest artistic form by Thomas Middleton's city tragedies – emerged during the 1620s. See Heinemann, op. cit., pp. 172-199. The conclusion which Butler draws – that the drama of these elite theatres was an 'opposition' drama – doesn't necessarily follow from his premise about the social composition of audiences. Whether the ideological messages carried by the plays were Cavalier or Puritan, court or country is almost irrelevant. Butler has already made his central point, which is that the theatres had an oppositional social function.

79 This corresponds with what is commonly viewed as the 'decadence' of Caroline revenge tragedy. See M. C. Bradbrook, *Themes and Conventions of Elizabethan Tragedy* (Cambridge: Cambridge University Press, 1935), pp. 240–67 and Fredson Bowers, *Elizabethan Revenge Tragedy 1587–1642* (Princeton: Princeton University Press, 1940), pp. 217–58. Walter Cohen gives a superficial Marxist gloss to this line when he treats Ford as ideologically residual, arguing that his plays dramatize 'the feelings of a class, a section of a class, when it senses that it no longer has a social function, that history has passed it by,' Walter Cohen, *Drama of a Nation: Public Theater in Renaissance England and Spain* (Ithaca: Cornell University Press, 1985), p. 372. For Cohen's larger interpretation of 'pathetic tragedy', see pp. 357–404. Everything written off as a corruption, enervation or dissipation of an earlier vital tradition should instead be seen as a refinement of manners.

80 A term of abuse first popularized by the playwright Thomas Dekker in 1606. See Gurr, op. cit., p. 38.

81 This is to restate in broader form Harbage's conception of the 'rival traditions' of the public and private theatres. Keith Sturgess makes the point in succinct fashion

when he observes that 'the private playhouses became a club, an academy and an art-house, while its public counterpart became notable for rowdy behaviour and, on-stage, an over-dependence on jigs, fighting and horseplay', Keith Sturgess, op. cit., p. 4. Sturgess associates private drama with the plays of Ben Jonson, Thomas Middleton, John Webster and John Ford.

82 'A tragicomedy is not so called in respect of mirth and killing, but in respect it wants death, which is enough to make it no tragedy, yet brings some near to it, which is enough to make it no comedy.' Quoted in Jacqueline Pearson, *Tragedy and Tragicomedy in the Plays of John Webster* (Manchester: Manchester University Press, 1980), pp. 17–18.

83 Muriel C. Bradbrook, 'Marlowe's Doctor Faustus and the Eldritch Tradition' in Richard Hosley (ed.), *Essays on Shakespeare and Elizabethan Drama in Honour of Hardin Craig* (London: Routledge, 1963), pp. 83–90. For similar observations, see also Nicholas Brooke, *Horrid Laughter in Jacobean Tragedy* (London: Open Books, 1979).

84 See Heinemann, pp. 237–57; Butler, op. cit., p.136.

85 Joseph Addison commented in the *Spectator* during 1711: 'But among all our methods of moving pity or terror, there is none so absurd and barbarous, and which more exposes us to the contempt and ridicule of our neighbours than that dreadful butchering of one another, which is so very frequent upon the English stage. To delight in seeing men stabbed, poisoned, racked, or impaled, is certainly the sign of a cruel temper.' Quoted in Lily B. Campbell, *Scenes and Machines on the English Stage During the Renaissance* (Cambridge: Cambridge University Press, 1923), p. 273.

86 Quoted in G. E. Bentley, *The Profession of Dramatist in Shakespeare's Time, 1590–1642* (Princeton: Princeton University Press, 1971), p. 160.

87 Foucault, *The History of Sexuality*, pp. 122–127.

88 Eight corporations controlled the American motion picture industry throughout the 1930s and 1940s. They were known as the Big Five – Paramount Pictures, Loew's Inc (parent company of Metro-Goldwyn-Mayer or MGM), 20th Century Fox, Warner Bros and Radio-Keith-Orpheum or RKO – and the Little Three – Universal, Columbia and United Artists. The Big Five were fully vertically integrated, whereas the Little Three concentrated on production and exhibition. See Douglas Gomery, *The Hollywood Studio System* (Basingstoke: BFI, 1985). Gomery offers a salutary corrective to the usual obsession with all things Hollywood. 'Historians' interest in competition for maximum box-office revenues (i.e. the differences between films) has only served to ignore the total and necessary corporate cooperation which existed on the level of distribution and exhibition. The inordinate interest in production has also focussed too much attention on Hollywood as the centre for movies, when in reality throughout the studio era officials in New York "called the shots",' ibid., p. 193.

89 As Jean Baudrillard observes, 'the idolatry of stars, the cult of Hollywood idols, is not a media pathology but a glorious form of the cinema, its mythical transfiguration, perhaps the last great myth of our modernity,' Jean Baudrillard, *The Evil Demon of Images* (Annandale: Power Institute of Fine Arts, 1984), p. 26.

90 Richard Sennett, *The Fall of Public Man* (London: Faber, 1986; orig. 1977), pp. 206–7.

91 Mike Davis, *City of Quartz: Excavating the Future in Los Angeles* (London: Verso, 1990), p. 227. Davis sees Los Angeles as an urban laboratory for the invention of new crowd control techniques. 'To reduce contact with untouchables, urban redevelopment has converted once vital pedestrian streets into traffic-sewers and transformed public parks into temporary receptacles for the homeless and wretched. The American city ... is being systematically turned inside out - or, rather, outside in. The valorized spaces of the new megastructures and super-malls are concentrated in the center, street frontage is denuded, public activity is sorted into strictly functional compartments, and circulation is internalized in corridors under the gaze of private police,' ibid., p. 226.

92 Jean Baudrillard, 'Design and Environment' in his *For a Critique of the Political Economy of the Sign* (St Louis: Telos Press, 1981; orig. 1972), pp. 185–203. Baudrillard plausibly argues that Bauhaus design 'institutes the universal semantization of the environment in which everything becomes the object of a calculus of function and of signification,' ibid., p. 185. The logical conclusion to the Bauhaus project is a cybernetic society of total simulation.

93 For the relationship between Hollywood movie production and the new technologies of distribution and exhibition in the Eighties, see Douglas Gomery, 'Hollywood's Hold on the New Television Technologies', *Screen*, vol. 29, no. 2, (Spring 1988), pp. 82–8.

94 Kim Newman, *Nightmare Movies: A Critical History of the Horror Film, 1968–88* (London: Bloomsbury, 1988; orig. 1984).

95 For a full account of the video nasties scare see Martin Barker, 'Nasty Politics or Video Nasties?' in Martin Barker (ed.), *The Video Nasties: Freedom and Censorship in the Media* (London: Pluto, 1984), pp. 7–38.

96 Quoted in Barker, op. cit., p. 10.

97 Stallybrass and White, op. cit., p. 198.

98 See Paul Virilio, *Speed and Politics: An Essay on Dromology* (New York: Semiotext(e), 1986; orig. 1977). A series of extended footnotes to this text are added in Paul Virilio, *Popular Defense & Ecological Struggles* (New York: Semiotext(e), 1990; orig. 1978). Other translated works are Paul Virilio, *War and Cinema* (London: Verso, 1989; orig. 1984); idem., *The Lost Dimension* (New York: Semiotext(e), 1990); idem., *Aesthetics of Disappearance* (New York: Semiotext(e), 1990). A good introduction to his major concerns – speed, urbanization, the logistics of war – is provided by the series of interviews he gave in Paul Virilio and Sylvere Lotringer, *Pure War* (New York: Semiotext(e), 1983).

99 This analysis is based on Gilles Deleuze's and Felix Guattari's conceptualization of Virilio. See Gilles Deleuze and Felix Guattari, 'Treatise on Nomadology – The War Machine' in their *A Thousand Plateaus: Capitalism and Schizophrenia* (London: Athlone, 1988; orig. 1980), pp. 351–423. 'Virilio's texts are of great importance and originality in every respect. The only point that presents a difficulty for us is his assimilation of three groups of speed that seem very different to us: 1 speeds of nomadic, or revolutionary, tendency (riot, guerrilla warfare); 2 speeds that are regulated, converted, appropriated by the State apparatus (management of the public ways); 3 speeds that are reinstated by a worldwide organization of total war, or planetary overarmament (from the fleet in being to nuclear strategy). Virilio tends to equate these groups on account of their interactions and makes a general case for the 'fascist' character of speed. It is, nevertheless, his own analyses that

make these distinctions possible,' ibid., p. 559.

100 *Speed and Politics,* p. 30.

101 Ibid., p. 14.

102 Ibid., p. 89.

103 Ibid., p. 88.

104 Ibid., p. 30.

105 See Mullaney, op. cit., p. 44.

106 Virilio, *Speed and Politics,* op. cit., p. 15.

107 See Michael D. Bristol, *Carnival and Theater,* op. cit., pp. 140-155. Bristol comments on how the clown is allied to the devil in his refusal to participate in the authorized cultural fantasy of the main plot of an Elizabethan play, surviving by resorting to the practice of 'refusing to understand'. Typical elaborations of this device include 'partial deafness, inattention, ignorance of the correct meaning of words, mispronunciation and severely diminished intelligence', ibid., p. 141.

108 Virilio, *War and Cinema,* op. cit., p. 10.

109 Foucault, *Discipline and Punish,* op. cit., pp. 135-169. 'Historians of ideas usually attribute the dream of a perfect society to the philosophers and jurists of the eighteenth century; but there was also a military dream of society; its fundamental reference was not to the state of nature, but to the meticulously subordinated cogs of a machine, not to the primal social contract, but to permanent coercion, not to fundamental rights, but to indefinitely progressive forms of training, not to the general will but to automatic docility', p. 169.

110 Virilio, *Speed and Politics,* op. cit., p. 31.

111 See R T Maddock, *The Political Economy of the Arms Race* (Basingstoke: Macmillan, 1990); Miroslav Nincic, *The Arms Race: The Political Economy of Military Growth* (New York: Praeger, 1982).

112 Virilio, *Speed and Politics,* op. cit., p. 99.

113 'History shows that the decay of the enclosed bourgeoisies necessarily marks the decline of the productive masses and the rise in the State of methods of military proletarianization', Virilio, ibid., p. 31. One such method, operative in certain regions of the States, is workfare, or labour-for-dole. This represents, in the sphere of production, a kind of militarized Taylorism, with teams of unemployables picking up litter or counting lamp-posts for a pittance. Its counterpart in the sphere of consumption is drug addiction, which represents a similar mobilization of maximum effort to a minimum end. Both activities are heavily monitored by the state. Add them together and you get the zero-degree figure of Fordism.

114 Virilio, *Speed and Politics,* op. cit., p. 78.

115 Mike Davis observes that bum-proof benches and random-assault sprinklers have been constructed in Los Angles as a means of keeping the Fourth World out of the city's bus shelters and public parks and on the move. See Davis, *City of Quartz,* p. 233.

116 'Endo-colonization: the colony has always been the model of the political State, which began in the city, spread to the nation, across the communes, and reached the stage of the French and English colonial empires. And now it backfires, which we knew the moment there was decolonization. Decolonization is not a positive sign, it's an endo-colonial sign. If you decolonize without, you'll colonize all the more intensely within', Virilio, *Pure War,* op. cit., p. 157.

117 The 'minimum state' is a political concept derived from monetarist economic

policy. See Virilio, *Popular Defense & Ecological Struggles*, op. cit., pp. 60–61. The 'intercept policy' of the 1984 Police and Criminal Evidence Act seems to be a trailer for this new social order. It allows the police to stop anyone they like on the roads, if they believe there is a real and imminent danger of a breach of the peace, and has so far been used against such 'enemies within' as striking miners and hippy convoys. Its purpose seems to be to keep out the new poor from the new heartlands.

118 See Mike Davis, *City of Quartz*, op. cit., pp. 267–322. A version of this chapter, 'Los Angeles: Civil Liberties Between the Hammer and the Rock', originally appeared in *New Left Review* 170 (Jul/Aug 1988), pp. 37–60.

119 Quoted in Martin Barker, op. cit., p. 10.

120 Arthur Kroker, 'Baudrillard's Marx' in Arthur Kroker and David Cook, *The Postmodern Scene*, op. cit., pp. 170–188. See p. 185.

121 Virilio, *Speed and Politics*, op. cit., p. 33.

122 Beard, *Logic Bomb*, op. cit., pp.163–204.

123 See, for example, Mark Poster's introduction to Baudrillard's *Selected Writings*, where he comments that de Certeau's 'position on resistance seems more heuristic and more sensible than Baudrillard's,' Baudrillard's *Selected Writings*, op. cit., p. 7.

124 Michel de Certeau, *The Practice of Everyday Life* (London: University of California Press, 1984), pp. 15–28.

125 Ibid., p. 25.

126 George Yudice, 'Marginality and the Ethics of Survival' in Andrew Ross (ed.), *Universal Abandon?: The Politics of Postmodernism* (Edinburgh: Edinburgh University Press, 1988), pp. 214–236. See p. 216.

127 De Certeau, op. cit., pp. 29–42.

128 Ibid., p.40.

129 Bristol's obvious indebtedness to de Certeau in his elaboration of this tactic is underlined when he proposes that clowning cannot be considered a mere dramatic device because it belongs to the 'bigger, extra-literary context of everyday life', Bristol, *Carnival and Theater*, op. cit., p. 143.

130 Virilio, *Speed and Politics*, op. cit., p. 123.

131 Ibid., p. 122.

132 Virilio, *Pure War*, p. 93.

133 Ibid., p. 92.

index of names

index of concepts

LIGHT READINGS
Film Criticism and Screen Arts

Chris Darke

I n *Light Readings*, leading film critic Chris Darke re-visits
his writing over recent years to address important questions
emerging out of the changes effecting film
and digital media. Was the 1990s the
decade in which cinema as a medium and
collective experience finally became sub-
sumed within a converging universe of
multiple media? Should the term 'cinema'
be reconsidered to accommodate the new
possibilities of the moving image? This
insightful collection of reviews and essays
also includes interviews with Atom
Egoyan, Bill Viola, Olivier Assayas, Jacques
Audiard, and Xavier Beauvois.

208 pages

1-903364-07-8   £12.99

Chris Darke is a regular contributor to *Sight and Sound, mute*
and *The Independent*. His other activities include screenwrit-
ing, cinema programming and producing arts reportage for
television.

"An inspired collection of essays on the interface of new medias and their
mutual interfaces."

Film Comment

MOVIE WARS
How Hollywood and the Media Conspire to Limit What Films We Can See

Jonathan Rosenbaum

In *Movie Wars* leading film critic Jonathan Rosenbaum cogently explains how movies are packaged, distributed and promoted and how at every stage in the process, the potential moviegoer is treated with contempt. Along the way it exposes industry secrets such as that Miramax often buys distribution rights to movies it then fails to distribute, thus ensuring that its competitors don't get them. And it shows for the first time why the corporate ownership of movie theatres defies antitrust laws and precedents stretching back over fifty years. Using examples ranging from *New York Times* coverage of the Cannes Film Festival to the anticommercial practices of Orson Welles, from the American Film Institute to the major studios Rosenbaum identifies "the media-industrial complex" as a powerful force in the process of ruining our precious cinematic culture and heritage.

Jonathan Rosenbaum is a film critic for the for *Chicago Reader* and is author of *Moving Places, Placing Movies, Placing Movies, Movies as Politics, Dead Man*, and other books. He is a frequent contributor to *Film Comment* and *Cineaste*.

208 pages
1-903364-48-3   £12.99

"Jonathan Rosenbaum is the best Film Critic in the United States —indeed, he's one of the best writers on film of any kind in the history of the medium."
James Naremore author of *More than Night: Film Noir in its Contexts*